THE REMINISCENCES OF
Vice Admiral William I. Martin
U.S. Navy (Retired)

INTERVIEWED BY
John T. Mason, Jr.

U.S. Naval Institute • Annapolis, Maryland

Copyright © 2013

Preface

Shortly after World War I ended, Bill Martin was nine years old and one day was spreading fertilizer on a cornfield in the Ozarks of Missouri. His chore was interrupted by the sight of a barnstorming biplane that flew low over the field and then turned around to double back and fly over Martin again. The pilot, whose white scarf was flowing in the wind, waved to the youngster. Martin was hooked then and there. He aspired to a career in aviation and later achieved his dream.

Along the way, he became a naval aviation pioneer, especially in the area of instrument flying at night and in bad weather. He not only mastered the skill himself but also became expert in teaching it to others. During World War II he had several tours of duty on board the fabled aircraft carrier *Enterprise*. Among many other events, he managed to survive the sinking of the carrier *Hornet* in 1942 during the Battle of Santa Cruz Islands. He was later shot down during a bombing run in support of the amphibious assault on the island of Saipan in 1944. He was rescued and soon returned to duty. Later that year, as the *Enterprise* began specialized work as a night carrier, he commanded her air group. His desire for new experiences led him to serve as a test pilot right after World War II. He flew the Navy's newest planes and those it was considering.

In the memoir that follows, Martin relates an assessment from senior officers that he himself agreed with—perhaps with too much modesty. The admirals told Martin that he was adequate in jobs ashore but exceptionally capable at sea and in the air—the essence of the naval profession. One admiral who was particularly impressed by Martin's capabilities was Arleigh Burke, who had first encountered him during the air-sea operations of the World War II Pacific. Another was Admiral Arthur Radford, who was Commander in Chief of the Pacific Fleet. He sent Martin to Washington in 1949 to testify on behalf of naval aviation—and against the Air Force—during the testy inter-service squabble that marked congressional hearings on the Air Force's B-36 bomber. Burke later arranged other billets for Martin, including serving as Burke's executive assistant and senior aide in the mid-1950s when Burke was Chief of Naval Operations.

In his various jobs at sea, Martin sought out opportunities for tactical development and improvement and continued to preach the benefits of instrument flying. When he was a student at the Naval War College, Martin had an unofficial collateral duty as instrument instructor for his fellow students who had not yet qualified. In his first seagoing flag billet, Martin commanded an antisubmarine carrier division during the Cold War, a time when the Soviet undersea threat was developing. He also commanded an attack carrier division with his flag in the recently commissioned *Enterprise*, the nuclear-powered namesake of the carrier from which he had flown during World War II. In the early 1960s, Martin commanded a task force comprised of the *Enterprise*, cruiser *Long Beach*, and frigate *Bainbridge*—the first nuclear-powered group to operate together. Martin and his staff planned an around-the-world cruise for the three ships, seeking to enhance the tactical advantages inherent in nuclear power and rebuffing efforts by Admiral Hyman Rickover to make the cruise essentially a public relations show. Martin was understandably disappointed when he had to leave the carrier division command before the famous cruise took place.

Instead, he reported back to the Pentagon to serve as the number-two admiral in OP-05, the naval aviation section of the OpNav staff. From there he went to one of the choicest operational commands in the entire Navy, the Sixth Fleet in the Mediterranean. Dr. John Mason, my predecessor as the Naval Institute's oral historian, conducted the interviews that comprise this memoir. In reading them, I concluded that the admiral and the interviewer essentially made a prior agreement that Martin would express no opinions on the Six-Day War of June 1967, a conflict between Egypt and Israel. A controversial part of that war was Israel's devastating attack on the communications intelligence ship *Liberty*. Admiral Martin discussed the Sixth Fleet's operations at that time only briefly and with a strict just-the-facts approach.

Admiral Martin wound up his long active career by serving as Deputy Commander in Chief of the Atlantic Fleet, retiring soon after the advent of Admiral Elmo Zumwalt's tenure as Chief of Naval Operations. Throughout the entire oral history, the reader learns a good deal about Martin's passion for aviation and how it can best serve the profession. One also is reminded again and again of the remarkable capability and achievements of Admiral Arleigh Burke, for Martin worked with him closely and developed a great deal of admiration for him.

I greatly regret that it has taken so long for the admiral's memories to become publicly available. As he wrote in a letter many years ago, he procrastinated in sending back the transcript with his perfunctory changes and additions. Then, because of competing priorities and changing circumstances, I procrastinated in doing the remaining work, which involved some additional editing, fact checking, annotation with footnotes, and indexing.

As the project finally comes to a close, making available the work on which Dr. Mason and Admiral Martin collaborated, I thank Janis Jorgensen of the Naval Institute staff who coordinated the printing and binding of the finished history.

In completing the volume, the Naval Institute expresses its gratitude to the Tawani Foundation and the Pritzker Military Library of Chicago for their generous financial support of the oral history program that produced this memoir.

Paul Stillwell
U.S. Naval Institute
January 2013

VICE ADMIRAL WILLIAM INMAN MARTIN
UNITED STATES NAVY (RETIRED)

Born: 5 May 1910 in Ava, Missouri

Died: 29 March 1996, Alexandria, Virginia

Chronological Record of Commissioned Service:

Jun 1934-Jun 1937	USS *Idaho* (BB-42)
Jun 1937-May 1938	Naval Air Station, Pensacola, Florida, under instruction
May 1938-May 1940	Scouting Squadron Two (VS-2) on board USS *Lexington* (CV-2)
May 1940-May 1940	Cruiser Scouting Squadron Four (VSO-4) on board USS *Northampton* (CA-26)
May 1940-Aug 1940	Scouting Squadron Two (VS-2) on board USS *Lexington* (CV-2)
Aug 1940-Feb 1941	Naval Air Station, Pensacola, Florida, instructor
Feb 1941-Jul 1942	Naval Air Station, Corpus Christi, Texas, instructor
Jul 1942-Jun 1943	Scouting Squadron 10 (VS-10) on board USS *Enterprise* (CV-6), executive officer/commanding officer
Jul 1943-Jul 1944	Torpedo Squadron Ten (VT-10) on board USS *Enterprise* (CV-6), commanding officer
Jul 1944-Jun 1945	Commander Night Carrier Air Group 90 (CAG-90) on board USS *Enterprise* (CV-6)
Jun 1945-Sep 1945	Headquarters, Commander in Chief U.S. Fleet, assistant for air control in Special Defense Section
Sep 1945-Aug 1948	Naval Air Test Center, Patuxent River, Maryland, director, Tactical Test Division
Aug 1948-Jun 1950	Fleet All-Weather Training Unit Pacific, executive officer
Jun 1950-Jun 1951	Naval War College, Newport, Rhode Island, student

Jun 1951-Jun 1953	Office of the Chief of Naval Operations, Washington, D.C., all-weather flight coordinator, Air Warfare Division
Jun 1953-Aug 1955	Fleet All-Weather Training Unit Pacific, commanding officer
Aug 1955-Jan 1956	USS *Saipan* (CVL-48), commanding officer
Jan 1956-Jun 1957	Office of the Chief of Naval Operations, Washington, D.C., executive assistant and senior aide to the CNO
Jun 1957-Jul 1958	Carrier Division Five, chief of staff and aide
Jul 1958-Dec 1959	Commander Airborne Early Warning Wing Atlantic/ Commander Fleet Air, Argentia, Newfoundland, Canada
Dec 1959-Aug 1960	Commander Carrier Division 19
Aug 1960-Oct 1961	Military Assistance Advisory Group (MAAG), Federal Republic of Germany, deputy chief
Oct 1961-May 1963	Chief of Naval Air Reserve Training, Glenview Naval Air Station, Illinois
May 1963-Apr 1964	Commander Carrier Division Two
Apr 1964-Mar 1967	Office of the Chief of Naval Operations, Washington, D.C., Assistant CNO (Air)
Mar 1967-Aug 1968	Commander Sixth Fleet and Commander Naval Striking and Support Forces, Southern Europe
Aug 1968-Jan 1971	Commander in Chief Atlantic Fleet, deputy and chief of staff and chief of staff Atlantic Command

Dates of Rank:

Midshipman: 12 June 1930
Ensign: 31 May 1934
Lieutenant (junior grade): 31 May 1937
Lieutenant: 1 July 1941
Lieutenant Commander: 1 March 1943
Commander: 1 February 1944
Captain: 1 July 1953
Rear Admiral: 1 July 1959
Vice Admiral: 10 April 1967

1 February 1971   Retired from active duty

Medals and Awards:

Distinguished Service Medal with two gold stars in lieu of second and third awards
Silver Star Medal
Legion of Merit with one gold star in lieu of second award
Distinguished Flying Cross with two gold stars in lieu of subsequent awards
Navy Commendation Medal
Presidential Unit Citation awarded First Marine Division Reinforced
Presidential Unit Citation awarded USS *Enterprise* (CV-6)
American Defense Service Medal with fleet clasp
American Campaign Medal
Asiatic-Pacific Campaign Medal
World War II Victory Medal
National Defense Service Medal with one bronze star in lieu of second award
Philippine Liberation Ribbon
Philippine Republic Presidential Unit Citation Badge

Foreign Decorations:

Knight Commander of the Royal Order of King George I (Greece)

Special Qualifications:

Designated Naval Aviator (Heavier than Air), 21 April 1938
Graduate of the Naval War College, 1951

Memorandum for the Record

Although Vice Admiral Martin did not sign a formal deed of gift to authorize release of the material in the following transcript, he did agree to do the interviews with the intent that they be made available for public use. He also signed a letter that referred to the oral history and included the following words, "You have my consent to do whatever you wish with it."

Paul Stillwell

Paul Stillwell
21 January 2013

Interview Number 1 with Vice Admiral William I. Martin, U.S. Navy (Retired)
Place: Admiral Martin's home, Alexandria, Virginia
Date: Tuesday, 30 October 1979

John T. Mason Jr.: I have been looking forward to this series with you, having pursued your career, which is a very illustrious one. I am sure you have many, many points to make which will be of use and interest to historians.

Would you begin a talking biography in the proper way by telling me where you were born, when you were born, and something about your family background.

Admiral Martin: I was born on the fifth of May 1910 in the heart of the Ozarks, Missouri. This is very close to the center of hillbilly country. My father was a cattleman, and so I spent much of my youth on horses, on trips with my father to buy stock in Arkansas, Oklahoma, and our part of Missouri. We shipped them into Chicago, Kansas City, St. Louis.

My father also had considerable acreage. He would bring the stock into his acreage and fatten it up and then ship it on to the market. He raised his own feed for the winter. At the age of nine, I was fertilizing a field of young corn. It was the first time my father had shifted from barnyard fertilizer to commercial fertilizer. It was an extremely hot day—I can still picture it vividly—and it was windy. When I would dip this mealy fertilizer to put it next to this stalk of corn, the wind would blow it up in my eyes. It was toxic, and this had been going on for a couple of hours, I guess.

In the distance I heard an engine that I just knew right away was an airplane. It was coming from the southeast, and I knew it was going to pass over this field I was in. I ran out into the middle of the field, dropped this bucket of fertilizer I had strapped around my neck, and I waved. It was a barnstormer. It was an old biplane, a typical barnstorming airplane, just the one person in it. He saw me, and he made a turn back the other way, and he waved. I could see that long white scarf, and it just looked so exciting, and I immediately compared his position with mine. There he was, 500 or 1,000 feet up in the air—that nice, fresh air—and here I was down here in this dust and heat and the fertilizer. I really decided at that moment—and it never left me—that someday I was going to be an aviator.

John T. Mason Jr.: That really was a dramatic moment.

Admiral Martin: It was really, and my intense interest in aviation, my commitment, really started then.

John T. Mason Jr.: Up to that point, I suppose you hadn't thought of a career of any kind, had you?

Admiral Martin: Not too much. My father wanted me to stay with him, of course.

John T. Mason Jr.: Were there other children in the family?

Admiral Martin: Yes, I had an older sister and a younger sister, and they still live. I was the only son. There had been doctors in the family, and he wanted me to be a doctor.

In the meantime, I read all the books about aviation, and I was intrigued with naval aviation, because it offered such a variety. They had small planes and large planes, land planes, seaplanes, lighter than air. And the thing that really intrigued me was the aircraft carrier. To fly on and off an aircraft carrier, I thought, would be the most exciting thing that a person could do.

John T. Mason Jr.: There was only one aircraft carrier in existence at that time?

Admiral Martin: Yes, there was. They were at that point just coming out. I guess it was just about the time I was coming out of high school.

John T. Mason Jr.: The old *Ranger*, wasn't it?

Admiral Martin: No, the *Langley* was the very first one.[*]

When I was finishing high school and it came time to go to college, which my older sister insisted that I do, Father said that I was to be a doctor. So I went to the University of Oklahoma the first year as a freshman and then to the University of Missouri the second year as a sophomore.

John T. Mason Jr.: Why did you switch, because there was more opportunity for pre-medical?

Admiral Martin: To be closer to home for one reason, and also I had some friends that were in the University of Missouri that I liked to be with. Father was sending me enough money to go to school but not enough money to go out to the airfield on weekends (they had little airfields—grass strips—at both of them) to fly.

John T. Mason Jr.: Probably smart—he kept you on a taut rein, right?

Admiral Martin: Yes, he did. I worked on weekends, at night, first in the laundry at the University of Oklahoma, to get extra money. As a sophomore at the University of Missouri, I worked at a drugstore at night delivering orders to the fraternity and sorority houses, to get the money to fly on weekends. In the spring of my sophomore year, I had a long talk with Dad about my going into naval aviation. The congressman from our district was a very good friend Dewey Short.[†] His family had been a close friend of my family.

John T. Mason Jr.: I knew Dewey Short.

---

[*] USS *Langley* (CV-1) was originally commissioned as the collier *Jupiter* (AC-3) in 1913 with Commander Joseph M. Reeves, USN, in command. She was later converted to the U.S. Navy's first aircraft carrier. She was commissioned as the *Langley* in 1922 with Commander Kenneth Whiting, USN, in command. USS *Lexington* CV-2) was commissioned 14 December 1927. USS *Saratoga* (CV-3), a *Lexington*-class aircraft carrier, was commissioned 16 November 1927.
[†] Dewey J. Short, a Republican from Missouri, served in the House of Representatives from 1929 to 1931 and from 1935 to 1957.

Admiral Martin: He was a remarkable man, still living, and he comes out here frequently.*

I asked Dad if he would write to Dewey and back me up on this to get an appointment. Dad said, "No, I really want you to be a doctor." So I wrote to Dewey Short, and Dewey came back, as I expected, and said, "If your father is supporting you in this, I'll make sure you get an appointment. I can give you a West Point appointment outright, but if you want to go to the Naval Academy, you will have to take the competitive examination." So I took the competitive exams, barely passed them, but that was the beginning.

John T. Mason Jr.: What was the attitude of your mother?

Admiral Martin: Mother preferred that I be a doctor. She really didn't want me to get into the military. I think mothers are usually this way; they don't want their sons to get into the more dangerous things.

John T. Mason Jr.: Especially when it means flying.

Admiral Martin: Yes, especially. So, as I say, I took the competitive exams, and I barely passed them.

John T. Mason Jr.: Were you able to assure Dewey Short that your father would back you?

Admiral Martin: No, I wasn't, but Dewey promised me that if I would take the competitive exams and pass them, I would probably get an appointment. So I did, and that was the beginning. I finished the year at the University of Missouri. Then I heard that I was supposed to enter the Naval Academy about a week or so after they had started accepting people. But I was so eager to get over there that I hitchhiked from Missouri to Washington, D.C., early, and that gave me a chance to look around Washington. That

---

* Short died at age 81 on 19 November 1979, three weeks after this interview.

was in 1930. I was so eager to look at Annapolis that I went on over. I found some of my friends who had been in prep school back in Columbia, Missouri, were there to go in the first day of acceptance.* It was suggested that I might be able to enter that first day. I inquired, and, yes, I could, so I entered that first day.

John T. Mason Jr.: You had more than the equivalent of prep school in that you had two years of university.

Admiral Martin: Well, that's a maturing experience, but I must say that there was no math involved in it, and a premed course is not really good preparation for the Naval Academy. That's another reason that I barely passed the exams.

To go back on that first day, I was skinny then. I had been out for the cross-country team at the university and was working late at night and studying quite a bit, and I was very skinny. I weighed about 129 pounds.

John T. Mason Jr.: You were underweight?

Admiral Martin: Yes. The medical board accepted me only on the provision that I gain eight pounds from that time until the beginning of the academic year. I gained 12 pounds.

John T. Mason Jr.: You must have drunk milk with each meal.

Admiral Martin: The Naval Academy has its own dairy, and that cold milk was so good, and I was having to go to bed. You know, you turn out the lights at a specified time, and I was getting more sleep and more of the right kind of nourishment, and so I gained 12 pounds. Then I thought I was big enough to go out for football, which I tried. My second day I got hit by two people much larger than I was. As a matter of fact, one was

---

* The University of Missouri is at Columbia.

Butch Harbold, who is at the Naval Academy now, a classmate of mine.* Johnny Waybright was the other.† They were about to collide, and I was in the middle. I spent a little time at the hospital, and I was advised then by the medical people that I should stay out of contact sports until I had gotten bigger and stronger. They strongly advised that I go out for the swimming team. This I did, and that was very good; later it saved my life on a couple of occasions.

So there is not too much outside of the normal routine for me at the Naval Academy.

John T. Mason Jr.: How did you take to the routine and the regimen and all that?

Admiral Martin: I enjoyed it. I certainly enjoyed it; I could see the reason for it, and everything was so new. It was then that I began to see why a naval aviator should be a naval officer first, and this is what naval aviation teaches us. To get all of this background that you would get at the Naval Academy, I could see would be very helpful no matter what.

John T. Mason Jr.: Engineering and those things?

Admiral Martin: Yes. I did not find the course easy; I had to work very hard. I think it was because my little high school back in the Ozark hills of Missouri hadn't had too much math and science.

John T. Mason Jr.: They didn't in those days; I know from my own experience.

Admiral Martin: And then the two years of college had somewhat dimmed my memory of what I had learned, because the premed course had absolutely nothing that contributed to the Naval Academy course. But despite working very hard and studying very hard, I

---

* Midshipman Robert P. Harbold Jr., USN, was a 200-pounder who participated in football, lacrosse, and boxing at the Naval Academy.
† Midshipman John J. Waybright, USN.

enjoyed it. I enjoyed the second year much more than the first; the third year was even better.

I was put on report the first day I was in the Naval Academy for "indecent exposure." My roommate and I were changing clothes, getting out of civilian clothes into the white works uniform, and we were too close to the window which overlooked the park. An upperclassman saw us and put us on report. So that was my introduction to demerits.

John T. Mason Jr.: How many demerits does one get for that?

Admiral Martin: I think we got ten each. I forget exactly. The man who put us on report was a second classman. He became a very good friend later, but at the time I thought he was too picayune.

The rest of the four years at the Naval Academy was enjoyable hard work.

John T. Mason Jr.: Was there much hazing at that time?

Admiral Martin: Yes, there was a lot of it the first year. This was back when there was a belief that your plebe year should put all of the plebes at the same common denominator.[*] No matter what their background was, whether they were affluent or the underprivileged, they tried to give them all the same experience so that they would come out equal. I think it was a strengthening thing. The class who had all gone through the same thing came out of it very close. And my class has been very, very close from the very beginning—good friends.

I think my last year was the most enjoyable, but I was very surprised that they made me a two-striper. I was told that the reason they made me a two-striper—a platoon commander—was that they were going to put me in a platoon which needed a little bit of discipline, and that they would probably do everything that I asked them to do because I was one of them.

---

[*] A midshipman in his or her first year is called a plebe; second year, youngster or third classman; third year, second classman; fourth year, first classman.

On graduation—

John T. Mason Jr.: First go back and tell me about your summer experiences there, the cruises and so forth.

Admiral Martin: Well, the first summer was a wonderful cruise. We were on two battleships, the *Arkansas* and the *Wyoming*.* At about halfway across there was a ship in distress. It turned out that Sir Hubert Wilkins was trying to take a submarine under the ice to the North Pole.† The submarine was in trouble. They left the *Arkansas*, that I was aboard, to stay with them until they solved their problem, or to take them aboard. It was impossible for them to put the submarine back into operating condition, so we spent four or five days more than we had anticipated at sea, towing this submarine back to England.

John T. Mason Jr.: It must have been thrilling for the midshipmen, however, wasn't it?

Admiral Martin: Well, it was rough as the dickens. I was seasick, and many of my friends were seasick. It was a very rough time in the North Atlantic. We were missing some time at a very interesting port. We were going in to Scotland, and the port was a very short distance from Loch Lomond. I made side trips to Edinburgh, and then the cruise went to Copenhagen and from there, side trips down to Germany, into Berlin. It was later that we realized that the Hitler movement had already begun.‡ Then we came back around through the English Channel to Cadiz, Spain. From there side trips to

---

* USS *Arkansas* (BB-33), lead battleship of her class, was commissioned 17 September 1912. Following modernization in 1925-26 she had a standard displacement of 26,100 tons, was 562 feet long and 106 feet in the beam. USS *Wyoming* (BB-32) was commissioned as a battleship in 1912 and served in that role until being demilitarized as a result of the 1930 London Treaty on the limitation of naval armaments. She was redesignated a miscellaneous auxiliary, AG-17, on 1 July 1931 and thereafter served into the mid-1940s as a training ship for gunnery and for midshipman cruises.
† Sir Hubert Wilkins (1888-1958) was a noted British explorer. In 1931 he attempted operations in the Arctic in an ice-cutting submarine named *Nautilus*. As the USS *O-12* (SS-73), she had been commissioned by the U.S. Navy in 1918. She was decommissioned in 1924 and struck from the Navy List in 1930. While on the Wilkins expedition she foundered in mid-June of 1931. She had to be rescued by the USS *Wyoming* (BB-32) and was towed to Queenstown, Northern Ireland. After her ill-fated service as a civilian submarine, the *Nautilus* was returned to the Navy and sunk in a Norwegian fjord on 20 November 1931.
‡ Adolf Hitler was Chancellor of Germany from 1933 until his death by suicide on 30 April 1945.

Seville and from there over to Morocco. Those were the only ports that we hit, but they were very interesting ports. It was an extremely broadening experience.

John T. Mason Jr.: The advent of the Depression hadn't yet affected the cruises, had it?[*]

Admiral Martin: No, they hadn't been affected.

John T. Mason Jr.: Would you comment on the broadening experience of a summer cruise—this sort of thing of introducing you to Europe and other places?

Admiral Martin: Of course, the experiences aboard the ship were very valuable, too, because on your first cruise you were doing the duties of the enlisted men, which I think is extremely valuable. To go into foreign ports and observe the different customs, to take a stab at their language, is also valuable. You would practice it before you would go in there. It is strange how knowing just a few of the common words and phrases you could strike up a conversation and actually form some interesting acquaintances in those countries.

John T. Mason Jr.: What sort of preparation did you have in advance on the customs?

Admiral Martin: As I recall, before we would go into a port they would give us a mimeographed brochure which gave you the information you needed to know on the money exchange, the customs of the people. Before we went into Spain, for example, we were cautioned about the water, which gave us an excuse to have some wine and bottled soft drinks. They were very broad: the points of interest, the libraries, the works of art, and the things they thought would be valuable for us to see, and some things not cultural—like the bullfights in Spain, and that was an experience.

---

[*] Following the crash of the New York Stock Exchange in late October 1929, the United States was plunged into the Great Depression, from which it did not recover until the nation geared up for World War II at the beginning of the 1940s. The Depression was marked by high unemployment and many business failures.

John T. Mason Jr.: You were, in effect, minor ambassadors, weren't you?

Admiral Martin: Yes, we were cautioned on that and advised that not only our Naval Academy was going to be judged by the way we deported ourselves, but our ship as a whole, and it takes only a few who don't have good behavior to give the entire crew a bad name, but also that we were, as you say, young ambassadors or our country, and in many cases our country would be judged on how we presented ourselves. I think most of us took that very seriously. We did try to form friendships and some very interesting friendships—some that I continued to correspond with after I got back.

John T. Mason Jr.: You were very privileged, too, were you not, in meeting some of the nicer people at these ports, they were entertaining you?

Admiral Martin: Yes, they were, and I think that was an introduction to the responsibilities that come later on in life. As you advance, you get into situations where your diplomatic duties are almost as important as your naval duties. This was certainly true when I had the Sixth Fleet.* About half of the job included contacts with important people, and this is something which my wife handled beautifully, because she had language which were very helpful, and she knew how to entertain. Those early beginnings—the next time you are in a situation like that, you feel more at ease. I think it's like almost anything else, just the experience and breaking in and dealing with people who do not speak your language, who have different customs, and so on, to have a respect for their customs. It becomes a mutual respect, and that is where friendships begin, and some of them are very lasting.

John T. Mason Jr.: Did you have any instruction on board the battleship? Were any of the faculty members from the academy with you?

Admiral Martin: Yes, we did. There were academic sessions that were related in most cases to the practical aspects of what we were taking. We learned something about the

---

* Vice Admiral Martin commanded the Sixth Fleet from 10 April 1967 to 14 August 1968.

boiler rooms, the firerooms, before we would go down there. It was a good balance of the introduction through the academics of the technical side of the practical things you were doing. This was true in the engineering areas, the gunnery areas, the fire control, the damage control, in addition, of course, to the seamanship and the ship handling and so on. I thought it was very well balanced.

John T. Mason Jr.: Did this heighten your interest in becoming a sailor?

Admiral Martin: Well, I knew I was going to like it. It wasn't contributing to my primary interest in aviation, but I knew that if I was going to be a carrier aviator I had to know the ship side of the thing too. I was very good about it. I kept my journal. I did it all myself. I climbed through the double bottoms and made my own drawings. I thought it was very valuable, that it was a good practical introduction to life at sea, life aboard a ship.

John T. Mason Jr.: That experience with the whole body of midshipmen on board a battleship is quite different from what the midshipmen now do. Would you comment on that.

Admiral Martin: It is.

John T. Mason Jr.: Now their training is much more specialized.

Admiral Martin: I really can't say. The situation today I am not too familiar with.

John T. Mason Jr.: Some of them go to submarines, some of the go to destroyers or cruisers.

Admiral Martin: I guess you are right; there is a need for specialization now, which we didn't get too much of. We were introduced to all phases of it, and we were expected to be able to take over. This was basic learning of what the crew does and what the senior petty officers would do, which would give you the basis for a junior officer when you go out.

In our second summer we had an aviation period; we went around to the bases. We didn't have the cruise to Europe.

John T. Mason Jr.: You had experience with seaplanes?

Admiral Martin: Yes, we had them right at the academy. It was termed aviation summer, which was the general aspect of it.

John T. Mason Jr.: You didn't really learn a great deal from it, did you?

Admiral Martin: No, not a great deal. You became familiar with being up in an airplane other than the airliners, but it was informative. We had some very good instructors. I remember there was one called Artie Doyle, who later became a three-star admiral.[*] He was a very good instructor, and those who showed an interest in it he would go out of his way to talk to you about aviation and familiarize you with it and try to keep your interest.

I thought it was a very good summer, and, of course, the second classmen that summer were more or less running the organization—the Naval Academy. We were indoctrinating the plebes, giving them a little taste of what we had had when we were plebes. It was a very good summer, which added at that level to the learning that we were going to need as junior officers when we got out.

My last year at the Naval Academy was my most enjoyable one and one in which I had responsibilities which I enjoyed.

John T. Mason Jr.: What abut the cruise that came after aviation summer?

Admiral Martin: The first class cruise was aboard the *Wyoming*, and we went to the Madeira Islands for about four days and then back to Gloucester, Massachusetts, and to Newport, Rhode Island. Of course, on that cruise we were taking the places of junior

---

[*] Lieutenant Austin K. Doyle, USN.

officer and were treated as such so far as our responsibilities were concerned, both on the ship and our responsibilities ashore. It was very good training for the junior officer level. The social events in Newport were outstanding. We got there just in the middle of their busiest social season, and so we were invited to some beautiful homes and some beautiful social occasions. It was very enjoyable.

Then, as I say, my last academic year at the academy, I was a platoon commander. I think that might have helped to keep me out of trouble and taught me a lesson that I was able to use later—that if you have someone, a sailor who is inclined to get into trouble, if you give him some responsibilities, that frequently straightens him out. I knew of one sailor who was terrible as a fireman. He was very smart and always passed his exams. When we finally made him a third-class petty officer, that responsibility straightened him out. I think that was similar to the experience I had that last year, and I was able to stay out of trouble with the executive department.

John T. Mason Jr.: You mean you didn't go over the wall?

Admiral Martin: No, I didn't go over the wall, and I don't think I got any demerits at all my last year there. Maybe it was because I was so busy with some of my good friends who were in my platoon as I was trying to keep them from getting into trouble.

John T. Mason Jr.: At that stage how much time were you allowed out of the academy? How much time did you have in town?

Admiral Martin: Much more. The plebe year was very constraining, of course, and each year would give you more liberties and on weekend later hours for tattoo.* Just a general loosening up, which I thoroughly enjoyed. My last year had as much liberty as I wanted.

John T. Mason Jr.: What did you do for the holiday vacations, Christmas vacation, did you go home?

---

* Tattoo is a warning sounded shortly before the lights go out at night at taps.

Admiral Martin: I'd go home, back to Missouri, on the long vacations. The shorter ones like Thanksgiving and Easter I had friends in the area, girlfriends, who would invite me into their homes. At times when there was enough time I would go back to my home in Missouri.

John T. Mason Jr.: In that day it was by train, was it not?

Admiral Martin: No, there was an airline that would take me from St. Louis down to Springfield, Missouri, our nearest airport. It was a Ford Trimotor.[*] It was pretty primitive, didn't seem so to me at the time. It was very exciting, and the last time I went back, the senior pilot, knowing I was interested in aviation, let me come up into the cockpit and showed me all about it. It was possible to fly home at that time.

John T. Mason Jr.: Did you have any relations with the superintendents during your period there? Tommy Hart was there part of the time.[†]

Admiral Martin: Yes, he was. First it was S. S. Robison, then Tommy Hart.[‡] I had a very early experience; I was put on report for having sideburns.

John T. Mason Jr.: Sideburns?

Admiral Martin: They weren't really sideburns, but they were a little thicker than you were supposed to have. They came down about midway of my ear, and I had to go see

---

[*] The Ford Trimotor aircraft, nicknamed the "The Tin Goose," was designed to bring airline travel to the public. To overcome concerns of engine reliability, industrialist Henry Ford specified three engines and added features for passenger comfort, such as an enclosed cabin. Ford Motor Company built 199 Trimotors from 1926 to 1933.

[†] Rear Admiral Thomas C. Hart, USN, was superintendent of the Naval Academy from May 1931 to June 1934. His oral history is in the Columbia University collection.

[‡] Rear Admiral Samuel S. Robison, USN, served as superintendent of the Naval Academy from June 1928 to May 1931.

the executive officer, who was W. W. Smith, Commander Smith.* He asked me if I was trying to look like Captain P. V. H. Weems.† You know the name?

John T. Mason Jr.: Pappy Weems! I knew him.

Admiral Martin: A man I greatly admired. He was different. What a talented man he was; he taught Lindbergh his navigation.‡ Anyway, off came the sideburns, which meant that I was almost shaven above the ears. But that was back when it was desired that the hair be very short. Crew cuts were fine and were usually what men wore at that time. As for running into problems with the superintendent or commandant, no. I saw them frequently. I was in both of their quarters at what we would call a tea fight on Sunday afternoons, but I held them in awe as I held even ensigns in awe at that time. I had no problems with the executive department. I learned early to stay out of trouble.

John T. Mason Jr.: Now tell me about the graduation and the events surrounding that and your assignment to the *Idaho*.

Admiral Martin: The *Idaho* was my first assignment.

John T. Mason Jr.: Was this your choice?

Admiral Martin: Yes, I preferred a battleship, because even at that time we were operating small seaplanes from battleships and cruisers, and I wanted a battleship or cruiser where I could get close to aviation. I was assigned to the *Idaho*, which was a

---

* Commander William Ward "Poco" Smith, USN.
† Lieutenant Commander Philip Van Horn Weems, USN, had graduated from the Naval Academy in the class of 1912 and retired in 1933 as a captain. He was later recalled to active duty in 1942-46 and 1960-61. He was an expert in navigation and ran his own navigation business in Annapolis while not serving in the Navy. He died in 1979.
‡ Charles A. Lindbergh became a national hero when he made the first solo flight across the Atlantic Ocean in May 1927. The light cruiser *Memphis* (CL-13) brought Lindbergh and his plane back to the United States, arriving at the Washington Navy Yard on 11 June.

complete modernization program at Newport News.*

I will never forget how disappointed I was the first time I saw her. She was in the Navy yard, and the whole topside was painted with red lead paint, couldn't see any of that nice gray anywhere.† They were doing things with the turrets, and the guns were not even parallel with each other; they were all askew. There was so much painting and welding going on that we couldn't live aboard. We lived aboard an auxiliary ship which served as a barracks until the *Idaho* was ready for its shakedown after this complete modernization.‡ As I recall, that modernization was so very extensive and expensive—it cost $12 million, which was a lot of money at that time.

John T. Mason Jr.: Horrendous! Well, it was equipped with blisters for torpedo protection?

Admiral Martin: Yes, they put blisters on for protection against torpedoes. They put in an entirely new power plant, and they put in the very latest fire control system and some instruments that were forerunners of the computer. It was a complete overhaul, and her shakedown cruise was almost like for a new ship. We went to Guantánamo Bay, went through all the exercises of the day.§

John T. Mason Jr.: Who was your skipper?

Admiral Martin: Captain Forde Todd was the first one, and the exec was Dallas Laizure.** After a year, when we had left the Atlantic for the Pacific, our captain was

---

* USS *Idaho* (BB-42), a *New Mexico*-class battleship, was commissioned 24 March 1919. She was modernized at the Norfolk Navy Yard from 1931 to 1934. Among the most noticeable changes was the replacement of her cage masts with a tower bridge. As modernized, her standard displacement was 35,000 tons. She was 624 feet long and 106 feet in the beam, and maximum draft of 31 feet. Her top speed was 22 knots. She was armed with 12 14-inch guns, 12 5-inch broadside guns, and 8 5-inch antiaircraft guns. She was eventually decommissioned in 1946, following World War II service.
† Red lead is the nickname for an orange-colored anti-corrosive primer paint applied to bare metal before the regular paint is put on.
‡ The modernization of the *Idaho* lasted from September 1931 to October 1934. Shakedown is the term for a period of crew training for a new ship—in this case a substantially rebuilt ship with a new crew.
§ Guantanamo Bay, on the south coast of Cuba, near the eastern end of the island, for many years provided a fleet anchorage and training area for U.S. Navy ships.
** Captain Forde A. Todd, USN; Commander Dallas C. Laizure, USN.

Arthur Curtiss Stott, a wonderful man. It was at that time our exec was Laizure; under Todd it was Leland Jordan.*

My experience on the battleship was what you would expect of any junior officer—nothing really exceptional to it, but every time I got a chance to fly in the back seat, I would do it. So I went through all of the departments.

John T. Mason Jr.: Did you get encouragement in terms of you prospective career in aviation?

Admiral Martin: Yes, here again the senior aviator was Lieutenant Artie Doyle.

John T. Mason Jr.: Was he as dynamic at that time as he was later on?

Admiral Martin: Very much so, and a practical joker who almost gave our exec Jordan ulcers, and ulcers on his ulcers. He and Paul Ramsey and Emerson Fawkes and Ford Taylor were in the aviation department, and I thought all of them were very classy aviators.†

John T. Mason Jr.: It was very fortunate, wasn't it, to get thrown in with a crew like that?

Admiral Martin: Indeed it was, because I was to see them all later on in my career, especially Doyle and more especially Ramsey. I was Paul Ramsey's exec on two occasions and his assistant when he was Deputy Chief of Naval Operations for Air.‡ Ford Taylor was also a very humorous fellow, and there was never a dull moment for the junior officers on the *Idaho*, because between Doyle and Ramsey and Taylor there was some practical joke always happening. On the long cruises and the times away from home in the States, there was always a lot of humor and things occurring that they would start, which would relieve the situation.

---

* Commander Leland Jordan Jr., USN.
† Lieutenant (junior grade) Paul H. Ramsey, USN; Lieutenant (junior grade) Emerson E. Fawkes, USN; Lieutenant (junior grade) Ford N. Taylor Jr., USN.
‡ Vice Admiral Paul H. Ramsey, USN, served as Deputy Chief of Naval Operations (Air) from 31 March 1965 to 1 October 1966.

I applied for aviation. At that time my class was not permitted to go into aviation or submarines immediately after graduation from the Naval Academy.

John T. Mason Jr.: What was the time period—three years?

Admiral Martin: Two years. Also, we were not permitted to marry during those two years. There is an interesting statistic on that. As I recall, my class ran a study of this: 85% of the class would have married on graduation, if they had been permitted. At the end of two years, when they could marry, 85% did marry, but only 10% did marry the girl they would have married two years before.

John T. Mason Jr.: And that was precisely the reason for the regulation.

Admiral Martin: It sort of proved the value of the rule—that young men getting out of the Naval Academy should have a couple years' experience before they choose their life partner.

John T. Mason Jr.: And then they would be more likely to choose one who would fit into the Navy picture more readily?

Admiral Martin: I think so. Maybe that isn't true at the Naval Academy today, because the midshipmen get a lot more liberty, a lot more association with the civilian environment than they did at that time, and they are permitted to marry upon graduation. But I still think it's a good idea to wait for a couple of years before marriage.

During my second year aboard the *Idaho* I had, just by luck, a great deal of success in controlling the main battery. It was called spot one; it was in the foremast, where they had big binoculars, and they would actually visually control the fire of the main battery. I had had such good success at it filling in for Lieutenant Whelchel, who was ill that day. This was Billick Whelchel; he had been a football player, and he was the football coach aboard ship.* He and his assistant were both ill, and so on the day of the

---

* Lieutenant John E. Whelchel, USN.

annual battle practice I had control of the main battery fire. We did very well, so well that the commanding officer of the ship would not forward my application for aviation. He thought it was best for me that I stay, so I stayed for the third year. It was a disappointment to me, but I don't think it hurt me too much later on. So I had three years on the battleship before I was permitted to go on to aviation.

John T. Mason Jr.: They used planes for spotting for gunnery practice, did they not?

Admiral Martin: Yes, they did, for scouting and for spotting fire.

John T. Mason Jr.: What was the retrieval of the planes?

Admiral Martin: The system was called cast recovery.* The battleships and the cruisers that had aircraft had what was called the aviation crane, which was near the deck edge. It was a big, high-capacity crane which would swing out from the edge of the ship and would tow, on cable, a sled which had a wire netting on the end of it. The idea was for the seaplane to land in such a way that it would be able to taxi up while the ship was making a turn into the wind. The plane would taxi up at high speed onto the sled, cut the gun. Then there was a hook on the bottom of the float that would catch in the wire netting, and at this point the ship was pulling the sled while also pulling the plane. As I recall now, the sled was towed by a boom that stuck out there. Then the crane would swing out, lowering its hook on the cable, catch the wire that was intended for hoisting the plane, and hoist it out of the water, and aboard and up onto the catapult. There was one catapult on both the upper and the lower on the top of the turret so they could swing around. It was a nifty idea.

John T. Mason Jr.: It sounds rather complicated, however. Were there any miscarriages?

Admiral Martin: I don't recall that we had any on the *Idaho*. As I say, there were some very fine pilots on there, and they knew how to do that. But it required some skill. It

---

* "Cast" represented the letter C in the phonetic alphabet of the time.

required that the ship be handled correctly, too, especially if you were in a very choppy sea, because the ship would make a turn in such a way as it came out of the turn it would leave a slick behind, which would be smooth. The pilot would land on that slick and taxi up as the ship was going ahead at 12 knots or so and would be up on the sled, cut the gun, and then would catch this wire net that was behind so it could be lifted aboard.

John T. Mason Jr.: In other word, the ship made a landing area for the plane?

Admiral Martin: Exactly. It actually smoothed out the sea temporarily from where it had been in this turn. If they did it exactly right, the pilot would land into the wind and taxi into the wind until it had caught the netting—a very interesting operation.

John T. Mason Jr.: How were the pilots treated on board? Did they stand watch? Had they other duties?

Admiral Martin: Yes, they did. They stood officer of the deck watches, just as the ship's other officers did. They would stand officer of the deck in port and officer of the deck under way, and in some ways the aviation part of their duties had the aspect of extra duty.

John T. Mason Jr.: Secondary duty?

Admiral Martin: I have heard some stories where the aviators didn't fare well, because they were a bother to the first lieutenant who had to clean up the deck after they were brought aboard, things like that. There were some stories that aviators weren't too popular aboard and also where they would sometimes bang up the planes and sometimes bang up part of the ship. But on the *Idaho* it was just a very good ship, and it seemed to me that the commanding officer of the ship, the exec, and all the heads of the departments had appreciation for their aviation unit, and they got along fine.

Shall we now go to flight training?

John T. Mason Jr.: Yes, indeed, flight training down at Pensacola. You finally got your ambition, or it was about to be realized.

Admiral Martin: Well, it was in 1937, in June, that I was in flight training in Pensacola. As you say, this was the realization of my desire from the time I was nine years old, to get into flight training. So I really thoroughly enjoyed flight training.

John T. Mason Jr.: Tell me about the course of study

Admiral Martin: We had about six weeks of indoctrination and the early phases of ground school before we were permitted to take flight training. There were various tests at that time. Of course, the physical exam was much more extensive and demanding with less tolerance than any physical exam you had had up to that time.

John T. Mason Jr.: They could afford to be selective, couldn't they?

Admiral Martin: Very much so. The requirements for the eyes and the whole physical exam were much more rigorous and much more detailed than any previous exam. Also there were some psychological exams that we had, and they used to amuse us, questions like, "When you are in high places, have you ever had the urge to jump off?"

There were some that failed. One of my best friends failed it, because he decided at that point that he really didn't want to be a pilot. He was a junior Marine officer, so when they asked him if he was ever in a high place and wanted to jump off, he said, "Yes, and I did." He was sent home.

Paul Stillwell: Did you have any experience with gliders? Were they using those at that time?

Admiral Martin: No, your instruction prior to solo at that time was in small two-place seaplanes, which I thought was very good, because it kept you in naval aviation, as distinct from other aspects of aviation. It made a lot of sense for other reasons, too, because you were over water. The seaplanes were on the beach, of course, and all of the operating areas were over water. So if you had engine trouble you were on floats, and you could make an emergency landing anyplace; you didn't have to look for a field.

John T. Mason Jr.: You felt more confident?

Admiral Martin: Yes, you did. It was just a very interesting operation. That was the first phase. The second phase was in the smaller land-plane variety, similar to those on the cruisers and battleships, but these were on wheels rather than floats. Actually, the same manufacturer made them. There were a lot of common elements in them.

Then the third squadron of flight training was the big twin-engine seaplanes. They looked awfully big then. Of course, they are awfully small now. They would compare roughly with the NC-4 that was the first ship to cross the Atlantic.[*]

The last squadron was in fighters, high-performance aircraft at that time. We were flying the Boeing aircraft.

John T. Mason Jr.: Dive-bombing was not perfected as a technique at that point, was it?

Admiral Martin: I think the Marines had done some of it. Yes, dive-bombing was a recognized technique, and we did some of it in training.

Now, I have left out one aspect of the training. The first squadron was of small seaplanes. The second squadron was the small land planes but still trainers. The third squadron was land planes that were of combat type. The fourth squadron was the big seaplanes, and the final, the fifth squadron, was instrument flying and the fighters. So there were five squadrons, each one of them with graduated complications and requiring more skill, more skill, and finally building up to actual missions that you would have when you got out to your squadron, whether it was seaplanes or land planes or a carrier.

---

[*] In May 1919 three Navy/Curtiss flying boats—the NC-1, NC-3, and NC-4—set out on a transatlantic flight from Trepassy, Newfoundland, to the Azores. Two of the aircraft dropped out, but the NC-4, whose crew was headed by Lieutenant Commander Albert C. Read, USN, became the first plane to fly nonstop across the Atlantic. See Richard K. Smith, *First Across* (Annapolis: Naval Institute Press, 1973).

John T. Mason Jr.: How many men were enrolled originally in this class?

Admiral Martin: As I recall, there were about 100 in my class, and these were made up of both naval and Marine junior officers and officers who had come in from the civilian side as well. They were taking in aviation cadets at that time; this was the very beginning of the aviation cadet program.*

John T. Mason Jr.: Were there any of the men who had graduated in '33 and didn't get commissions and went in the Army Air Corps and then came back?†

Admiral Martin: Thirty-three was an unusual class, because when they graduated only half the class could be commissioned. The Congress hadn't voted enough money to commission all of them, and the half that didn't get commissions later were offered commissions in about four categories. For example, those who had married in the meanwhile were the last ones they permitted to come in. The Navy finally allowed all of them that wanted to come back in. Some of them had the same desire to fly that I had but weren't offered commissions. They went into the Army, took that course, and became Air Corps pilots.

John T. Mason Jr.: But then I understood that some of them came back into the Navy and had to take a refresher course at Pensacola.

Admiral Martin: They did. It was the year after that when they started coming in; none of them were in my class.

John T. Mason Jr.: What sort of attrition was there in your class?

---

* The aviation cadet program was instituted in 1935. Individuals enlisted in the Naval Reserve, then were trained as aviators and sent to the fleet in cadet status until later being commissioned as officers. In 1939 the program was modified so that individuals were commissioned upon successful completion of flight training.

† As an economy measure, in 1933 only the top half of that year's Naval Academy graduating class received Navy and Marine Corps commissions the year of graduation. Some members of the class were subsequently commissioned in 1934 and 1935. Still others joined the reserve and served on active duty in later years. And some were commissioned in other branches of the service.

Admiral Martin: About 40% to 50% attrition. I was told at the time that they wanted that amount of attrition, because they had enough applicants, and they wanted the best. This, I think, the Naval Academy has done for years and still does. They have many more applicants than they have vacancies, which is a very good thing. They get the very high-caliber applicants. I still do some evaluations for the Naval Academy, so I sort of keep track of that.

There is really nothing that I recall that is so unusual that occurred to me down there.

John T. Mason Jr.: Did you have any downs or anything of that sort?[*]

Admiral Martin: I had no downs until I got into squadron three; this was just before Christmas vacation. Squeak Tuzo was my check pilot instructor, and he was renowned for giving downs.[†] He used to roll two dice, they said, once a month, and if it came up two sixes—boxcars—he would give one up that month. Of course, that wasn't really true, but he was a very tough check pilot. I thought I had flown a good flight on my check, but he gave me a down, he told me later, it was time I was running into trouble. He said, "Martin, you've had no downs up to now, and it's time you had some trouble."

So I got a down, having felt that I had flown enough. So on my next check I got a pilot who was considered the Santa Claus of all check pilots; Conn was his name.[‡] And on that occasion I didn't do anything right. He tried to give me an up, but he had to give me a down. On Christmas leave I went back to Missouri on what they called squadron time. I had to have extra instruction before I took the next check. So that wasn't a very happy Christmas.

John T. Mason Jr.: The psychological factor really got you down, didn't it?

---

[*] A "down" was an unsatisfactory grade given by an instructor during a check flight with a student pilot.
[†] Lieutenant Paul B. Tuzo Jr., USN.
[‡] Lieutenant Lannie Conn, USN.

Admiral Martin: But then I went back, and I had an excellent instructor, a fellow named Ed Quilter; he just died recently.* He was a wonderful instructor, and after I had had six hours of extra instruction from him I had enough confidence that I knew I could fly enough even for Squeak Tuzo. So I did get an up and progressed from squadron three to squadron four in what at that time we called big boats. These were the twin-engine flying boats that were in squadron four. It was a thrilling experience to get into a plane that large, the largest I had been in.

John T. Mason Jr.: Were they the Mars?†

Admiral Martin: No, they were smaller than that. They were on one big float with wing pontoons—small ones at the wingtips, and they had twin engines and were the forerunners of the PBMs and the PBYs that we had later.‡ That was a happy squadron.

John T. Mason Jr.: Did you have any close calls at any time during the training?

Admiral Martin: I had one. Many of the things we practice had to do with precision. One was to cut the engine, take the throttle all the way off, make a 360-degree turn, and land into the wind. You were judged by how smooth a turn you could make and how precisely you would come out on the heading at just the time your hull would hit the water. At exactly the end of the turn you should be hitting the water. I was with a fellow I was very fond of, but it turned out his depth perception wasn't very good. He was a junior Marine officer. We were practicing together. The two of us would go out, and each of us would take half the hour and a half at the controls.

When he was doing his 360-degree turn from 1,000 feet down, he was descending too fast. He still had about 45 degrees to go in the turn when we should have been sitting down. I had to take over the controls on that occasion to keep us from what might have been a crash. Maybe he would have come out of it all right, but this shook him up too.

---

* Lieutenant (junior grade) Edward S. Quilter, USNR.
† The Martin-built PB2M Mars was a four-engine Navy flying boat that first flew in 1942. It was later redesignated JRM.
‡ The PBM Mariner and PBY Catalina were Navy flying boats used in World War II and afterward.

He just hadn't been scanning his instruments and keeping track of his altitude. He was going to make that 360-degree turn whether he was ready or not. That shook us up a little, and we did a lot more practice on that one before we came back. The last ones he did on that were very good, because he was using his altimeter, and he was keeping it lined up with his readings on his heading. That's the only close one I had on that one.

John T. Mason Jr.: You showed that you were quite adept at instrument flying?

Admiral Martin: This is really when I became most interested in instrument flying, because I just realized that after I had finished that course that I wasn't really a capable instrument pilot. This built up after I went to my first squadron, which was the old *Lexington* air group, into dive-bombers.* Every year I would have to re-qualify as an instrument pilot, which meant that I would go up with one of the senior pilots. Of course, they had to be judged also. Finally, the commanding officer would be the one to check the most senior people in the squadron. The pilots who had been out there for some time, who had been graduated years before I had, weren't good instrument pilots either. They considered they were doing very well if they could fly on instruments for just a few minutes without spinning in. We had a hood over us that would simulate instrument flying.

Because of that, I decided then that I was going to become a competent instrument pilot. I concentrated on that full time after I had graduated from flight training, and I was in this dive-bomber outfit on the *Lexington*. When I was ordered back to become a flight instructor at Pensacola, everybody who checked in at that time had to go into primary, basic flight instruction where you were teaching the youngster to solo.† I really didn't want to do that. I stayed on the sick list for about a week until the instrument squadron opened up, so that I could become an instrument instructor.

John T. Mason Jr.: You were dragging your feet.

---

* Lieutenant (junior grade) Martin served in Scouting Squadron Two (VS-2) on board the aircraft carrier *Lexington* (CV-2) from May 1938 to May 1940.
† Lieutenant Martin was an instructor at Pensacola Naval Air Station from August 1940 to February 1941.

Admiral Martin: I know it wasn't an admirable thing to do, but I really was determined to become an instrument instructor and a good instrument pilot. That gave me a very concentrated dosage of instrument flying as I was teaching it. But even there I was permitted to take an airplane from Pensacola, Florida, back to my home in Missouri for the Thanksgiving vacation at the time. I got into an instrument situation which I really wasn't competent to handle, and I was very lucky to get into Memphis without crashing. That further impressed me that if this was going to be my full career, I had better learn to do this well.

John T. Mason Jr.: In order to survive. And did it look like the wave of the future?

Admiral Martin: It did, and I was impressed at the time, because on aircraft carriers we were really not capable of carrying out night missions. We just weren't able to do it. So this became my desire. Also, something that came up during my last year as a flight instructor—radar. That was introduced to us as something that was coming; by that time we had it in our PBYs, and some of the large aircraft had it.[*] This would be 1940-41. It was also in the summer of '41 that two people came out who were being sent around by Admiral John Towers to introduce the naval aviators to what they called altitude instrument flying.[†]

Prior to that time we were doing what we called "needle-ball airspeed." The needle gave you your direction; the ball told you if you were out of a coordinated situation. The ball would slide over to one side and tell you that it was there, and the airspeed was for the climb-out, the cruise at whatever speed you wanted to make. It would give you the position of your nose to see if you were doing it just right. If you were making too much speed, you knew your nose was down for that power setting. If you were making not enough speed, then your nose was up for that power setting. It was not an easy thing to do. It took a long time to accomplish that, whereas with the gyro system the altitude system would permit you to have a gyro horizon, as they called it, and

---

[*] The PBY Catalina was a twin-engine flying boat that performed extensive service before and during World War II. Built by Consolidated, it first entered fleet squadrons in 1936. The PBY-2 model had a wingspan of 104 feet, length of 65 feet, gross weight of 28,400 pounds, and top speed of 178 miles per hour. Cruising speed was 103 mph.
[†] Rear Admiral John H. Towers, USN, was Chief of the Bureau of Aeronautics from 1939 to 1942.

this would give you your attitude as far as your wings level or not—lateral—and also in pitch. If your nose was below that artificial horizon, you were diving.

John T. Mason Jr.: It was a great advantage to know that?

Admiral Martin: Very much easier—also the directional gyro, which was something you could set from you compass and get exact readings.

Some of the aircraft had those instruments in there, but the Navy considered them unreliable and wouldn't permit them to be used.

John T. Mason Jr.: Why were they there then?

Admiral Martin: Because somebody felt that maybe someday it would become reliable, I guess. I really don't know. I couldn't figure it out myself, because it was a thing that was so much better. We did find that if you did preventive maintenance with these instruments that they could become quite reliable. The first squadron I went to after I had become a flight instructor, we started using them. The war was started by this time, and we just took off the masks and started maintaining them and using them. We found that if the gyro instruments had the proper preventive maintenance they were quite reliable.

John T. Mason Jr.: To do that showed great initiative.

Admiral Martin: I wasn't the only one who had that feeling about it. One was a Marine lieutenant colonel, Karl Day, who had been an airline pilot for some time.[*] He had written a book about it and was very good at this sort of thing. The other one was a fellow named Ward Davis, who was a lieutenant commander. Those two people became very well known to naval aviation. They came to Corpus Christi while I was an instructor there and taught us this new system of attitude instrument flying.[†] There were no books then on attitude instrument flying, so during the first year of the war I wrote the

---

[*] Lieutenant Colonel Karl S. Day, USMCR, assigned to the Bureau of Aeronautics. Day eventually retired as a Marine Corps lieutenant general. His oral history is in the Marine Corps collection.
[†] Lieutenant Martin was an instructor at Corpus Christi Naval Air Station from February 1941 to July 1942.

first instruction book on this subject. It was considered to be very good; I named it *Instrument Flying for the Carrier Pilot*, because there were certain aspects of it that were unique to the problems of the aircraft carrier. I submitted it, and the Bureau of Aeronautics published it.

John T. Mason Jr.: This is something you did on your own initiative?

Admiral Martin: Yes, when the war started, I was an instrument flight instructor at Corpus Christi, Texas.

John T. Mason Jr.: Was this what you did immediately upon graduation—upon getting your wings?*

Admiral Martin: I got my wings and went to a dive-bomber squadron on the old *Lexington*.†

John T. Mason Jr.: Was King there then?

Admiral Martin: He was Commander Aircraft Battle Force, called ComAirBatFor, and he was real tough.‡ He came out with an order that nobody would ground-loop. A ground loop is rather an ordinary thing. When you are landing, if you are a little out of the wind and you don't handle it just right, the wind will catch one wing and put it up, and it will drag the other wing. Of course, we were flying biplanes, you see, and frequently you'd go into a loop. It didn't do very much damage usually, but it was rather an ignoble thing to do. So the order came: "No more ground loops."

John T. Mason Jr.: But it wasn't done intentionally, was it?

---

* Lieutenant (junior grade) Martin was designated a naval aviator in 1938.
† USS *Lexington* CV-2) was commissioned 14 December 1927. She had a standard displacement of 33,000 tons, was 888 feet long, 106 feet in the beam, an extreme width of 130 feet on the flight deck, and had a draft of 24 feet. She had a top speed of 33.5 knots and could accommodate approximately 60-70 aircraft. She was originally armed with eight 8-inch guns that were later removed in World War II.
‡ Vice Admiral Ernest J. King, USN, served as Commander Aircraft Battle Force from January 1938 to June 1939. During World War II he was Chief of Naval Operations and Commander in Chief U.S. Fleet.

Admiral Martin: Oh, no, that's why it was such an unusual order to tell you that you weren't going to do it. It was always accidental.

After two and a half years on the *Lexington*, then I went back to become an instrument instructor.[*]

John T. Mason Jr.: Now, with that time on the *Lexington*, can you evaluate the contribution those experiences made in the development of your own career?

Admiral Martin: Well, it was all there except the ability to do it at night or in bad weather. I thought the experience for training, for bringing us up as competent dive-bombers, was very good for daytime. But for nighttime it really bothered me; it bugged me that we weren't able to do it in bad weather or at night. I had already decided when I was in flight training that this was what I wanted to specialize in. Then, when I went back as a flight instructor, I was able to carry on that specialty and become a competent instrument flier.

John T. Mason Jr.: When you were with the dive-bombers had the Norden bombsight come in use?[†]

Admiral Martin: Yes, they were in the torpedo planes at that time. The torpedo planes were actually using that Norden sight, and they worked out the tactics for horizontal bombing. I really don't know of any instance where it was actually used during the war. Next to making a torpedo attack, it was the most dangerous tactic you could use. In horizontal bombing you had to stay very carefully at the same altitude, same speed, and you were very vulnerable to antiaircraft fire. I think a torpedo attack is even more vulnerable, because you're getting so much closer in, and you are at altitudes and speeds that they know. It's not difficult to determine what the altitude and speed are, because you are just 250 feet above the water. That's why, when later I had a torpedo squadron, I

---

[*] Martin was a member of Scouting Two (VS-2) while on board the *Lexington*.
[†] The Norden bombsight was a precision optical device developed in the early 1930s by Carl L. Norden, a civilian consultant employed by the Navy, together with Lieutenant Frederick L. Entwistle, USN. Its gyro-stabilized automatic pilot kept the bomber straight and level during bomb runs. It was used in both Navy and Army bombers in the 1930s and 1940s.

didn't drop any torpedoes except on one occasion. That wasn't the only reason; the torpedoes weren't reliable either.

John T. Mason Jr.: You were talking about that period when you were with the *Lexington* and the dive-bombers.

Admiral Martin: I would say that because of this drive I had toward night operations and bad-weather operations from the aircraft carriers, that the principal thing in my thinking and tactics at that time, and my effort even then, was to get a little capability—just enough to do it on occasion—to be able to defend the force, if that was the principal thing that was needed. Or if there were targets of opportunity, especially the ones that are found in the last day of the daytime missions that they come back, and they tell you about a "fat target," to be unable to go out and strike that at night bothered me

So I started writing my ideas as to what the tactics would be to just introduce it and just the basic fundamentals of a standard night attack from a carrier, taking into account the problems of rendezvous, which are more complicated than taking off from a field because there are interruptions. When the airplane goes down on the catapult, there is delay, and you just can't make a rendezvous pattern before departure for the target that is reliable. And there are other aspects of it involving the carrier. It is not going to be where you think it is when you get back—a few things of that kind—not being able to use lights. The ship must be darkened or almost darkened. There are some real complications, and I was thinking these things all through. I wrote my first letter on night tactics that we should be working on while I was in this dive-bomber squadron.

John T. Mason Jr.: You were a lone eagle, so to speak, in this endeavor?

Admiral Martin: Yes. I was not getting very much encouragement, and the fact is I was getting considerable discouragement from some.

John T. Mason Jr.: Didn't the superior officers see the wisdom of this development?

Admiral Martin: Not many of them. On the first proposal I wrote, I would say the first encouragement that I got was at John Towers's level. This was in '42, and after I got back with that dive-bomber squadron, I had asked to be transferred to the command of a torpedo squadron, because they were the only attack aircraft that had radar. We had a few night-fighter detachments at the time—four planes per carrier, no more, and some of them didn't have that.

John T. Mason Jr.: You didn't, up to this point, know much about radar?

Admiral Martin: Not very much, except what it was supposed to do. I was never interested too much in the technicalities, but what they could do operationally was very important to me.

John T. Mason Jr.: There were so few you weren't exposed to it?

Admiral Martin: No, but if by this time you have become a competent instrument pilot and you can fly at night and in bad weather and you know you can train others to do it, then the idea of radar that could provide you with eyes to see through this weather and see through the darkness was just an actual marriage of the two. The things that you could do with just a few pilots who could handle the flight part of it, of taking off, going from A to B, making an attack, and coming back—it just gave you an additional capability that was gong to use the other half of the day.

It would give you some capabilities that were really bonuses—the things that you could do by night by paralyzing an airstrip. We could take off an airplane if we knew there were potholes in the runway that would wreck this aircraft. The Japanese might have been a little more daring than that, but that aircraft could paralyze an airfield as long as he is over it. And there is the idea of keeping their antiaircraft people, everybody at their base, awake all night. A man who has been awake all night isn't going to be as sharp on the guns the next day. So it had some direct effects and some side effects that just looked so very attractive.

John T. Mason Jr.: It seems like a degree of wisdom that was beyond the ordinary. It's the sort of thing that I remember in Jimmy Thach's story—the innovative things that he engaged in because he saw a need.* You were seeing a need.

Admiral Martin: The Thach weave and so on. That's it; he certainly filled that one.

The thought was there, and I think that was valuable to get that information out, to get the proposal out even if it is going to get a down. Just to sow the seed. The next year when I had this torpedo outfit, we were training in Seattle.†

John T. Mason Jr.: Where was that based?

Admiral Martin: It hadn't been determined what carrier it was going out on, although as it later turned out, fortunately, it was going out on the *Enterprise*, where I had been the year before.‡ And these pilots were turning around to go back with me. It was like going back home to go back to the *Enterprise*, because we had such good friends back there, and it was just such a wonderful ship and so tremendously cooperative with the air group. We trained at Seattle, and because we were a "torpedo" squadron we had to practice torpedoes, and we did. We should have been the very best, because by this time they were all competent instrument pilots, and they could fly a path at an altitude and a speed more accurately than those who are not trained for instrument work, because they are used to it. They are used to flying by their instruments and even with dropping those torpedoes under the most careful conditions, I don't think a single one was dropped that was beyond the tolerances of the prescribed method for dropping a torpedo. Out of 30-some-odd, only one ran hot and reasonably normal; it didn't run straight. This was a real discouragement so far as torpedoes are concerned. I determined that we would become extremely good at low-level bombing instead of low-level torpedoing.

---

* The Thach Weave was developed shortly before World War II by Lieutenant Commander John S. Thach, USN, commanding officer of Fighting Squadron Three. It was a means of enabling the F4F Wildcat to counter the better-performing Japanese Zero fighter. Thach, who retired as a four-star admiral, described the origin of the maneuver in his Naval Institute oral history.
† Lieutenant Commander Martin commanded Torpedo Squadron Ten (VT-10), July 1943-July 1944.
‡ USS *Enterprise* (CV-6) was commissioned 12 May 1938. Her World War II history, including extensive coverage of Martin's exploits, is reported in Edward P. Stafford's *The Big E* (Annapolis: Naval Institute Press, 1988). See also Barrett Tillman, *Enterprise* (New York: Simon & Schuster, 2012).

John T. Mason Jr.: You had an alternate. A submariner didn't.

Admiral Martin: That's right, we did, and during the war we were finally given permission to make a predawn attack at Truk. It turned out to be a real classic.

John T. Mason Jr.: What year was this?

Admiral Martin: I think it was February of '44.*

John T. Mason Jr.: Truk was still considered the bastion, wasn't it?

Admiral Martin: Truk was the one that raised terror in everybody's mind, because it was supposed to be heavily defended, and it was. There were 12 planes that went in to Truk from Torpedo Ten. It wasn't a night outfit yet, but we trained at night, and the 12 planes that went in to Truk for the purpose of attacking the shipping that was in Truk lagoon were very careful to note that there might be a hospital ship in there. Each one of the pilots was trained to make repeated attacks until he was sure to get a hit on a ship. The radar displays at that time required an operator to learn it from the beginning. It was a little like learning a new language that you hadn't known one word about before. Because instead of it being a radar plot, looking down on it like a map, this cathode ray tube just gave you indications that there was something out there. After considerable practice, you'd get so that you knew there was a ship out there and approximately its size.

John T. Mason Jr.: You related the blip to the image?

Admiral Martin: Exactly, and this is how we trained, by making repeated runs over the target that we could find. At Truk we did make repeated runs; some of them made as many as four runs. They had two 500-pound bombs; they had a number of 100-pound bombs, I think up to ten, and rockets. In this lagoon there were little hummocks, little

---

* On 17-18 February 1944, planes from nine carriers attacked Truk Atoll in the Carolines chain, and surface combatants later made a circuit around the atoll. All told, U.S. forces destroyed most of Truk's airstrips and sank a number of warships and merchant ships—a total tonnage of some 200,000.

islets that would give a radar return that looked a little like a ship. There were some pilots who realized they were making a run on a hummock at the last minute and wouldn't drop. They would go back and make another run in sequence.

John T. Mason Jr.: This was wasted if they dropped it on a hummock.

Admiral Martin: Exactly, and this explains why 12 planes got 13 confirmed hits—13 ships either sunk or burning and were out of commission.

John T. Mason Jr.: Because they were discriminating in their target.

Admiral Martin: They were, and that's about what you would expect. That number of hits is what you would expect from four or five times the number of day attacks in a similar situation.

John T. Mason Jr.: What about the flak?

Admiral Martin: It was pretty thick, but out of the 12 planes there was only one that was lost, and we are not absolutely certain about that. This is one of the things about night work that adds a lot of the mystery to it; you never see what happens. You deduce it from the information that you have. I can't be sure this man was lost to antiaircraft, but in my own mind am quite certain that he was shot down.

John T. Mason Jr.: You mean you lost a flier?

Admiral Martin: Yes, he was lost, and this is what you would expect from an airplane being hit, and the fire from it was observed.

John T. Mason Jr.: I was interested in what you said about being very certain that they didn't have a hospital ship in the lagoon. You were meticulous about the Geneva Convention?

Admiral Martin: Yes, that's right, and there was one in there.

John T. Mason Jr.: Was it properly lighted?

Admiral Martin: Yes. I wasn't on that strike. I had a broken arm, and I went through tests to see if I could manage the controls. Did you ever hear the name of Tom Hamilton?

John T. Mason Jr.: Yes.

Admiral Martin: Tom Hamilton was the exec of the ship, and he put me up in the cockpit to see if I could turn the controls.* I couldn't do it well enough to pass his test, so I could not go on that flight. However, it had this added advantage. They were so well trained and the tactics were sufficiently workable that they went out without me—the first time they had ever been out without me at night—and they did a terrific job.

John T. Mason Jr.: They went out without the teacher.

Admiral Martin: Well, that's proof in itself, and that helped along the selling, if you will, of the proposal that we have a night carrier and a night air group.

John T. Mason Jr.: Was this proposal closed by various commanding officers? I think of Mitscher; now, Mitscher was receptive to the idea, wasn't he?†

Admiral Martin: Not initially, no. When I say initially, I am talking about what was written in '42. Now, this classic attack on Truk was really what turned the corner. They began to see. This was a demonstration, you see, and that is really what did it.

John T. Mason Jr.: How ironic that you proposed this and couldn't take part in it.

---

* Commander Thomas J. Hamilton, USN, later rear admiral, is the subject of a Naval Institute oral history.
† Vice Admiral Marc A. Mitscher, USN, served as Commander Task Force 58, the fast carrier task force, in 1944-45.

Admiral Martin: I know. It really broke me up. I hated to miss that attack, but it was a great satisfaction to me that these youngsters were able to carry this thing out so beautifully. It was just that they had become extremely competent pilots in utter darkness and in the worst of weather. And they were the only ones in the whole fleet who had this capability on the carriers at this time. Now, our land-based aircraft were doing instrument work all the time and were very good at it, but the carrier air groups were not at that time. What it took to sell it was a demonstration that first you could train the pilots to do it, and the tactics that we worked out with this crude radar.

For example, when your radar operator says, "I'm over the target, would you give me a mark over the target?" the pilot would say, One alligator, two" and push the pickle, and that was it.* I don't know who thought up "One alligator, two," but it's just the right amount of timing to drop the bomb so that if you are at the proper altitude and on the proper speed, you would hit the waterline, which is where you want it to explode. If you hit at the waterline, a lot of water is going to get in there quickly. If that's your point of aim, and let's say you drop a fraction of a second too early, you are still going to have a hit, or if you drop a fraction of a second late, you are still going to get a hit on the ship. But to do the damage and get the water inside that ship so it will sink, you must have the aiming point at the waterline, as that is the most effective moment.

John T. Mason Jr.: What kind of action, what kind of protest, did naval aviation offer in terms of the defective torpedoes?

Admiral Martin: I really don't know. Everybody was complaining about them.

John T. Mason Jr.: The submariners certainly did.

Admiral Martin: Yes, and the aerial torpedo was even worse.

John T. Mason Jr.: It was the same breed, wasn't it?

---

* Martin was flying a TBF Avenger, a torpedo bomber with a crew of one officer pilot and two enlisted men.

Admiral Martin: Yes, except that the impact of the torpedo hitting the water offered the possibility of more damage than coming out of a torpedo tube, because the impact is considerable from an altitude. I know there was a big effort to improve that torpedo, but to my knowledge it did not come about while the war was going on.

I told you my squadron did drop torpedoes on one occasion; we couldn't talk our superiors out of it. The loading was torpedoes, and we took them and making a run on a destroyer—I think this was Truk as well—the destroyer was outside the lagoon. The ships sunk in the night attack were inside the lagoon. This destroyer outside of the lagoon on which we made a torpedo run—there were nine on that attack, and not one of them ran hot, straight, and normal.

John T. Mason Jr.: How distressing.

Admiral Martin: The dive-bombers came in and got some hits. A good friend of mine got a hit and got sucked down in the same dive. He was in Bombing Ten. He was an all-American basketball player named Stubby Pearson from either Cornell or Fordham, but he was lost of course.*

John T. Mason Jr.: The defective aerial torpedo must have had some effect on the morale of the pilots, did it?

Admiral Martin: There were none of the torpedo pilots that wanted to drop the torpedoes.

John T. Mason Jr.: That's understandable.

Admiral Martin: You know you are really taking great risks to make a torpedo run on a ship.

John T. Mason Jr.: They are risking their life, so they want it to be something effective.

---

* On 30 March 1944 Lieutenant (junior grade) Charles B. Pearson, USNR, was killed while flying an SBD Dauntless in a dive-bombing attack on Japanese destroyer near Palau Island. He was from Dartmouth.

Admiral Martin: That's why we developed the dive-bombing techniques with the torpedo plane, and the torpedo plane fortunately was made by what they called "the Ironworks." The Grumman Company built those planes, and they built them so they were very, very rugged. You could dive-bomb the TBF just like a dive-bomber; it would hold together.*

John T. Mason Jr.: Did this enhance the dive-bombing technique as a result—using the torpedo planes?

Admiral Martin: I don't think it did, because the SBD that we started the war with, and I had flown it—the Douglas Dauntless—the first year of the war.† That was probably the best dive-bomber, so far as the pilot is concerned, that has ever been developed. So I don't think we enhanced the dive-bombing techniques by using it, but the TBF was a good dive-bomber. In fact, when I was shot down in Saipan by antiaircraft, I was in a vertical dive, and that doesn't happen very often. A vertical dive rarely gets hit by antiaircraft, because it presents the people on the antiaircraft gun with the problem of getting straight up. You've got one man controlling an azimuth and another controlling it for elevation, and when you are near the top, neither one knows which way to turn. It is very difficult, and that's why we would try to dive vertically.‡

After the attack on Truk, we began to get other missions on a bad-weather day. For example, going into Hollandia—we went in there under conditions that the other squadrons, the daytime people, were not flying, although they did fly in there when the

---

* The Grumman-built TBF Avenger was the U.S. Navy's standard carrier-based torpedo bomber from mid-1942 through the remainder of World War II. The TBF-1 model had a wingspan of 54 feet, length of 40 feet, gross weight of 15,905 pounds, and top speed of 271 miles per hour. It was armed with one .30-caliber machine gun (two .50 caliber in the TBF-1C). The first TBF-1s reached the fleet in the spring of 1942. The General Motors-built version of the Avenger was designated TBM.
† The Douglas-built SBD Dauntless, which entered fleet squadrons in 1941, was a most successful dive-bomber in the early part of World War II. It was instrumental in the sinking of four Japanese aircraft carriers in the Battle of Midway. The SBD-5 model had the following characteristics: length, 33 feet; wingspan, 42 feet; gross weight, 10,855 pounds; top speed, 245 miles per hour.
‡ This incident was on 13 June 1944. For details, see Stafford, *The Big E*, pages 374-382.

weather was better.* But there was very bad weather in there, and when there was bad weather we would go.

When we were in the South China Sea, when the whole carrier task force was there, we were the ones that went over to Cam Ranh Bay and Pratas Reef.† When the weather was really stinking, that's when we were permitted to go. It opened up a lot of opportunities for us to do what we were trained to do, once we had had that success. Of course, the following year they had approved the proposal of designating at least one carrier as a night carrier, and its air group would be called a group, instead of a wing as they were called at the time. The air group would be designated a night air group. When we went out on that one, we were aboard the night attack carrier *Enterprise*, and our group was called Night Air Group 90. Then we were made up entirely of night-competent pilots.

John T. Mason Jr.: Then that avoided a lot of difficulties, didn't it, I mean, concentrating on one carrier for night operations?

Admiral Martin: It worked out quite well, because we would permit, in the task force, taking over all the night duties would give some relief to the day carriers. Where it would put us when we would operate, that took some experimentation, whether we would operate inside the total task force or operate outside of it. At that time I wasn't too much worried about the carrier division commander's problems. If we got outside the task force, we would try to get back in it by daylight.

There was one period, off Iwo Jima I think, where we had planes in the air constantly, 24 hours a day.‡

John T. Mason Jr.: This was made possible by the night carrier development?

---

* On 22 April 1944, U.S. Army troops invaded Hollandia, New Guinea. The *Enterprise*'s air group provided pre- and post-landing air support. See Stafford, *The Big E*, pages 357-362.
† This operation was in January 1945.
‡ On 19 February 1945, U.S. Marines invaded the island of Iwo Jima, approximately 660 miles south of Tokyo, and captured it in a fierce campaign. The objective was to provide a forward airfield—an emergency landing site—to support the U.S. bomber offensive against Japan.

Admiral Martin: We had airplanes constantly in the air for a week, 176 hours, and the *Enterprise* was operating all night.

John T. Mason Jr.: How did the enemy stand up to this? Did they have night operations that were comparable?

Admiral Martin: They had more capability than we had at night, or at least they were doing more of it. Now, I don't know what their operational losses were. They were operating from airfields that were not getting attacks at night and that sort of thing. Nothing was interfering with their night operations on their bases.

John T. Mason Jr.: They had had some experience prior to the war with night operations, hadn't they?

Admiral Martin: I guess they had. They were doing some of it, and there were some threats at night.

John T. Mason Jr.: The irony of it was this was reported to the people in Washington, but we didn't take any steps.

Admiral Martin: It was known?

John T. Mason Jr.: Yes.

Admiral Martin: Well, they became a threat, and there were bogeys on the screen at night, and that's why Butch O'Hare and John Phillips tried to devise this means of providing some defense against it. You know the story of Butch O'Hare and John Phillips, with Phillips flying the torpedo plane that had radar and taking two fighters with him.* The three would be the night fighter defense, and it was just sort of a last resort really to provide some defense, because even if it had worked as well as you thought it wouldn't be too effective, because the fighters didn't have any radar. They were operating on instructions from the torpedo plane that did have radar. Very early in those experiments Butch got shot down and probably was shot down by the tail gunner in the torpedo plane.† There was a need for defense and a capable defense—one that you knew would work. Some of our night fighter detachments were quite successful in their night defense. There were a number of night shoot-downs before we had the night air group. We weren't the very beginners of the night fighter business. We were the beginning of the night attack.

John T. Mason Jr.: What about the Japanese use of flares? They had exceptional flares, did they not?

Admiral Martin: Yes, and they had a technique that wasn't too bad, of dropping flares on one side of the fleet and making their attacks against the silhouettes on the other side. It was not a bad scheme. I just don't think though that at the point their instrumentation and their training of the pilots were good enough to carry it out as well as it might have been.

John T. Mason Jr.: Is it more than a theory that they lost their first-line pilots a little bit earlier down in the Guadalcanal area, and they didn't have sufficient backup?

---

* Lieutenant Commander Edward H. O'Hare, USN, was killed the night of 27 November 1943. He was the pilot of an F6F Hellcat while it flying with a radar-equipped TBF. See Eugene Burns, "Butch O'Hare's Last Flight," *The Saturday Evening Post*, 11 March 1944, page 19, and Steve Ewing and John B. Lundstrom, *Fateful Rendezvous: The Life of Butch O'Hare* (Annapolis: Naval Institute Press, 1997). Lieutenant Commander John L. Phillips Jr., USN, was the commanding officer of Torpedo Six (VT-6) in November 1943, at the time O'Hare was killed. For a participant's account, see Alvin B. Kernan, *Crossing the Line: a Bluejacket's World War II Odyssey* (Annapolis: Naval Institute Press, 1994). Kernan was a crew member of Phillips's plane.

† The Ewing-Lundstrom book asserts that O'Hare was shot down by a Japanese plane, not by tail gunner Kernan.

Admiral Martin: I don't think they did have sufficient backup. By this time, after Midway, they had lost an awful lot of their first-line pilots.* They never got as good again, as they had been at Midway. They weren't wiped out, but they weren't as good.

John T. Mason Jr.: This would bear out, I suppose, Yamamoto's statement that if they got in the war they had to win it within the first year.† I'm not sure this was his statement, but somebody made this statement.

John T. Mason Jr.: Yes, and I don't think he was too far wrong, because they did have very capable pilots when the war started, and they had their carrier wings filled out with them. Their big losses at Midway, and then later, after the "Turkey Shoot," they were almost wiped out of experienced people, but they began to seriously dilute them, I think, after Midway.‡

John T. Mason Jr.: Would you talk about some of the specific operations in which you were involved?

Admiral Martin: Yes, I was involved, about this time when we were operating as a night carrier and providing the all-night fighter defense for the entire task force, and also the night scouting missions and the weather hops and things of that kind.

During that period, the *Enterprise* was operating all night, it had planes in the air, its own planes in the air day and night. At the same time they were making more day landings of other aircraft of the task force than any other carrier. During that seven-day period—I think this is accurate—even during the daylight hours the *Enterprise* had more landings than any other carrier in the task force, because they were designated to take the cripples, the ones that were damaged, and the stragglers, the ones that came in too late to

---

* From 4 to 6 June 1942, U.S. and Japanese naval forces fought a battle northwest of Midway Island in the Pacific. After Japanese bombers had struck the island, carrier-based U.S. dive-bombers attacked and sank the Japanese carriers *Hiryu*, *Soryu*, *Kaga*, and *Akagi* and the cruiser *Mikuma*. U.S. ships lost were the carrier *Yorktown* (CV-5) and the destroyer *Hammann* (DD-412). The battle was both a tactical and strategic victory for U.S. forces.
† Admiral Isoroku Yamamoto, IJN, was Commander in Chief of the Japanese Combined Fleet.
‡ The "Great Marianas Turkey Shoot" took place on 19 June 1944 while U.S. carriers were supporting the invasion of Saipan. That day U.S. planes shot down more than 300 Japanese aircraft.

get aboard during the landing cycle of their own carrier, and they sent them over to the *Enterprise* to land. So that ship during that period was going almost full tilt, day and night. Really, I greatly admired that ship and that crew. They had such ability and such endurance. The commanding officer of the ship would be the CO at night, and his navigator would take the captain's duties on the captain's bridge during the daytime. They had two different teams that were doing this.

John T. Mason Jr.: The same principle as the Third and Fifth fleets?*

Admiral Martin: Very similar.

John T. Mason Jr.: Your experience with the *Enterprise* encompasses almost the whole Pacific War actually, going back to Guadalcanal.

Admiral Martin: The first action we got into was shortly after Midway. I was not in the Midway action. We were designated to go aboard the *Enterprise*. We were in Hawaii, but we got there a little too late to go out on that operation, and so we continued training.† We went out on the next one, and our first combat was at the Battle of Santa Cruz.‡

At that time, there were only two carriers that were operational, the *Enterprise* and the *Hornet*. As we joined up on the *Hornet* just the day before the Battle of Santa Cruz, the *Enterprise* had taken down out of Pearl Harbor several additional airplanes. We even had them hoisted up in the overhead of the hangar deck, and they were intended to replace the losses that the Marines had had at Guadalcanal. Meanwhile, the *Hornet*, before they left the Guadalcanal area, had sent all the replacement aircraft that they could afford over to the Marines. So when we joined up with the *Hornet*, we had nine aircraft that were intended for the Marines, in which case we were to deliver them to the *Hornet*, because they had already delivered them. I was put in charge of that flight to go over

---

* Admiral William F. Halsey, Jr., USN, Commander Third Fleet, March 1943-November 1945. Admiral Raymond A. Spruance, USN, Commander Fifth Fleet, April 1944-September 1945.
† From July 1942 to June 1943, Lieutenant Martin was executive officer of Bombing Squadron 10 (VB-10).
‡ On 26 October 1942, U.S. and Japanese carrier aircraft were involved in the Battle of the Santa Cruz Islands, near the Solomons. The *Enterprise* (CV-6) and *Hornet* (CV-8) faced the Japanese carriers *Shokaku*, *Zuikaku*, *Zuiho*, and *Junyo*. The *Hornet* was sunk as a result of the encounter, and the *Shokaku* badly damaged. Martin was on board the *Hornet* for the battle.

there and take these nine planes and land them on the *Hornet*, which we did. A destroyer was designated to take us back to the *Enterprise*. I remember so well, because we were back there waiting for it, all nine of us. The destroyer was coming up and was almost making its approach on the carrier to stay alongside so we would be sent over on the boatswain's chairs, when the Japanese Fleet was sighted, so this destroyer was told to resume its position in the screen, and we were aboard for the sinking. That's a miserable feeling for a pilot to be aboard a ship. If he's flying, he's got so much to do, and it's so exciting, and he has something that he can do.

John T. Mason Jr.: But here you were just a passenger.

Admiral Martin: Yes, a passenger. It's a miserable thing, and that was a vicious attack, all day long. Very early the *Hornet* got three torpedoes altogether, as I recall, all on the starboard side. It started to list to starboard, and the third hit knocked out, jammed the rudder. It was at full throw. The *Northampton* tried to take the *Hornet* in tow, and it was almost impossible to do. It just wasn't working out; the *Hornet* had lost all power, and at that time we didn't have auxiliary power. Later they put diesels on there to give you auxiliary power to give you lights throughout the ship where you might need them and to put pressure on the fire mains to continue to fight the fires. We were fighting the fires on the *Hornet* by dipping the water from over the side. That's a long way to get water, about 55 feet.

John T. Mason Jr.: With a modern ship that's difficult.

Admiral Martin: It's hard to do, but we were doing it and getting ahead of the fire. The nine of us in the air crew had a job to do, and you don't get so frightened while the attack is going on. Finally, it was realized it was a hopeless situation, and I think the conclusion had been reached that the Japanese probably had a better job of taking the *Hornet* in tow than we did, and we decided to destroy her, and we started abandoning ship. Those who were still fighting the fires stayed on to keep on fighting them, and we got off just before dark onto a destroyer. We were on that destroyer, and late at night the destroyers put several 5-inch shells into the *Hornet* and finally put some torpedoes into her and sank her. She wasn't easy to sink.

John T. Mason Jr.: Just in time, too, was it?

Admiral Martin: Yes, just in time.

John T. Mason Jr.: What destroyer were you on?

Admiral Martin: It was the USS *Russell*—I thought I'd never forget this but almost drew a blank on it. I can see the skipper so well.* I didn't know him well, but he was one hell of a good skipper, and we picked up people that were in the water. A lot of them were so black when they came to the surface from the oil that was still around there, they were hard to find. We stayed around there until it was dark. The Japanese came in on their last attack that day. This destroyer had about 250 injured people, some of them just terribly burned. Somebody saw a movement down there in a blob of oil just as the Japanese were coming in for their last attack. We got this guy aboard, had just gotten him out of the water, when the Japs made their attack. You could see in the last of the sunlight—they are up in the sun, and you could see the reflections—they would push over on their dive, and they were shooting on their way down. And they would keep on shooting, shooting at the escorts as they pulled out across them. This one guy that we just pulled out of the water got a bullet right through the head. After all that, what an unusual situation. We were about to go off and leave there anyway, to his certain death, and getting him aboard, and he got shot right through the head.

John T. Mason Jr.: Fate had ordained that.

Admiral Martin: Yes. But that was our first fire—the Battle of Santa Cruz. Then, as you know, the *Enterprise* was the only carrier (there is a book written about it, and I have it

---

* Lieutenant Commander Glenn R. Hartwig, USN, commanded the destroyer *Russell* (DD-414) from 12 July 1941 to 14 January 1943.

here someplace) the only operational carrier that the United States had at that time, and we would make great efforts to be seen and settled in places to give the impression we were more than one.

From there we went back in to support the Guadalcanal effort, and some of us went into Guadalcanal before we had intended to. I had to go in there, because I couldn't get suction on one tank and couldn't get back across that equatorial front—the equatorial front that rolls across the equator. I couldn't get through there to the carrier. I didn't have enough gas that I could use with the one tank that I couldn't get suction on. So I went in to Guadalcanal.

John T. Mason Jr.: Henderson Field there?*

Admiral Martin: Yes.

John T. Mason Jr.: That was a hairy operation, wasn't it? Wasn't it under fire?

Admiral Martin: Yes, it was, and the Marines at this time were really trigger happy, and I made every turn I could think of, lowered my wheels, made a turn to the right and a turn to the left, and they continued to shoot at me going in there. I finally got in—

John T. Mason Jr.: Didn't they see the identification marks?

Admiral Martin: They didn't believe it. I wasn't on their schedule; I wasn't supposed to go in there. But I have great admiration for the Marines for that effort on Guadalcanal.

John T. Mason Jr.: How did you convince them that you were legitimate?

Admiral Martin: I guess because I just kept on coming, and fortunately they didn't shoot me down before I got there. I began to raise and lower my wheels to signal them. You

---

* Henderson Field was the U.S. Navy-Marine Corps airstrip on Guadalcanal. It was named in honor of Major Lofton R. Henderson, USMC, who was lost in action during the Battle of Midway.

see if I had gone in there intentionally the *Enterprise* would have given me the recognition signal of the day. I would have gotten in there without any trouble, but I hadn't had the slightest idea that I would go into Guadalcanal.

John T. Mason Jr.: You had no other option?

Admiral Martin: No, I didn't. I had to go in there. They found the stopped-up line soon after I got there. The Marines were very busy. Every airplane that came in there that would fly, they would load it and get it ready to go. I went out on a mission just as soon as I got there, and they got it loaded. I went over and talked to General Geiger and was wondering where I was going to sleep that night.* He said, "Don't worry about that, son. We'll worry about that when you get back from this next mission." That was an exciting time. The Seabees let me sleep in their foxhole that night.† Also, they had some brandy, which was acceptable.

John T. Mason Jr.: Was this on Guadalcanal or an adjacent island?

Admiral Martin: Guadalcanal.

John T. Mason Jr.: What was your mission at that point?

Admiral Martin: They had four Japanese transports that were trying to unload at Guadalcanal, and we were trying to destroy them before they could get in there and do it. Night was coming on, and if they had gotten in there without damage they would have been able to unload before daylight.

John T. Mason Jr.: Was this in Augusta Bay?

---

* Major General Roy Geiger, USMC, was commanding general of the Second Marine Air Wing at Henderson Field on Guadalcanal in 1942.
† Seabees is the nickname applied to members of the Navy's mobile construction battalions (CBs).

Admiral Martin: Just opposite from Savo Island. They were unloading on the beach at the northwest corner.

John T. Mason Jr.: Of course, it was part of the island they occupied.

Admiral Martin: Sure. They had all of the island except those two strips, the fighter strip and Henderson Field, the bomber strip. The torpedo skipper, whose name was Coffin, a classmate of mine, had some torpedo planes there from the *Enterprise*, and we worked for about four days there before we went back to the ship.[*] Then we were back there on two more occasions.

John T. Mason Jr.: Were you simply lost to the ship those four days, or did they know your whereabouts?

Admiral Martin: They knew where we were the next day. They were a little concerned, as they didn't know until the next day.
    Where shall we go now? I've been jumping around.

John T. Mason Jr.: I think in order perhaps you should talk about the operations at New Guinea.

Admiral Martin: That was one of the first places where I thought we were showing our value for the all-weather preparations that we had been making while we were in training at Seattle. The weather was very bad from the task force into New Guinea, to Hollandia. We were able to get through there, and we could take a number with us. We would take them in to the target and would bring more out. There were some able to get through to the target and were not eager to go through that tropical front to go back.

John T. Mason Jr.: Would you talk about that hazard, the tropical front?

---

[*] Lieutenant Albert P. Coffin, USN, commanding officer of Torpedo Ten (VT-10).

Admiral Martin: The tropical front is something that wallows on both sides of the equator, and this was close enough. I don't know exactly how close New Guinea is to the equator, but it's not very far.*

John T. Mason Jr.: What is it, thunderstorms?

Admiral Martin: No, it's just a wallowing cloud that is not very turbulent, but there is no visibility through it. Completely heavy, and if you are flying through it at right angles to it, it takes from 10 to 15 minutes to penetrate it and to get back on the other side.

John T. Mason Jr.: How does the plane react?

Admiral Martin: The plane doesn't know it. As a matter of fact, the engine probably runs better, because it is getting more water injection, you see. The added humidity probably makes the engine run a little better. We know that used to be one technique of getting more power out of an engine on takeoff, and that one thing was water injection. The only problem was for the pilot and his skill to fly the plane accurately and safely until he could get to the other side.

John T. Mason Jr.: Was this a thing you could train for? Could you simulate this condition?

Admiral Martin: Oh, sure. It's just a matter of visibility itself, really, so far as the frontal condition, because anytime you are flying and you cannot orient yourself by looking at the ground, you are on instruments, and you have got to fly the instruments. That's the only way you can fly an airplane safely and go from point A to point B. The difficulty of flying was not bad; for us it was no problem. We were able to fly through it and locate the target.

---

* Hollandia, New Guinea, is at about 2½ degrees south latitude.

This takes me back, the places we got into where there was some weather a qualified instrument pilot is not worried about being able to go back home, back to the carrier. A pilot who cannot fly the instrument is a little afraid to penetrate even a cloud that he is going to be in for some time because he's got to fly straight and level purely on instruments, and there weren't many people who could do it at that time. While he is attacking the target, his mind is on, "How am I going to get through this thing and get back home?"

We made repeated runs at Hollandia, and we caught a lot of planes on the ground, and we got some attacks from them. They had some fighters that were a problem, but we were able to penetrate it, and, as I have said, there was a clearance just at Hollandia where you could make the attack visually. But when you left Hollandia to return to the task force, which was east of there over 100 miles, there was a matter of flying the instruments until you had gone through the weather—this equatorial front. All of my planes had planes from other squadrons that were joining up on them to fly formation back to the carrier. That frequently happened. When there was bad weather, they would come in and fly formation back to the carrier.

John T. Mason Jr.: One would think that instrument flying would have come into its own much sooner because this was a realistic situation.

Admiral Martin: They were doing it, but once the war had started, there was hardly an opportunity to get the training. We were trying to turn out pilots as fast as we could in the training command. It took me longer than seven years, you see, from the time I went to Annapolis, to get my wings. Just before the war started, when I was a flight instructor, we were turning out pilots in seven months. This gives you some idea. And when you are turning them out so fast and there is a need for them in the fleet, you can't extend the training time very well to give them more instrument training, because there is a need for them.

John T. Mason Jr.: To be realistic, too, about it, I suppose the instruments weren't there—they were coming on stream, weren't they?

Admiral Martin: No, by this time all of the planes had these instruments, but they hadn't all taken the masking tape off the gyro instruments as we had. The pilots hadn't had the opportunity to learn this new method of instrument flying, what we called the attitude system. They hadn't had the opportunity to learn that. It took a while. After the war was over, I think there was an intensity then to establish some all-weather training organizations as they did in Hawaii and on the East Coast at Atlantic City, specifically for this type of all-weather training. During the war is not a very good time to do that; there is hardly time for it.

John T. Mason Jr.: You wanted to go back to Group Ten, to Hawaii, after your second engagement.

Admiral Martin: That was the second deployment of Air Group Ten, in which this nucleus of night people were going out with Torpedo Ten, and it was during that period of the attacks on Truk and Hollandia and others you have there that take us up to 1944, when they finally approved the proposal for a night carrier and a night air group.

John T. Mason Jr.: Let me ask, who finally pushed this thing through?

Admiral Martin: I can't really answer that as to actually did it, except that it was getting favorable endorsements from the fleet, up through Captain Gardner, who was the commanding officer of the carrier, and through ComAirPac—I'm not exactly sure who ComAirPac was at that time—and on up through and to Admiral Towers, who was at this time on the CinCPac staff, and on into Washington and the Navy Department.*

They agreed to designate a carrier, and they designated the *Enterprise*, fortunately for us, to be the night carrier. We had been on her two deployments before, and I think it was very fortuitous that that happened, because the problems of a night carrier, as I have already indicated, are very difficult ones. Unless they can organize themselves and have

---

* Captain Matthias B. Gardner, USN, commanded the aircraft carrier *Enterprise* (CV-6) from 7 November 1943 to 10 July 1944. Rear Admiral Charles A. Pownall, USN, served as Commander Air Force Pacific Fleet from 28 February 1944 to 17 August 1944. Vice Admiral John H. Towers, USN, served as Deputy Commander in Chief Pacific Fleet from February 1944 to July 1945.

the endurance to operate both day and night, it can be very difficult. Fortunately, since the *Enterprise* knew us and knew we were coming back, it was like inviting us back into they family, and they were willing to endure these changes that had to take place to operate at night. There were some big changes: the shops, the spare parts, the total logistic setting, the eating arrangements, and that sort of thing had to be turned around so that we could have our breakfast at night and our dinner before dawn. It is not an easy situation. But they did it most admirably.

Now, the night fighters had been out before, and they were pretty well shaken down with radar and their tactics, but on the night attacks nothing had been done. The airplane we had to use for night attack was pretty heavily loaded for the daytime situation. It was fully loaded with ordnance and fuel. It was just about the max gross weight to take off from the carrier, and almost invariably it would settle at the bow after takeoff, which means it wasn't quite flying as if left the carrier.

John T. Mason Jr.: What plane was this?

Admiral Martin: It was the TBF, the Avenger. The Avenger was designed and built by Grumman, but then later in the war General Motors started building that design, and they called it a TBM. TBF – Grumman, TBM – General Motors. They were building the TBM the last year and a half of the war that I know of. To configure this plane so that it was a reasonably safe proposition to operate at night, we wanted to unload as much stuff as we could spare to take more gas and full ordnance. We took out the whole turret assembly. We took out the tail gun, and this left us no defense except our forward guns.

John T. Mason Jr.: Wasn't this somewhat hazardous?

Admiral Martin: A little, if you are going to be caught in daytime, but at night we didn't consider it a real threat. We didn't consider the antiaircraft really as too much of a problem at night. Their fire control was just not that good. Their radars were not that good.

John T. Mason Jr.: For a long time they didn't have radar, did they?

Admiral Martin: Well, I don't know just when they got it, but they started getting surface radar, and we started observing the kind of control of an entire battery around a defensive position during the second year of the war. We also, on this torpedo plane, the Avenger, took out all of the bottom armor plate. We would have taken out this heavy armor that was back of the pilot, but that was just too complicated. We were getting into a lot more complications than we were able to deal with. We only had ten days to do this before we deployed.

John T. Mason Jr.: It was a matter of balance, wasn't it?

Admiral Martin: Yes, it was a problem, and that leads up to a story that has been considered fairly amusing. What we did to that airplane—unloading it of its defensive capabilities—I had made this proposal a number of times to ComAirLant that this was what we wanted to do, and they had said that it had been disapproved.[*] There were two reasons for it: that the airplane would not fly if you did all those things to it, because it would shift the center of gravity so far forward that you couldn't get the tail down, and also it would take too long.

The overhaul and repair did all the modifications to aircraft, and they estimated it would take over a month even with a high priority—to do just these 24 aircraft we were to take with us in ten days. And so—by this time we were not called a torpedo squadron, we were the Night Attack Squadron—that squadron, overnight, took the turret out, took out the armor plate, took out the stinger gun in the tail, and did the things we wanted to do so far as unloading it was concerned—did it overnight.

The next day I went back to ComAirPac to give a final approval to do this. It finally got up through Admiral Forrest Sherman to Admiral Towers.[†] Admiral Towers knew me by this time, and I was able to see him, and he said something to the effect, "Martin, I admire your persistence, but this proposal I don't think I can approve because

---

[*] ComAirLant – Commander Air Force Atlantic Fleet.
[†] Rear Admiral Forrest P. Sherman, USN, an aviator, was head of war plans on the Pacific Fleet staff.

our aeronautical engineers tell me the airplane won't fly like that. And they tell me it can't be done, that the O and R capacity won't permit it to be done before you have to deploy.* Also, they tell me the plane won't fly if you do to it what you have proposed."

And that's when I said, "Admiral Towers, I request permission to borrow a jeep, so I can go back to Barbers Point.† I flew one of those airplanes over here, and if it really won't fly, I sure don't want to fly it back."

He said, "Let's go look at it." So he took some of these aeronautical engineers that were on the staff down there. And, sure enough, they checked to see what we had done in taking off the turret and so forth. Things weren't put back in place like they should have been, but we had unloaded that thing.

John T. Mason Jr.: All except the protective armament to the fire.

Admiral Martin: All except this back armament, and we would have taken that out, because from a very practical point of view the operational hazard was a far greater risk operating an overloaded aircraft aboard an aircraft carrier at night, than the enemy's night fighter and the enemy's antiaircraft at night. And so it made a lot of sense, plus the fact that we could then take a full load of ordnance and more gasoline.

One thing they had come through with was a half of a bomb-bay fuel tank that permitted us to take 500 gallons more fuel than we could otherwise take. It gave us much greater range and endurance. So they went down to take a look at it. I must admit the airplane was difficult to land because the center of gravity had been moved so far forward they were very difficult to get the tail down. But we found out that by putting only 14 pounds of lead all the way in the tail, it restored the center of gravity within workable limits.

John T. Mason Jr.: You didn't find this out overnight?

---

* O&R – overhaul and repair.
† Barbers Point was the site of a naval air station at the southwest "corner" of the island of Oahu, Hawaii.

Admiral Martin: No, we didn't, but we started getting some information that we knew this could be done, and we got the aeronautical engineers working toward this, and Admiral Towers gave this such a high priority, particularly since we had done this ourselves overnight, the modifications and configurations. They knew then it could be done, and we got enough priority that all 24 of those aircraft were so modified, and ten days later, when we had to go aboard the *Enterprise* and go back into the Western Pacific, they were all in shape. We had a wonderful priority, and it worked. The result of that was it turned out it was really the thing that needed to be done to make this torpedo bomber into a very capable and reasonably safe operating aircraft from an aircraft carrier at night. We needed that additional endurance, and we needed that additional range. It put a lot of targets within range of us at night that we couldn't otherwise have reached.

John T. Mason Jr.: It was persistence on your part that achieved this?

Admiral Martin: By this time I had a lot of help. I had these youngsters who were willing to turn around three times to go back with me. I don't think it would have worked if we hadn't had a corps of very capable and very dedicated young patriots that were willing to go out on a third deployment. None of them really had to go; they had had two deployments. That's the way it worked out.

Having the additional endurance that we did would permit us to go over Kyushu. We were able to go in there and stay over the target for three and four hours at night, not permitting them to show a light. The Japanese at this time were using the hours of darkness to prepare for the next day. They would move their aircraft from field to field and work on them at night and get them ready to go for a dawn flight the next day. They can't do that without lights, and by staying over an hour we could keep every airdrome within 50 to 75 miles—we could keep them paralyzed by constantly harassing them. One plane with sufficient endurance to stay there would accomplish this. We would replace them, and then just before dawn the night attack aircraft would leave, and then the dawn attack of the day people would come in as we were leaving.

John T. Mason Jr.: This was a vengeance many times over in comparison with their earlier use of what they called "Washing Machine Charlie," when they came every night to harass an encampment.*

Admiral Martin: If we had had just one good night fighter pattern in there, we'd have shot him down every time he came over.

---

* "Washing Machine Charlie" was an American nickname for a noisy, generally non-attacking Japanese aircraft that would fly over U.S. positions at night as part of psychological warfare to keep people awake.

Interview Number 2 with Vice Admiral William I. Martin, U.S. Navy (Retired)
Place: Admiral Martin's home in Alexandria, Virginia
Date: Thursday, 8 November 1979

John T. Mason Jr.: We will begin interview number two with your account of being shot down during the Saipan operation, was it not?*

Admiral Martin: It was two days before the amphibious operations were scheduled to begin. For two days before the amphibious operations we had gone in and had operated against the shipping that was in sight and had been successful in sinking everything we saw. I remember this vividly because the battleships and cruisers had closed in to a point where the softening-up process was to begin, and while I was in the air they were firing over my head.

A large part of the fleet was there, and the air forces that they were going to put on that target to soften it were very large. Bob Isley commanded one of the groups that were to go in to strike at dawn, and I had the second group.† My group was the northernmost one that took in Charan Kanoa airstrip and the air defenses that we knew about around it. Bob Isley's group was taking the southern tip of the island, surrounding and including Aslito Airfield, which was later named after him. Today it is called Isley Field.

We had planned this thing on tactical radio with signals back and forth how to coordinate it, and it was a beautifully coordinated attack, approaching from the east. Our intention was to commence our pushovers into our dives at exactly the same time in order that the antiaircraft defenses that were between these two positions—and could fire either way—would be divided. They couldn't concentrate on one and then concentrate on the other. It was very well coordinated. As we approached it and got within range, the

---

* On 15 June 1944, U.S. Marines and U.S. Army soldiers mounted an amphibious assault on Saipan in the Mariana Islands.
† On 13 June 1944, Lieutenant Commander Robert E. Isley, USN, commanding officer of Torpedo Squadron 16 (VT-16) from the carrier *Lexington* (CV-16) was shot down and killed by antiaircraft fire on Saipan. Martin was shot down the same day.

antiaircraft fire appeared in front of both of us at the same time. When he said he was ready to push over, so was I, and we wanted to make as steep a dive as we could. I was coming down about as vertically as you can make it. My radioman would always call out the altitude, so as he called out 2,500 feet, which was the desired release point—

John T. Mason Jr.: At what speed were you going?

Admiral Martin: Don't know exactly. It was almost terminal speed for the TBF, which was well over 300 knots. He called out 2,500 feet, and I was on target at that point, so I released. I not only pushed the electric release, but also I pulled the manual release so that I would make sure my ordnance was going to leave. I still had that toggle in my hand for the manual release when there was a terrific blast. A Japanese 5-incher, or the closest thing to that that they used for antiaircraft fire, had hit my plane right in the middle. It burned the hair on the back of my neck; it was that close. I'll never know how I got out of that airplane, because they figured out it takes just over three and a fraction seconds from the point where I was to the deck. But I pulled the ripcord before I released the safety belt, which is probably another thing that let me get out in time, because the chute opened and didn't even swing, and I hit the water. The chute was badly ripped. There were two panels that were badly ripped, and so I hit pretty hard. A lot of things go through your mind on that.

Paul Stillwell: You retained consciousness?

Admiral Martin: Yes, I did, and I was in about four feet of water just 100 yards off the beach. There were lots of Japanese soldiers over there. If I had known one of them, I could have recognized him; I was that close. A lot of things were very fortunate about getting out that low; if I had descended slowly from some altitude, I would probably have been killed—being a good target for some time. After I landed, I looked up, and large pieces of my plane were still falling. The after part of the plane was doing a falling leaf. I was told it was chopped half in two by the blast, and it was falling in flames. Just 30 or 40 feet from me, the forward part of the plane that I had just bailed out of was there burning, and I had to move away from it because the gasoline was burning on the surface. It was coming toward me, so I had to move away. I realized that this "zip-burp, zip-burp" that I was hearing was the firing from the beach. They were not hitting me, but close enough that I could hear it and it would hit the water.

John T. Mason Jr.: They were aiming at you?

Admiral Martin: Oh, yes. I stayed under water then and was just pulling in what was left of my parachute, because I had some idea I might need it later. I had a one-man rubber boat, but I couldn't begin to inflate it at that point; I would have been a target. I had to stay under water except to come up, when I had to, to stick my nose out to breathe and try to move away from that.

John T. Mason Jr.: Was there much surf?

Admiral Martin: No, not within the lagoon. I was inside the lagoon, just south of Garapan town. Garapan town is on the northern end of the lagoon, and Sugar Mill is on the southern end of it. The Charan Kanoa airstrip was just inboard between the two. I continued to move out, away from the beach and away from the small-arms fire. I realized I was in a position to observe some antiaircraft that we didn't know was there. We knew very little about that place. As a matter of fact, it was a very hot place, and the reports we had from reconnaissance were very sketchy. I learned later that the frogmen who were supposed to go in there—Draper Kauffman, do you know him?[*]

John T. Mason Jr.: I know him very well.

Admiral Martin: Draper and I hadn't met at this time. He had tried to get in there, and it was too hot for them.

---

[*] Lieutenant Draper L. Kauffman, USN, headed an underwater demolition team. The oral history of Kauffman, who retired as a rear admiral, is in the Naval Institute oral history collection. See also Elizabeth K. Bush, *America's First Frogman: the Draper Kauffman Story* (Annapolis: Naval Institute Press, 2004).

John T. Mason Jr.: He told me that story. This was the first operation they were involved in.

Admiral Martin: Their first? I didn't know that. There were reports later that Draper and I saw each other there. We didn't actually. We saw each other later at the War College. We were in the same class, and he asked me if I was this crazy guy that volunteered to bail out and get this intelligence at Saipan. I told him I was neither that crazy nor that brave.

To finish the story, gradually I got out of there. It was close to 1,000 yards out to the reef that enclosed the lagoon. When I got over halfway out there, the small-arms fire stopped as I was out of their range. When I got to the reef, I was sitting there realizing that I had some intelligence that was of some value. I took bearings on the southern coast of Saipan, as against Tinian, and was able later to know exactly where I was. Therefore the reports on the antiaircraft and other things of interest could be accurately located.

John T. Mason Jr.: I would say this showed remarkable presence of mind in your circumstance to think of observing these things.

Admiral Martin: Don't think I wasn't frightened. As I was on my way out, I saw a boat approaching from Garapan town, and I wondered then what I would do. I had a .45 with me.

John T. Mason Jr.: It wasn't waterlogged?

Admiral Martin: Of course, it was wet. Whether it would fire or not, I don't know. Only two of us were coached on the operation—the air corps and the amphibious leader—for the following day. The only two of us were Killer Kane, the fighter squadron commander on the *Enterprise*, and myself.[*] We had spent almost the previous week with

---

[*] Commander William R. Kane, USN, commanding officer of Fighting Ten (VF-10).

Captain Whitehead and the amphibious people coaching us and preparing us to be air coordinator for the amphibious operations on the following day.*

John T. Mason Jr.: So you had all that knowledge?

Admiral Martin: We had it all, and this was what frightened me most, knowing this and because of our rank they would expect that we would know a great deal about the amphibious operation, and they would put all kinds of torture on us to find that out, probably up to the extent of killing us. I really had decided that if they came up, I would sure try out my gun and take as many as I could with me. As it turned out, the next strike—we were on Strike Able, the first one of the day—Strike Baker came in, and they had been cautioned that someone had seen a parachute. Only one person had seen the parachute, because it was open for such a short period of time. It was someone pouring down after me in a dive who thought he had seen it. So all the pilots in Strike Baker, the second strike, were cautioned that there might be somebody alive in there—and not to drop anything in the water. I was able to see where they dropped, and they were dropping very accurately. The boat turned around and went back.

John T. Mason Jr.: Was it an enemy boat?

Admiral Martin: Yes, then later there was another enemy boat coming up from—I presume they were enemy, because there was nothing but enemy in there. The enemy really occupied Saipan at this time. The boat approached from the Sugar Mill side, the southern end of the lagoon. He got about halfway there when the battleships and cruisers which had gotten within range—within 30,000 yards—began firing at the beach over my head. That's quite an experience too. Each one of them sounded like a freight train going over.

But this was very fortunate too. They had been instructed, as I found out later, that nothing should be short. If they were going to err, they should be on the other side.

---

* Captain Richard F. Whitehead, USN, Commander Support Aircraft, directed operations from on board the amphibious force flagship *Rocky Mount* (AGC-3).

Their fire was extremely accurate from my point of view, and nothing did fall short. Nothing hit in the water while I was there, except for the antiaircraft that was shooting back at them. This was falling down on me, and there was lots of shrapnel falling around me. I finally got to the reef, as I had said, and positioned myself. I sat there with just my eyes above the water, observing what was going on and making mental notes reviewing what I had seen on my way out there. There were no manmade obstacles; there were a lot of coral heads.

John T. Mason Jr.: Under water? That's what Draper and his crew were concerned with, and the demolition of them.

Admiral Martin: Yes, that's right. Sometime in the afternoon planes from my own squadron and fighters from the *Enterprise* came in there with the intention of finding a survivor if there was one. I shone my mirror, and that's what they saw. I also released—let me go back a way. The reason I left the reef was because the Japanese had also spotted me, and they opened up with something that seemed to me like a 40-millimeter. One shot was off to the left and short; it splashed water on me. The other was just to the right of me and long.

John T. Mason Jr.: They were getting the range.

Admiral Martin: So they had bracketed me, and I wasted no time. I gathered up my parachute, got up and ran across that live coral. It took about 15 steps to get completely across it, and then there was deep water on the other side. I had to get farther out before I could inflate my rubber boat. When I thought I was far enough out, where they could no longer reach me with the small arms, I inflated the rubbed boat, and it took some time to get in it. I swallowed enough seawater so that I was nauseated; it acts as a laxative too. I was throwing up and suddenly had diarrhea and cramps. The intelligence people who questioned me later said, "That's splendid, splendid. It is a wonderful shark repellant."

John T. Mason Jr.: That's some consolation, isn't it? Isn't it surprising the Japanese spent so much time focusing on you, a single object, when they must have had other things to occupy their sights?

Admiral Martin: Of course they did, and that is why these boats went back. They didn't want to get where I was. Obviously, they would have liked to take a prisoner, to have gotten some information.

When the *Enterprise* planes came looking for me, there was a fellow named Gibby Blake who survived it all; I saw him just last week.[*] He is in good health and lives down in Florida. There was also a fighter pilot named Taddeo.[†] They saw this flash of light from the mirror and came down and dropped another life raft to me, and I knew that I had been spotted. After that I could relax, because the wind was from the island, blowing me to the westward, and that's where our ships were.

John T. Mason Jr.: That must have been your first moment of confidence.

Admiral Martin: Yes, it was. I was confident that I was going to survive that ordeal, and all I had to do was sail then. So I pulled in my parachute and let out enough of it to act as a sail. The wind was breezy enough that I was kicking up a little wake as I went westward from there. When I got a mile or so from the island, a seaplane came in and landed close enough to taxi up. A young fellow named Ensign Townsend was the pilot of that seaplane. He was from Admiral Spruance's flagship, and he picked me up.[‡]

I wanted to take my chute and my life raft with me. He said, "No, sir, Commander. You get in this airplane; we're going to get out of here real fast." He took his .45 and put holes in the rubber boat. He was correct in doing it, because otherwise it would have floated out, and our people would have wondered about it and spent some time on it. So he very correctly sank it with my parachute.

---

[*] Lieutenant (junior grade) Albert P. Blake, USNR
[†] Lieutenant (junior grade) Alfred Taddeo, USNR.
[‡] Admiral Raymond A. Spruance, USN, Commander Fifth Fleet, embarked in the heavy cruiser *Indianapolis* (CA-35), was the operational commander for the invasion of the Marianas.

I got in the back seat of that seaplane. It was his first encounter with antiaircraft, his very first. To get off, we had to go right into the wind, which meant we were going right back in to the island and the antiaircraft fire. We finally rocked it off, and we in the air, and that old SOC was so slow.* Fortunately, it was the first time I, or anybody, had ever seen the Japanese over-lead—their lead was way ahead of us. Usually they were behind us, but the plane was so slow they were leading it excessively. So none of it hit us, and he finally was able to turn away from Saipan, and we made a Cast recovery on the ship.

I was taken to Admiral Spruance, a fine gentleman. After I talked with him for a few minutes, he turned me over to his intelligence people, who spent the next several hours questioning me and gave me a plot on the amphibious operations I had seen before. Of course, I had memorized it, and I had been shot down at Beach Green One, which was to be the first wave of the amphibious operation; they were going in there. As it turned out, the information I had on the depths of the water and the obstacles, also the antiaircraft locations, turned out to be very helpful to them.

John T. Mason Jr.: This is a very vivid illustration of rescue operations. Would you comment in a more general way on the policy of our fleet people in rescuing pilots who were shot down—the attention they paid to this, the reactions it had upon the pilots themselves?

Admiral Martin: Actually, from the beginning this was a very comforting thing for the aviators, because so much attention was put into improving this, especially to improve the thing of picking up people that we knew had been shot down that might have been left behind at the end of the day. I know that Admiral Reeves—they call him Blackjack Reeves, who was in the *Enterprise* the second year of the war, spent a great deal of time on that project of organizing a seaplane rescue team protected by fighters to go in close to

---

* The Curtiss-built SOC Seagull was a biplane that first entered fleet squadrons in 1935, primarily in a floatplane version to perform observation and scouting missions for battleships and cruisers. It served through World War II. The SOC-1 version was 31 feet long, had a wingspan of 36 feet, gross weight of 5,437 pounds, and maximum speed of 165 miles an hour. It was armed with two .30-caliber machine guns.

the beach and pick up people that might be left behind because we had to leave the area.[*] It worked very well. I doubt if there was anything that occupied our planners' hours during an operation when our aviators were exposed like that, and you knew you were going to lose some of them to antiaircraft. The planning for search and rescue was very complete and very efficient. Usually there were submarines on station, too, just for that purpose.

John T. Mason Jr.: You are saying that this added to the morale of the pilot when you went out on a mission?

Admiral Martin: Yes, it did. And, of course, the pilots themselves—when these planes came in looking for me, Gibby Blake and a torpedo plane and Tad Taddeo, a fighter, were exposing themselves to antiaircraft fire just to locate us so they could tell the rescue plane where to come, and they did. So it was very comforting.

John T. Mason: And now, I suppose, in rescue operations the helicopter has taken the place of the seaplane. Is it more efficient?

Admiral Martin: Yes, that's right. The helicopter has some very special capabilities that a seaplane doesn't have. The fact that he could some in so low and hover permits him to operate in a lot of areas where a seaplane cannot operate. Especially this is true in shallow water and for someone who is already on the beach. The helicopters go in and pick people up out of the forests, out of the jungle forest. The Navy actually procures aircraft that are most capable in exactly that operation.

John T. Mason: In this instance were the other members of the crew lost?

Admiral Martin: Yes, they were. It was believed that they were killed immediately when the antiaircraft shell exploded.

---

[*] Rear Admiral John W. Reeves Jr., USN, Commander Task Group 58.1.

John T. Mason: How many were there?

Admiral Martin: Two, a fellow named Williams, who was the radio operator, and also a fellow named Hargrove, who was in the turret. They were both lost and their bodies never located.

I think I mentioned previously that in the night effort, it was very fortunate that some of us had been with the *Enterprise* from the first year of the war. She was already known as a wonderful fighting ship, and the crew were just great fighters. They knew when they had to pull up their guard like a good prizefighter. When they could relax, they relaxed, and when it was time for them to operate, it was with the greatest efficiency and up to maximum capability that they were able to do it. It was a ship of great endurance, and there were people on that ship the last year of the war who were there when the war started.

When it was decided to designate a night carrier, I think it was most fortunate that they did pick the *Enterprise* to do this because she was such a veteran. The fact that several of us had been on there before and knew the ship's officers and the ship's company was a decided asset for us, because the night operations were going to be a great inconvenience to the entire ship. The eating hours had to be changed, and the shops and parts and spares and all that sort of thing had to be available during the hours of darkness.

As it turned out, during the time that the *Enterprise* and Night Air Group 90 were operating together, the ship was designated, almost from our first day, as the ship to take aboard the planes that were damaged or the stragglers that were late coming from a target. At any time that their home ship was engaged with launching and they had already taken their aircraft aboard for that cycle, the *Enterprise* would be designated to take them aboard. As a consequence, the *Enterprise* was operating its own night air group during the hours of darkness, and it was actually performing more landing operations than the day carriers were in the daytime. This required a remarkable change in the operation of the ship. It required two separate crews to do some of the operations. For example, the commanding officer would handle the ship in the night hours, and the navigator would handle the ship during the daytime.

John T. Mason: There's a certain Fifth Fleet—same ship?

Admiral Martin: Very similar, but of course with some of those operations the same people function—the ship got so very good, so efficient, that the second team, (if you would like to call it that, the daylight team), became just as proficient as the so-called first team.

John T. Mason: This is just an observation—that particular ship became so very valuable because it incorporated the whole night-flying operation, and it was putting all the eggs in one basket, so to speak.

Admiral Martin: Well, until others came out—the *Saratoga* came out and operated for a few days, I don't remember for how long. But she caught another torpedo, which she was very good at, and was knocked out of action.* Until the *Enterprise* was knocked out of action by a kamikaze and except for the few days the *Saratoga* was there, the *Bonhomme Richard* arrived after the *Enterprise* had been knocked out of action in May of 1945.†

Of course, there were some of the day missions during this period where you needed to do some searching and some strikes that had to be carried out when the weather was so bad that they had to be conducted under instrument flying conditions, and the night air group aboard the *Enterprise* did those. We did all of the searches that were in such bad weather that the day people couldn't do them. It became an operation every night and during a large part of the day for its own air group.

John T. Mason: You might draw attention to all these remarks by fleet personnel as to the effectiveness of the night fighter and the *Enterprise* operation.

---

* Although the *Saratoga* (CV-3) was torpedoed twice in 1942, bombs inflicted the damage in 1945. The ship began night combat operations on 16 February 1945 in support of the invasion of Iwo Jima. Several Japanese bombs damaged the ship on 21 February and sent her back to the West Coast for repairs.
† The *Enterprise* was damaged by a kamikaze on 14 May 1945, ending her combat role in the war.

Admiral Martin: I am sure that all the other carriers were happy to see a night carrier in there, because it did take over the night fighter operations for the defense of the fleet and the night searches that the night aircraft carried out—also the bad-weather strikes. One strike, when we were in the South China Sea, we had gone down and hit Camranh Bay at night and were to strike Pratas Reef, which we knew had a large Japanese communications station on it, but they didn't know what else was there.[*] The weather was so bad that the night air group performed that operation. Yes, it is true, I am sure, that the other carriers were relieved that they didn't have to operate at night.

John T. Mason: Toward the end of the war, you were operating almost in Japanese home waters, weren't you?

Admiral Martin: Yes, we were. Staring in March, actually, and in April. Before we had actually gone in to the home islands, we performed a strike against Formosa, the northern end of which is known as Taiwan—Keelung. This was a remarkable flight; it was the longest range of any strike from an aircraft carrier at the time, and it was the kind of a strike that you couldn't do from a day carrier, because it required going close to Japanese-occupied islands en route and on the way home. We had a very successful operation so far as the damage we did to the enemy, but out of nine planes we lost half of them.

John T. Mason: What was the purpose of this mission?

Admiral Martin: The purpose was that we had a report that there was a concentration of Japanese shipping in Keelung Harbor, and we were sent in to get them as a surprise. And it was a surprise before they could get under way and escape us. It was a successful strike. The timing of these things would throw them out, because they had no idea—it turned out that the Japanese thought that we were much closer to them than we were. The night operations gave them a lot of problems that they hadn't had before. The idea of paralyzing an airport—the airfields—to damage them so they could not use them at

---

[*] The Camranh Bay strike was on 11 January 1945, and Pratas Reef was hit the following day.

night, and therefore they couldn't relocate the aircraft. It was their custom to redeploy at night to the fields from which they would be operating the next day. If we could hit those fields where most of the aircraft were, we could keep them paralyzed until our day fighter sweep would get into position, and then the day attacks would keep them down.

Once we got into operating against the Japanese homeland—and I think this is true—there were no strikes against the fleet for a long period of time and none from the airfields that we operated against at night. We know that to be a fact. The airfields where we had hit the night before, none of those operated against the fleet the next day, because they had been paralyzed during the night period. Our day strikes would hit there at dawn the next morning. The strikes against the homeland itself I thought were very effective. Here we were coming into the area where the residue of the aircraft that they had left were operating and to be able to go in and do enough damage during the night hours, and keep their gunners awake all night, had a very comforting effect on the other carriers and their air groups that were to hit during the daylight.

John T. Mason: The Japanese efficiency must have been declining at this stage of the war, whereas ours was improving.

Admiral Martin: Yes, both as to our quality and our quantity. Of course, the carriers were coming out the last year of the war, and we had four operating task groups. At one time we had five, including the night task group. Our pilots were all well trained, and the longer they stayed in the operation, the better they became. They were improving every day, and the Japanese fleet was not capable of countering our fleet again during that period.

John T. Mason: And the personnel on the mainland must have been losing efficiency, they were battered so much.

Admiral Martin: They were; it was a last-ditch thing. There is a figure of 8,000 that sticks in my mind. The Japanese were believed to have that many aircraft and pilots to put into a last-ditch kamikaze effort. If we had had to go into the Japanese mainland with amphibious operations, it would have been very costly. I am sure this was taken into account in planning the use of the atomic bomb.*

John T. Mason: Tell me about the damaging attack on the *Enterprise*.

Admiral Martin: This was in the middle of May—May 14, 1945. The night-before efforts were all back aboard the *Enterprise* when it was hit that day. I recall I was up on the captain's wing of the bridge, and the kamikazes were expected. There had been considerable kamikaze action the previous few days, and on this day it was so vivid watching this one aircraft that everyone had their eyes on and the antiaircraft, our own and that of the supporting ships' antiaircraft, were firing at this one that came across above the lower clouds. He passed over a number of ships before he got up to where he was near us, and it was our belief that his appointed target was the *Enterprise*, because he just kept coming and kept coming.

When he got into position to come in on his attack, he came right straight down on the *Enterprise,* and they were firing at him all the way. It appeared to us—we kept our eyes on him—that he was about to overshoot when he rolled over like he would do a split S. He rolled over on his back and pulled through, and he hit the very center of the flight deck, just aft of the number-one centerline elevator. His bomb went off in the elevator well, which people who know more about it than I do figured it acted as a gun chamber. It sent the elevator 400-and-some-odd feet in the air. They have photographs of it that they could scale off and determine what height it was. They don't know whether that elevator was still on its way up or on its way down, or whether it had hit the peak of its rise at the time of the photograph.

John T. Mason: He not only selected the proper target, but he selected the proper place in that target.

---

* In the first combat use of atomic bombs, U.S. B-29 bombers hit Hiroshima, on the island of Honshu, on 6 August 1945 and Nagasaki, on Kyushu, on 9 August.

Admiral Martin: He certainly did. It was a perfect place to put the ship out of commission.

John T. Mason: And he hadn't been hit by all of this antiaircraft fire?

Admiral Martin: I don't think so. Of course, there are many cases where they believe that the aircraft had been hit and probably wounded, but what did he have to lose? That was his mission anyway, to hit the ship with his aircraft, thereby destroying himself. It started fires. It buckled the flight deck into the center of the elevator. It couldn't have been placed more accurately so far as operating aircraft was concerned. After we got the ship's fires under control, we knew we were out of commission.

John T. Mason: Were there many losses in personnel?

Admiral Martin: I don't remember the number lost, but there was a large number of people that were lost.

John T. Mason: You personally were far enough removed from the explosion?

Admiral Martin: I had walked, before he hit, into the captain's bridge and closed the door, which is all that saved me, because others in exposed places on that side of the superstructure of the ship were killed. I had just gotten inside in time.

John T. Mason: You must have had a very active guardian angel during this whole period.

Admiral Martin: I think so. I had had a number of close calls; I don't know. I think most pilots have the feeling that even when they see their squadron mates fail to come back, or see their shipmates on the ship that had been killed or seriously injured, there is just the feeling that it's not going to happen to you. I am sure everybody takes as much precaution as they can, like you plan your approach to a target in such a way that you are coming out of the sun to give the antiaircraft a difficult sighting problem. Or you try to approach in such a way that you are under minimum exposure to antiaircraft, not only during your approach but during your retirement from the area. You plan all these things with an intent to carry out your mission and yet give you the best chance possible to survive, but you do get into a place where it is impossible to hit that target without considerable exposure to antiaircraft, and considerable exposure to enemy fighter opposition. You can minimize that sometimes, but you can't escape it.

John T. Mason: After a time I would think that this danger becomes sort of commonplace and you don't lie awake at night worrying about it?

Admiral Martin: No, I don't think so. I don't think you do, because, as I say, most pilots just think it is never going to happen to them. And the ship plans it so that when you have had losses and you are going to retire, as the fleet frequently did to places like Ulithi and Mogmog for a few days of licking your wounds and making your repairs and resting up for the next operation.* We would have our memorial services and burials at sea, but then when we would get back to the island, they would have recreation places where you could go in and relax and have some beers with some old friends that were still around. I thought the balance between the fighting and the rest periods was well timed.

There were people—Admiral Mitscher's and Admiral McCain's staffs—who spelled each other, but I used to marvel at their endurance, because there were really no times for them to relax.† An operation would just complete, and they would immediately turn to long periods of work, planning for the next operation. Those were always the kind to have a deadline that was too close, and sometimes the planning was not as complete as you would like to have it when you go into the next action. But, as I said, the tactics and the doctrine, so far as aviation was concerned on the carrier—a lot of that was worked out by the fliers themselves as time went along.

---

* Ulithi is an atoll in the Western Caroline Islands. It had a large lagoon that provided a sheltered anchorage for many ships after U.S. forces captured it without opposition on 23 September 1944. Mogmog is one of the islands in the Ulithi Atoll. During World War II, it provided recreation for naval crews ashore.
† Vice Admiral John S. McCain, USN, served as Commander Task Force 58, the fast carrier task force, in 1944-45. He and Vice Admiral Marc A. Mitscher, USN, alternated in that role.

We started the war with untested doctrine and untried tactics, so the staffs that were doing the planning for us were always happy to get our help, and they were wonderful about consulting the pilots on such things as the best approach and the best retirement and the ordnance loads to carry and the sizes of the force to take. I for one had great admiration for the staffs that I worked with—with Admiral Reeves and before him we had Admiral Ginder, Admiral Buddy Wieber, Admiral Glover.[*] And after Admiral Blackjack Reeves we had Admiral Matt Gardner the last year on the night carrier.[†]

John T. Mason: Who noticed any immediate benefit from intelligence efforts in some of these operations? I use as an illustration something Admiral Burke told me about their ability one time on operation the Japanese had an officer—I don't know what you call him, but he was a senior pilot type who was above the operation and was guiding his pilots.[‡] He was giving verbal instructions to the pilots, and they were reading all of this and using the information our side of the operation.

Admiral Martin: I don't recall getting any information from that source, although the intelligence that we got was usually very good. And if there was some doubt about it, if it was speculative, we would be told that. On the other hand, there were places they couldn't go in, like Truk—there was very little information on Truk before we went in there. There was very little information of value to the amphibious operation on Saipan, as I indicated.

John T. Mason: I remember Herb Riley telling me—he was in command of a CVE, I guess it was, at one point in the operation—about the special treatment afforded the pilots

---

[*] In 1944 Rear Admiral John W. Reeves Jr., USN, was embarked on board the *Enterprise* as Commander Task Group 58.1; Captain Samuel P. Ginder, USN, commanded the *Enterprise* from 16 April 1943 to 7 November 1943; Captain Carlos W. Wieber, USN, commanded the *Enterprise* from 7 April 1943 to 16 April 1943; Captain Cato D. Glover, USN, commanded the *Enterprise* from 29 July 1944 to 14 December 1944.

[†] Rear Admiral Matthias B. Gardner, USN, Commander Carrier Division Seven/Commander Task Group 58.5, 1944-45.

[‡] In late March 1944 Commodore Arleigh A. Burke, USN became chief of staff to Vice Admiral Marc A. Mitscher, USN, Commander Task Force 58. As a four-star admiral, Burke was Chief of Naval Operations from 1955 to 1961. His five-volume oral history is in the Naval Institute collection.

after their return from the operation.* They were given the privilege of what really constituted a cocktail hour—medicinal spirits. Did this happen on the *Enterprise*?

Admiral Martin: Yes, it did. I think, however, the squadrons and air groups took their own supplies on those. My first year out there was very dry. I was one rank behind the cold beer; I could get some warm beer. Having had that experience, during my second tour (here, again, it was aboard the *Enterprise*) we were well equipped. We had boxes marked "Handle with care, electronics." I recall the commanding officer found out that we had these boxes in the place that was designated to keep squadron gear. The executive officer was a very capable man, but he was fairly meticulous on rules, as he should have been. When I found out that he had discovered our supply of medicinal whiskey, I was with the commanding officer of the ship, Captain Budd Hall, and I told him the exec had found our supply.† The captain, I thought, was very nice about it. He said, "Well, there's probably a reason for it," and he permitted me to write the rules under which it would be dispensed. So I wrote that our air group flight surgeon would have to approve it, and the commanding officer of the ship would have to approve it. The captain had enough confidence in me so that he crossed out "commanding officer" and left it up to the air group commander and the air group flight surgeon. But in actual practice I always informed the captain that we were going to have a cocktail hour. Usually they would follow our memorial services, burials at sea.

John T. Mason: The emotional impact of that had to be alleviated some way.

Admiral Martin: And at no time did it interfere in any way. If there was to be an operation the next day, we never did that. We were always away from any expectation of combat flying the next day.

---

* In 1944-45 Captain Herbert D. Riley, USN commanded the escort carrier *Makassar Strait* (CVE-91). For details, see the Naval Institute oral history of Riley, who retired as a vice admiral.
† Captain Grover B. H. Hall, USN, commanded the aircraft carrier *Enterprise* (CV-6) from 14 December 1944 to 25 September 1945.

John T. Mason: It seems like a commonsense approach to that problem, in that when that rule was imposed on the fleet back in the dim dark ages of Josephus Daniels, you didn't have fliers who were in combat and who had to be handled in a very special way.*

Admiral Martin: I could see the effects of being able to relax a few hours was sort of a relief valve—a very prudent one, I thought. Of course, I think each ship handled it differently, but I think all of them either handled it as the *Enterprise* did or turned a blind eye. What did Nelson say, who had only one eye—that he would turn his eye away from something he didn't want to see?†

John T. Mason: There is something else I would like you to comment on, since we are dealing with these various subjects. Burke told me a story about showing real compassion for the enemy in times of burial service for those taken and some consideration for the survivors, and this tied in with a remark that a friend of mine made in a book. I checkmated it and told her she was in error. She said there were no signs of compassion with the enemy in World War II, that this had gone out of fashion after World War I.

Admiral Martin: No, that isn't true. As a matter of fact, on this occasion, when I was shot down at Saipan, when I got over to the destroyer, it was commanded by a man I hadn't met before but had heard of him, he was of the class of '32, and I was of the class of '34. He had picked up a Japanese survivor and had him aboard when I was transferred by highline from the cruiser over to the destroyer that was to take me back to the *Enterprise*. The Japanese was a captain that had been aboard the ship that my squadron had sunk the day before. One cheek of his buttocks had been shot off. He had lost a lot of blood, but the doctors had worked on him, giving him the same treatment as anybody else. When I was transferred back to the *Enterprise*, he went back with me in a stretcher.

---

* On 1 July 1914 a general order from Secretary of the Navy Josephus Daniels went into effect. It abolished the traditional wine messes on board U.S. Navy ships, resulting in a prohibition against drinking alcoholic beverages on board. The ban was relaxed in the 1980s to permit the serving of beer and wine—but not hard liquor—at official receptions on board.

† Lord Horatio Viscount Nelson (1758-1805), British naval hero of the Battle of Cape St. Vincent, 1797, Battle of the Nile, 1798, Trafalgar, 1805. In the 1801 Battle of Copenhagen his superior, Admiral Sir Hyde Parker gave Nelson the discretion to withdraw in a message sent by signal flags. Nelson disobeyed the order and succeeded in destroying many enemy ships. He quipped that he didn't see the order because he put the telescope to his blind eye.

There were two of them; I was going over in a breeches buoy, and he was going in a stretcher.* We both went over there together. He was queried by our intelligence people the same as I was when I got back, but I know he got as good treatment as was possible to give him. I have seen other cases of that where there were cases on both sides, of course, but the humane side of ours—that consideration was always there. This thing of shooting up people in their parachutes and things like that—you hear of spotted cases, and maybe it went on, but I never saw it. I never observed it.

John T. Mason: The *Enterprise* had been damaged and knocked out of any further combat operations, so you were detached and returned to the States, were you not?

Admiral Martin: I came back with the ship, which had to come back all the way for repairs. While this was going on, I got a set of orders from BuPers to go to the Bureau of Aeronautics, and with the help of the skipper of the *Enterprise* I got out of that set.† As a matter of fact, I had been asked to set up a course for squadron and air group commanders who were going out in combat. And I was asked to do it the way I wanted to do it and select where I wanted to do it, as long as it was on the West Coast. This I had really looked forward to and had really planned a lot of the material for it. I really wasn't anxious to leave the West Coast; I wanted to stay out there with my family, which had moved out there from Missouri. My boys were born on the West Coast, and I hoped to remain there.

John T. Mason: Where did you live?

Admiral Martin: In Coronado. I was really intrigued with the idea of giving a taste of combat to the training that the squadron and air group commanders were going to get, and if they had had it before on previous deployments, to bring them up to date.

John T. Mason: And this was to crystallize the knowledge you had obtained?

---

* A breeches buoy comprised a chair and harness suspended from a line between two ships and was used to transfer personnel.
† BuPers – Bureau of Naval Personnel.

Admiral Martin: Exactly. And this was strongly backed by ComAirPac and CinCPacFlt.* So I got out of the BuAer orders, and then another set came in to OpNav, and I was able to get out of those through the same support.† A third set came in ordering me to the staff of CominCh; this was when it became top hat.‡

John T. Mason: It didn't look like you could get out of that set of orders?

Admiral Martin: And I didn't have enough influence on the West Coast to get out of those, so I called my good friend Arleigh Burke in Washington. He was about to do something back there. I wasn't sure what it was, but I knew he was very close to the top.

John T. Mason: Where had you gotten to know him, from the Mitscher-Burke combination?§

Admiral Martin: Yes, he was a person who delved deeply into things. Every person in my squadrons and later in my air group had the highest regard for him, because he listened, and he took it aboard. If you had a serious recommendation, you were going to get some action from them. He would give you real good reasons why it shouldn't be done or couldn't be done, or he would tell you how long it was going to take.

John T. Mason: This respect that he had gained with the pilots was also due to the fact that he had acquired a certain knowledge about flying, was it not?

Admiral Martin: Yes, amazingly so. From the time I became closely associated with him during the war, it seemed to me that of all the flag officers that were running around with Navy wings, he deserved them as much as any of them. He just had that kind of an objective outlook on things that he didn't know; he wanted to know about naval aviation.

---

* ComAirPac – Commander Air Force Pacific Fleet; CinCPacFlt – Commander in Chief Pacific Fleet.
† OpNav—the extended staff of the Chief of Naval Operations.
‡ CominCh was the abbreviation used for Commander in Chief U.S. Fleet when Admiral Ernest J. King, USN, held that title from 1941 to 1945. He was promoted to the five-star rank of fleet admiral in December 1944.
§ Discomfort arose between Vice Marc Mitscher and Captain Arleigh Burke when Burke was ordered as chief of staff to Mitscher, who was in command of Task Force 58. The assignment was part of Admiral Ernest King's policy that aviation officers such as Mitscher would have surface officers as chiefs of staff and vice versa. Mitscher believed only an aviator could understand carrier operations at sea and wanted an aviator as second in command. The two reportedly hardly spoke to each other for several days, but Burke's qualities of leadership became evident and accepted by Mitscher.

Of course, the indoctrination he had gotten from such a wonderful man as Mitscher and other wonderful people that were on that staff, and he was just so wonderful taking aboard even the difficult ones. I knew that he would help me, so I called him on the phone. It took a while to get in touch with him. As I recall, my words to him were, "Commodore, I need your help. I got orders to OpNav, and with considerable help I got out of those. Now, there is some cantankerous person back there in CominCh who insists on my coming to Washington. Would you do what you can to get me out of these orders?" The commodore's reply was, "Come on back, Bill. I'm that stubborn, cantankerous SOB."

John T. Mason: Had he been back of the other sets of orders too?

Admiral Martin: Apparently not. The first set was inspired by the detailer in BuPers; the second one was from an OP-05 source that wanted me to relieve him.[*] But that third set was Admiral Burke's idea, and I knew that was it, so I started packing. I went back to Washington for duty. This was in June or the third of July, and it was a special group established by Admiral King. This was at a time when it was foreseen that we might go into Japan on an amphibious operation, and the subject of the kamikaze threat was a very serious one—to work on ways to deal with the kamikaze, both to keep them from coming out and to shoot them down if they did come out. It was a very worthwhile effort, and the admiral had picked a number of people. It was a good-sized staff.[†] I would say there were a dozen or more officers working on it, other than the clerical help that we had. There were many, many ideas that came up. The one that I was first involved with was some way of knowing that a kamikaze, even after he got some bullets in his aircraft and in himself, he was going to keep on coming, so how could we come up with a weapon that would do more than just put him full of holes—something that would disintegrate the craft. It was Admiral Burke's thought that the air-to-air rocket might be possible, using a large influence fuze on it.[‡]

---

[*] OP-05 – Deputy Chief of Naval Operations (Air).
[†] In the summer of 1945 Vice Admiral Willis A. Lee, Jr., USN, commanded Task Force 69, which conducted anti-kamikaze operational tests in Casco Bay, Maine. It reported to Burke's section n Washington.
[‡] The influence or proximity fuze in antiaircraft weapons was a device that would explode in the vicinity of an enemy aircraft and thus not require a direct hit.

John T. Mason: This was long before the Sidewinder?*

Admiral Martin: Yes, it was long before that. That seemed to be coming along fine, and he sent me and Pete Aurand. You may have heard his name.†

John T. Mason: I know Pete Aurand.

Admiral Martin: You know Peter. Burke sent us out to China Lake to see how they were coming along on their efforts in using the 5-inch rocket with influence fuze for air to air.‡ We hadn't used it for air to air before, and it was their finding that it wasn't going to be very successful. Now, Admiral Burke said scientists are wonderful people, but they are a peculiar breed. They are perfectionists, and they will have a solution which we would accept, but they won't let you know about it if it isn't close to 100%. In this case we would probably take even a 30% and certainly a 50% reliability.

John T. Mason: Under duress?

Admiral Martin: Yes, so we got out there, and they found the HVAR had a slow-burning propellant that attenuated the influence fuze, which was a very sensitive fuzing.§ You might get a premature from it occasionally, but more times you would have it so that the fuze would go off in the proximity of the target as intended. While we were there, we found they had a 4½-inch rocket made by Allegheny Ballistics that had a very high rate of burning propellant that did not give this trouble. It was giving better than 80% reliability, and it gave you a better aiming situation, because it was a faster rocket and therefore an aim-off target—to lead the target, a deflection shot, we call it. On the deflection shot it was a much more decent thing to handle, because you didn't have to aim-off as far from the target as you did with the HVAR, the 5-incher. It was good enough that Pete Aurand and I got seven out of eight hits the first time we went up to try it.

---

* Sidewinder is an air-to-air infrared-homing missile with a speed of approximately Mach 2.5. It has been operational, in various forms, since 1956. It was used extensively in the Vietnam War.
† Lieutenant Commander Evan P. Aurand, USN, later vice admiral.
‡ China Lake is another name for the Naval Ordnance Test Station at Inyokern, California.
§ HVAR – high-velocity aircraft rocket.

John T. Mason: That was more than 30%.

Admiral Martin: We were flying Corsairs, and it was not an airplane that I was very familiar with.* Yet that rocket was sufficiently accurate, good, and reliable that we each got seven out of eight hits. I am sure Commodore Burke was delighted with that, and it was his intention to get that out there as early as possible. I think it was 200,000 rounds that he wanted to get there within a very short period of time. As far as I recall, that was accomplished. While Pete and I were in California, we saw a B-29, had a high fence around it, very heavily guarded. This was the one that was on its way to drop the atom bomb.†

John T. Mason: Did you find out that was so?

Admiral Martin: No, it was so carefully guarded that either the people we were close to out there either didn't know or wouldn't tell. Once that second nuclear weapon was dropped, that war was over.

John T. Mason: Tell me what other approaches were made to the kamikaze problem, besides the one that you undertook when you went out to China Lake?

Admiral Martin: Well, that shows how short a time I had been on this project, and also how involved my part of it on the aviation side of it was. Other than to make sure that we had the launchers on our aircraft to accommodate the rocket and means of implementing that, I wasn't familiar with the other aspects of dealing with it.

John T. Mason: The war came to an end abruptly, and your project petered out with it, did it not?

Admiral Martin: Yes, it did. It was a very worthwhile one, but we still would have taken a lot of losses if we had had to go into Japan proper with amphibious operations. It is a happy thing that it didn't happen. I am sure that while there are some arguments against

---

* The Vought F4U Corsair was in production longer than any other U.S. fighter plane of World War II. It first entered fleet squadrons in 1942. The last Corsair was produced in 1953. The F4U-1 was 33 feet, 4 inches long; wingspan of 41 feet; gross weight of 14,000 pounds; and top speed of 417 miles per hour.
† In the first combat use of atomic bombs, U.S. B-29 bombers hit Hiroshima, on the island of Honshu, on 6 August 1945 and Nagasaki, on Kyushu, on 9 August.

the use of the atomic bombs that we used in there, I am confident in my own mind that not only more Americans would have been lost to do it otherwise, but also many more Japanese would have been lost as well in a long, drawn-out amphibious operations with the total invasion that would have been necessary.

John T. Mason: I suppose also, in the sense of looking at the world picture, it had to happen sometime or other that we had to know about the devastating effect of bombs of this sort.

Admiral Martin: Yes, I think that in itself has been a form of deterrent, don't you? If it had never been exploded, no one would have the fear of it that they do today, because they wouldn't know just what the extent of it was.

John T. Mason: So it has value in that sense.

Admiral Martin: I think so. Well, so the war is over.

John T. Mason: And you were deprived of your special assignment on the West Coast?

Admiral Martin: Well, that would have been gone too. What I had really wanted to do, from the time I became a fleet pilot, was to eventually become a test pilot back at Patuxent River, Maryland. When the commodore asked me what I wanted, I told him how strongly I felt about that, and so he supported me in it. Shortly thereafter, I received orders to Patuxent Naval Air Base in Maryland to be director of the tactical test division down there. It was a captain's job, and I was just a commander, so I felt very fortunate to have that assignment.[*]

John T. Mason: What was your motivation to become a test pilot?

Admiral Martin: I guess the same one that put me into the instrument and the night specialty—that you learn more and more, and you sharpen your skills with the things that are the most demanding. I always had such a great respect for our test pilots who had

---

[*] Commander Martin served as the Naval Air Test Center from September 1945 to August 1948.

been with us even back in the early days when they were operating out of Anacostia.* They were doing some very fine things for naval aviation, so it was rather a natural—and I think rather a common aspiration for fleet pilots today.

John T. Mason: Did you see it then as an opportunity to perfect the instrument-flying techniques—a further opportunity for you in this field?

Admiral Martin: Yes, I intended to pursue that. In fact, some of our most worthwhile projects down there were with that objective—night and all-weather. I must say that the ones we had written up ourselves—they didn't come to us. We thought them through and wrote them up as a proposal and took them with the necessary five copies, and so on, to Washington and got a BuAer signature on them.†

John T. Mason: Even then, the advocacy of these directions in naval aviation was not so widespread, was it? You had perfected the techniques out in the Pacific, but even so it wasn't all-pervasive in naval aviation, was it?

Admiral Martin: No, and as the war ended this was the desire of the top level of naval aviation—that there not be a specialized groups, that all carrier pilots would be capable of doing the night and all-weather business. That has continued today. With the advent of the jet that cannot fly low under the clouds and must go up into them, whatever is there—if there is an overcast, they have to go through it for reasons of fuel consumption, if not other. They operate most efficiently at high altitudes, from 35,000 on up. Consequently, the very necessity of having to go through whatever cloud layer is there and coming back down through it placed a higher requirement on the pilot's qualifications to handle that sort of thing. Of course, the fact that you do get upstairs so quickly in a jet meant that if you could get on top, you would do it in a much shorter time than with a propeller aircraft that has a much slower rate of climb.

---

* Anacostia is a section of the District of Columbia. It is across the Anacostia River from Washington. Until 1944, when the function was transferred to Patuxent River, Maryland, the air station at Anacostia was the site of the Navy's service testing of new aircraft.
† BuAer – Bureau of Aeronautics.

That was my desire, and when I first reported in to that tactical test division, I was the only one in that division who had what they called an unrestricted instrument rating. The Navy called it the "green card," which permitted the pilot with this special instrument rating to sign his own clearance. He didn't have to have someone else to sign an instrument clearance for him; he could sign his own.

John T. Mason: He's a privileged character.

Admiral Martin: He was privileged. I think usually he handled it a little more carefully. He planned the flight very carefully, he checked the weather; it was his full responsibility. I don't know of many cases where that privilege was abused. I set a time limit for my pilots to become instrument qualified. Many of them were youngsters. For example, the Deputy Chief of Naval Operations for Air, Vice Admiral Fred Turner—we called him "Foxy"—was a young jaygee in my squadron.* He and some other young tigers like him really picked up this challenge with zest, and it was only about six months until everybody was fully qualified on instruments.

Instead of being in a position that many outfits were of having to kick pilots out of the ready room to go fly in bad weather, I was in the enviable position of having to hold them back if the weather was too bad. But they became extremely competent as instrument pilots, and they took on the night and all-weather projects with enthusiasm. I considered our mission to be the most interesting one down there, because some of the test divisions were in a position of proving a manufacturer honest—that he has met his specification, and you were always dealing with production-type aircraft. Where in the tactical test division, our most important mission was to be able to advise the Bureau of Aeronautics and the Chief of Naval Operations on what kind of airplane they should be looking for in the future—what might its functions be.

Here's where Arleigh Burke came in. He was on the General Board at that time and also the most knowledgeable man in the service for across-the-board weapons. I

---

* Vice Admiral Frederick C. Turner, USN, served as Deputy Chief of Naval Operations (Air Warfare) from 6 October 1976 to 30 June 1979. As a junior officer, Turner served in tactical test and Patuxent River, Maryland, from June 1947 to November 1949.

asked him to come down and talk to our group to give us some advice on what we could expect in the future as to delivery of nuclear weapons—are there going to be enough of them that we should have all of our tactical squadrons equipped to deliver them, or will there be so few that we would need only a handful of special aircraft, like a possible conversion of the P2V or an aircraft of the A-3 variety?* The admiral came down and spent an afternoon with us and answered all of our questions. It was like taking a lost man out of the wilderness; we began to see in which direction we should be going on them, how much endurance the airplane should have. It practically sizes the airplane as to how large it will be, as to predictions how much this weapon is going to weigh.

The admiral was able to tell us then that they were going to make it much smaller and lighter than the "Fat Boy" that had to be carried in the bomb bay of that period, and that this was a capability that the Navy certainly should have.† It should not be an exclusive capability of any one single service, because our air capability at sea, at that time and even today, can reach areas in the world with capability of precise application that can't be reached now by land-based aircraft. That subject and many others of a conventional variety the admiral was able to cover, and they all turned out to be correct.

John T. Mason: That was very helpful, I am sure. Did you have anything to do with the school down there, the Test Pilot School?

Admiral Martin: Yes, I did. It certainly was not my idea, and I wouldn't be able to tell you whose idea it was.

John T. Mason: I think it was Trapnell, was it not?

---

* During the first half of the 20th century, the Navy's General Board was comprised of senior naval officers who helped shape strategy, policy, and ship characteristics. Commodore Burke had a 15-month tour of duty on the General Board in 1947-48.
The Lockheed P2V Neptune was a land-based patrol plane that first entered an operational squadron in March 1947. The Douglas A3D Skywarrior first entered fleet squadrons in 1956 as a carrier-based heavy bomber. It was reclassified as the A-3 in 1962.
† The nuclear bomb dropped on Hiroshima on 6 August 1945 was called "Little Boy;" it was 28 inches in diameter and weighed 9,000 pounds. The next bomb, dropped on Nagasaki on August 1945, was called "Fat Man;" it was 60 inches in diameter and weighed 10,000 pounds. The great size of these weapons was a concern to the Navy, because no carrier aircraft of the era had the capability of delivery. The Navy first experimented with carrier launching of the shore-based P2V-2 Neptune bomber and later designed the AJ-1 Savage, which was the first specific carrier aircraft capable of delivering a nuclear weapon.

Admiral Martin: Yes, Fred Trapnell, who was an exceptional man and one of the niftiest pilots I have ever flown with; he was just a natural.* There are three or four people that I knew very well who were better than I was, and he was one of them. He was just completely at home in an airplane; he knew what it was going to do. For example, Johnny Hyland, who recently retired as a four-star, was in an airshow when he hit a bird on a pass that seriously damaged the control surfaces in the tail.† Trapnell got in another aircraft and went up to see what the damage was. As I understand it, Trapnell—by looking over the exterior of the aircraft—was able to tell and advise Johnny Hyland as to how the aircraft would perform when he slowed down to landing speed, to approach speeds, and that it would be unsafe.

John T. Mason: That is precisely what Johnny Hyland told me.

Admiral Martin: That is exactly what happened. Johnny bailed out and was picked up without injury. Trapnell had an insight into aircraft and aircraft performance that was most unique, most unusual. We used to fly the Beechcraft back and forth between Washington and the Patuxent River. He would fly in one direction, and I would fly in the other, and he would, without giving it any thought at all—it was just as smooth as silk, on everything he did—his landings were just perfect three-point landings. I used to really work at it to be as good as he was, but I never was.

It probably was his initial idea that there should be a Test Pilot School in order to centralize the talent for instruction. So he and Captain Bill Davis and Tom Connolly and a fellow named Syd Sherby and a few others—there was a power plant man whose name I can't remember who was a lieutenant at the time.‡ These were officers who were on duty there who drew up the courses. They actually authored the courses and started the school. I think Syd Sherby was the principal lecturer, so to speak, and it might be that

---

* Commander Frederick M. Trapnell, USN, commanded test pilot programs at both Anacostia and Patuxent River during World War II. On 21 April 1943, at Muroc Army Airfield in California, he became the first U.S. naval aviator to fly a jet plane, the Bell XP-59A Airacomet. The official Test Pilot Training Program, with Captain Trapnell in command, was inaugurated at Patuxent in 1948.
† Admiral John J. Hyland, USN, served as Commander in Chief Pacific Fleet from 30 November 1967 to 5 December 1970. His oral history is in the Naval Institute collection.
‡ Captain William V. Davis Jr., USN; Commander Sydney S. Sherby, USN.

Tom Connolly was the first director of the Test Pilot School.* Of course, it was a big success—by concentrating the best of your talent.

---

* Commander Thomas F. Connolly, USN was the director of the Test Pilot School from 1948 to 1951. See *Naval Aviation News*, July-August 1983.

Interview Number 3 with Vice Admiral William I. Martin, U.S. Navy (Retired)

Place: Admiral Martin's home in Alexandria, Virginia

Date: Wednesday, 28 November 1979

John T. Mason: We are still at Patuxent Naval Air Base, and you were talking about your job as a test pilot.

Admiral Martin: That was the beginning of three wonderful years for me, because I was associated with some very high-caliber people. Apollo Soucek was the commander of the Naval Air Test Center, and Fred Trapnell—everybody called him "Trap"—was the chief of staff.[*] Captain Vosseller was there at that time, and later Captain Ned Hannegan came in to command the Naval Air Station.[†]

Shortly after I arrived, a week afterward, I was somewhat surprised—I knew I had received a recommendation for the Distinguished Service Medal, but I had no idea I would get it, because it was considered for flag rank only, and I was only a commander. But I was awarded the Distinguished Service Medal for the night carrier work I had done during three years of combat.

John T. Mason: That was so original and such a tremendous contribution that they reached down.

Admiral Martin: It was plowing a new field, so to speak. Also, it was an exciting time for flying, because the Navy had been able to get flyable aircraft that had been outstanding—well, some of them not quite so outstanding—during World War II, including the foreign models.

---

[*] Rear Admiral Apollo Soucek, USN, served as Commander Naval Air Test Center, Patuxent River, from 1947 to 1949. Captain Fred M. Trapnell, USN.
[†] Captain Aurelius B. Vosseller, USN; Captain Edward A. Hannegan, USN. From June 1945 to July 1946, Captain Hannegan served as commanding officer of the naval air station.

John T. Mason: The Messerschmitt 262-S?[*]

Admiral Martin: We had German types, the Italian, the British, and a number of the Japanese. We had their Emily, the flying boat; we had their Zero.[†] I think we had an Oscar and a Kate.[‡] There were at least five different types of Japanese aircraft there, so it was an exciting time.

John T. Mason: And they were all operational? What did you do about spare parts?

Admiral Martin: They were all operational. As to spare parts, in many cases they were machined; they were there. I think a little later the Japanese, as well as the Germans, were very cooperative in providing spare parts. In fact, the Germans gave us some of their scientists and some of their aeronautical engineers. They came over, and we had two that I recall at Patuxent River; they were very high type, fine technicians, aeronautical engineers—very helpful and very cooperative.

John T. Mason: As I understand it, for the Messerschmitt you had the 262-S, which was the very latest model in World War II. It wasn't a single plane? You had a number of them?

Admiral Martin: Yes, we did. In the test division where I was director of tactical tests, we had a spare Jumo engine. We had the Heinkel, which was a two-propeller aircraft; one was a puller and one was a pusher. No one really wanted to fly it, because if you had to bail out you'd be chopped by the prop behind you. The Germans had devised a very clever explosive hub so that if you were to bail out, you could electrically explode that hub on the rear propeller and get rid of it before you bailed out. This was something, however, that we had no real faith in; we didn't trust that hub.

---

[*] The German Messerschmitt Me 262 Schwalbe (Swallow) was the world's first operational jet fighter. It entered combat in mid-1944.
[†] Japan's Kawanishi H8K flying boat was known by the Allied code designation "Emily." The Mitsubishi-built A6M Zero was the best-known fighter plane in the Japanese Navy in World War II.
[‡] "Oscar" was the Allied code name for the Japanese Nakajima Ki 43 fighter plane. "Kate" was the Allied designation for the Japanese Nakajima B5N carrier-based torpedo bomber.

John T. Mason: Well, you didn't want to destroy the plane anyway.

Admiral Martin: No, you wouldn't, but if you are in the air and you have to bail out for one reason or another, you'd like to get rid of that propeller before you went over the side, because you would certainly get chopped up by that rear propeller.

John T. Mason: That was something that wasn't duplicated elsewhere, was it, in other models?

Admiral Martin: There was something like that; the Ryan Fireball came out a few years later.* It had a propeller in the front and a jet in the rear. It was not a successful airplane; it never got out of the experimental type. It was never produced. They put out three or four of them before they stopped, but that was a combination of a jet and a prop, and it was not a workable combination, mostly because of its lack of range and certain other troubles.

As I say, it was an exciting time to be a test pilot and have the opportunity to fly the foreign models as well as the ones we had been using during the war which had not yet completed their inspection and survey trials, and we had a number of these.

John T. Mason: These were new U.S. planes that we coming in?

Admiral Martin: No, these were the ones like the F6F.† The investigation and survey of the F6 hadn't really been completed—the things that go on to prove that the manufacturer had performed properly.

John T. Mason: That was one of your missions, wasn't it?

---

* The Ryan-built FR Fireball was a composite fighter plane that had a propeller forward and a jet engine in the rear fuselage. The FR-1 first entered an operational squadron in March 1945 in VF-66. The FR-1 was 32 feet, 4 inches long; wingspan of 40 feet; gross weight of 11,652 pounds, and top speed of 404 miles per hour. The plane was withdrawn from naval service following carrier-based exercises in 1946 and 1947.
† Grumman F6F Hellcat fighters first entered fleet squadrons in early 1943. The most commonly employed version of the airplane was the F6F-5, which was 34 feet long, wingspan of 43 feet, gross weight of 15,413 pounds, and top speed of 380 miles per hour.

Admiral Martin: It was the mission of all the five test divisions. Some got into it more deeply than others. I would say the tactical test got into it the least, with the least depth, because our mission, as I interpreted it, was more to determine the future and to advise the people in the Bureau of Aeronautics and the Chief of Naval Operations as to what types and performance we should be looking for in aircraft of the future. This is one of the reasons that very early I asked Arleigh Burke, who was then on the General Board, to come down and spend some time with us to advise us what we might expect, what might be the requirements for the Navy as a whole in the future, and what we might look forward to in order that we could adapt to the future of aviation and the types of aircraft, the performance we should have. It was a case of whether we should be looking for range and endurance or high performance with probably shorter range and endurance, and whether or not there would be enough nuclear weapons to go around after the Strategic Air Command was satisfied—that there would be atomic weapons, nuclear weapons, of a size and capability that the Navy could have that capability.[*]

In fact, that did come about, of course, so that the nuclear weapons became small enough and light enough that carrier-type aircraft—tactical aircraft on a carrier—could carry them. Before we got to that, though, we had come up with the P2V as a possibility of carrying the biggest—I think they called it Little Boy, which was the same type that was dropped at Hiroshima and Nagasaki.[†] It could actually carry it with a full load of fuel and could take off from the carrier. It couldn't come back and land on the carrier, but this did give us a capability to carry a nuclear weapon. Later we developed a twin-engine propeller-driven aircraft, and I believe it was designed with that particular mission, to carry a nuclear weapon with sufficient range to cover some of the more important targets in the southwestern parts of the Soviet Union and bloc countries in that

---

[*] The Strategic Air Command, based at Offutt Air Force Base near Omaha, Nebraska, controlled the Air Force's nuclear-capable bombers.
[†] The Lockheed P2V Neptune was a land-based Navy patrol plane that first entered an operational squadron in March 1947.
"Little Boy" was the nickname of the U.S. atomic bomb dropped on Hiroshima, Japan, on 6 August 1945. It weighed 9,000 pounds and measured 10 feet in length and 28 inches in diameter. "Fat Man" was the nickname of the U.S. atomic bomb dropped on Nagasaki, Japan, on 9 August 1945. It weighed 10,000 pounds and measured 10 feet, 8 inches in length and 5 feet in diameter.

area.* And it had enough range to go to the target and come back and could actually land back aboard with the weapon.

John T. Mason: You got Burke involved because the General Board at that time was making a very extensive study, and this was a portion of it, was that not so?

Admiral Martin: I'm sure they were. As I understood it, they were supposed to be the elder statesmen of the Navy, though I certainly would not put Arleigh Burke in that category.

John T. Mason: He was put there for a very specific purpose—as young blood, as a young Turk, so to speak.

Admiral Martin: I think that was the first time it was done.

John T. Mason: It was the first time, and he organized this vast study which incorporated the whole of the government. Typical Burke.

Admiral Martin: Typical. We were scratching our heads, really, until he came down and talked to us, and he put us on the path where we had some confidence that we were going to do some worthwhile predicting and be able to shape the performance requirements of the attack aircraft, the fighter aircraft, the need for the forerunners of the airborne early warning type of aircraft that gave the fleet an elevated radar that would reach over the horizon and keep track of everything on the surface as well as in the air. That was a successful endeavor from the beginning. Of course, there have been many improvements on that now. Today the Navy's AEW aircraft is almost as capable as the huge Air Force

---

* The AJ Savage was a propeller-driven carrier-based nuclear strike aircraft built by North American Aviation, Inc. It first entered the fleet in squadron VC-5 in September 1949. It was reclassified A-2 in 1962. The AJ-1 version was 63 feet long; wingspan of 75 feet; gross weight of 52,862 pounds; and top speed of 471 miles per hour. It had a maximum bomb capacity of 12,000 pounds.

aircraft, which is so much more expensive, but two of the Navy's AEWs will accomplish almost as much as the Air Force airborne early warning.[*]

John T. Mason: Did Radford come down? He was VCNO at that point.[†]

Admiral Martin: Yes, I was going to mention that.

Shortly after I arrived at Patuxent River, Admiral Radford sent word that he would like for me to see him at our mutual convenience. He was Vice Chief of Naval Operations at that time, so I went on up to the Pentagon and spent an hour or more reviewing with him what we planned to do on the all-weather business—what we had done and what we proposed to do. He was so impressed with this that he set out a schedule for me to proceed to all the major naval air stations to deliver a talk on all-weather and the requirements of all-weather for the future. He asked that I fly myself to these places in order that whatever the weather was I could take off and proceed.

John T. Mason: And you would be the actual demonstration?

Admiral Martin: Yes, this worked out with considerable excitement in some cases. Had this requirement not been on me, I might not have taken off in the weather that prevailed at times. I recall very vividly taking off from the naval air station at Memphis. Admiral Felix Stump was there at the time, and the weather was so terrible that there were a number of them who went out to the flight line to make sure that I took off in this weather.[‡]

I was flying an F7F Grumman twin-engine fighter that was intended to get out

---

[*] AWACS, airborne warning and control system, is an aerial look-down radar and tracking system carried on board the Air Force's E-3 Sentry, a modified Boeing 707 airliner with a rotating radome on top. The Navy's E-2 Hawkeye is a propeller-driven carrier plane that has a look-down radar in order to track and manage the air picture from aloft. Both were in use at the time of the interview.
[†] Admiral Arthur W. Radford, USN, a naval aviator, served as Vice Chief of Naval Operations from 3 January 1948 to 16 April 1949.
[‡] Rear Admiral Felix B. Stump, USN, was Chief, Naval Air Technical Training from 1945 to 1948.

there during the last year of the war, but it didn't quite make it.* It was a fine airplane, but it had no anti-icing and de-icing equipment, and there were icing conditions. I took off at dark and flew to Patuxent River. I had no more gotten off the ground until I started getting ice, and by this time though I knew if I could get 2,000 feet above the icing level or 2,000 below it, I wouldn't pick up a dangerous amount of it. So I climbed up on top of it. I was never really above the clouds, but I was above the icing level. By the time I got to Patuxent River, I was still in the static disturbance that you have on your radio, and it was useless to me, but the YE receiver that I had, that we used during the war, was giving me sectors that gave me a little better than just the general direction of the naval air station at Patuxent.† When I made my let-down there, I had an inch and one-half to two inches of ice on the wings and on the whole external body.

John T. Mason: Adding considerably to the weight.

Admiral Martin: That was a very exciting flight, because the F7F, as nice as it was, without droppable fuel tanks, had limited range, and when I let down at Patuxent River, I did not have fuel to go to an alternate field. I had to land there. I knew the officer who was in charge of ground-control radar, which turned out so successfully, and when I would ask for a practice let-down to touch down, he knew what I meant, and he would bring me in all the way and try to put me in the middle of the runway and tell me not to veer at all to the left. If you are going to err, don't err to the left, because that is where his radar shack was. He didn't want me over there.

On this assignment Admiral Radford asked me to take, it was very successful.

John T. Mason: How many stations were there that you had to visit?

---

* Grumman F7F Tigercat fighters first entered Marine Corps squadrons in early 1943. The F7F was the U.S. Navy's first twin-engine fighter to be produced in quantity. The F7F-3 version of the airplane was 45 feet, 4 inches long; wingspan of 51 feet, 6 inches; gross weight of 25,720 pounds; and top speed of 435 miles per hour. Grumman built 60 of the F7F-3N night-fighter model, which had a radome in the nose.
† YE-ZB was the designation for a radio direction-finding/homing device that enabled pilots to get a bearing to an aircraft carrier or shore base.

Admiral Martin: I went to Norfolk, to Jacksonville, to Corpus Christi, to San Diego, to Alameda, to Seattle, and to Glenview, which was the headquarters of the Naval Air Reserves at that time, and to Memphis.* There may have been some others like Squantum and some stations that are no longer in commission.† That sort of set the pattern that introduced to the pilots what they were expected to do in getting instrument qualifications. It stimulated a number of them so that they were able to go ahead and get what was called their standard instrument rating. And a few of them were sufficiently interested in it to go on and get their special instrument rating, which we called the green card. With that a pilot could fly on his own clearance; he didn't require the commanding officer's signature to take off under instrument conditions. He could sign his own clearance. I think that still holds even today.

John T. Mason: Did you have anything to do with the National Advisory Committee for Aeronautics.

Admiral Martin: The NACA they called it then.‡ We worked closely with them. The flight test division at that time was headed by Bill Davis, who later became DCNO (Air).§ Their work was more in the technical areas for flight—the technical areas of the performance of the aircraft, the control system, how it flew, etc. And they worked very closely with NACA, especially with the NACA plant at Langley Field.** I remember a fellow named Bill Groth, who became very important in NACA. They worked very closely together, and they were mutually helpful. This was before the space thing—before NASA. It was before the agency became very heavy on the side of space; in recent years they seem to be moving back to a little better balance where they put more

---

* Glenview, Illinois, in the northern suburbs of Chicago, was the site of a naval air station.
† Squantum Naval Air Station was in service from 1923 to 1953. It was on Squantum Point in the city of Quincy, Massachusetts.
‡ The National Advisory Committee for Aeronautics was the forerunner of the current National Aeronautics and Space Administration (NASA).
§ Captain William V. Davis Jr., USN. As a vice admiral he served as Deputy Chief of Naval Operations (Air) from 1 August 1956 to 22 May 1958.
** In 1916 the National Advisory Committee for Aeronautics recommended a joint aircraft providing ground. Langley Field, near Hampton and Newport News, Virginia, was established in 1917. In 1948 it was renamed Langley Air Force Base. It is now part of Joint Base Langley-Eustis.

time into the manned aircraft than they had for some time. But they have always been very helpful.

John T. Mason: You started to tell me last time about the relationship you had with the Test Pilot School down there.

Admiral Martin: Yes, right. There was no Test Pilot School when I reported in down there, and I really don't know whose idea it was for sure, but I think it was Trapnell who first conceived it. He was very active in establishing it; others that were very important in establishing it were Syd Sherby, who was an aeronautical engineer, and Tom Connolly, who was the first director of the school.[*] Those two and three or four others who mostly were in the flight test division actually prepared the course.

John T. Mason: There was one fellow, I guess a civilian whose name was Daniel Dommasch, an aerodynamicist.[†] He went on to teach at Princeton later on.

Admiral Martin: They had some power plant people: one named Nick Scobo, who was very good at power plants, and one named Zukrow. I really didn't have too much to do with them, because we were in a different field of endeavor.

I continued to pursue the night business. When I reported in, there were only two aviators who had the special instrument rating. None of the pilots who were in the test division had even a standard instrument rating. I made this a requirement and gave them six months to accomplish it, and they did. I was in the very favorable position then of not having to push them out of the ready room to go out and fly if the weather was a little bad. I was actually holding them back. There were two especially. One was Fox Turner, who was Deputy Chief of Naval Operations for Air until very recently when he retired.[‡] Fox Turner and Hugh Tate, both young jaygees, and Carl Dace.[§] I actually had to hold

---
[*] The oral history of Connolly, who retired as a vice admiral, is in the Naval Institute collection.
[†] Daniel O. Dommasch was the coauthor, along with Sydney S. Sherby and Thomas F. Connolly, of the book *Airplane Aerodynamics* (New York: Putnam, 1957). It has since appeared in updated editions.
[‡] Vice Admiral Frederick C. Turner, USN, served as Deputy Chief of Naval Operations (Air Warfare) from 6 October 1976 to 30 June 1979.
[§] Lieutenant (junior grade) Hugh J. Tate, USN; Lieutenant (junior grade) Carl C. Dace, USN.

them back. They wanted to go out into what were zero-zero conditions that were below the established minimum for the field. We did operate at much lower minimums than anybody else did, down to 50 feet and a quarter of a mile. I think even today no normal standard operations in any airfield go below 100 feet and a half mile.

John T. Mason: You must have had some accidents then?

Admiral Martin: There were some, but weather-caused accidents. I don't recall any except one case, a fellow named Joe Smith, who was a tremendous pilot. As a matter of fact, he was a graduate of the Empire Test Pilots' School, as well as the one at Farnborough, England. He came in for a landing—we had had heavy snows, and it had accumulated very much on the ground. There was heavy snow while he was in the air, and he picked the wrong track. It really wasn't his fault, but he landed into deep ruts that were in the runway, and he went over on his back. He wasn't injured, and the airplane wasn't seriously damaged. He was flying the F8F, the Grumman fighter of that time.[*] The Tigercat was the F7F, and the Hellcat was the F6F. The F8 was a very high performance, light fighter, single place, and a real performer. It came out just too late to get into World War II.

John T. Mason: You mentioned the Empire Test Pilots' School. Did you have a very intimate relationship with that English school?

Admiral Martin: Here again, the flight test division did have continuous relationships with them. Indeed, we had an exchange. We had some Royal Navy pilots in the program, especially after the Test Pilot School had started. We had one or two pilots who were selected to take that course over there.

John T. Mason: Is that school still in existence?

---

[*] Grumman F8F Bearcat fighters first entered fleet squadrons in 1945. The F8F-1 version was 28 feet long, wingspan of 35 feet, gross weight of 12,947 pounds, and top speed of 421 miles per hour. It was one of the best piston-engine planes ever to serve the U.S. Navy but had a short operational life because of the advent of jet fighters.

Admiral Martin: I'm sure it is, yes.

John T. Mason: Was there any relationship with the Naval Postgraduate School?

Admiral Martin: No direct relationship.

John T. Mason: The Naval Postgraduate School did have some concern for aeronautics, too, didn't they?

Admiral Martin: You would have expected that the tactical test division would have had a stronger contact there, because we were closer to fleet operations than the other test divisions. The other test divisions were service tests which really determined the maintenance of the aircraft, electronics tests of the electronic systems of the airplanes, ordnance tests for the guns and their installation and their effect on the flying characteristics, and in some cases the exhaust getting into the inlet ducts of the aircraft and the bomb-carrying devices, and launchers, and all that sort of thing. The pilot test divisions covered everything, and the other four divisions became more involved in the technical side than tactical test, which, as I say, was more in line of trying to predict future requirements.

Except for general coverage of learning, all we could from the foreign aircraft that we flew—and I think we did do a good job of learning what we could from that, I would say especially the British—we certainly didn't want to build the kind of airplanes that the Japanese were building, because they just were too vulnerable to enemy fire. The reason they were light and maneuverable was because they just didn't put any armor plate in there; the defensive things weren't there.

John T. Mason: Who was responsible for gathering all those foreign planes at that point?

Admiral Martin: I wish I knew that. We had some wonderful chiefs of the Bureau of Aeronautics during that period, and also Admiral Soucek at Patuxent River and, here again, Trapnell. Just who instigated that effort to accumulate all those—we should remember that the Naval Air Test Center was established shortly after World War II began, so it was a going concern during the last three and a half years of the war. They had some of these foreign models, especially the Japanese ones, German ones too. They had those in flying condition before the war was over.

John T. Mason: You haven't mentioned Russian planes.

Admiral Martin: No, we didn't have any of those.

John T. Mason: Then that wasn't an oversight?

Admiral Martin: No. One of the most exciting airplanes for me and one of the most interesting was the British twin-engine fighter.[*] It wasn't difficult to fly, but it was very difficult to taxi, because the brakes were hand brakes rather than foot pedals.

John T. Mason: You were flying the P-80s there, too, weren't you?[†]

Admiral Martin: Yes, we were. The very first jet that came to Patuxent River was the XP-80. I think it was about the third or fourth P-80 that was produced. I remember a very famous Marine pilot brought it in, Marion Carl, who later became a general officer in the Marine Corps.[‡] Marion Carl and Trap Trapnell were recognized as the most proficient test pilots at Patuxent River. They just seemed to be a cut above the others, knowing exactly what was going on in the aircraft.

John T. Mason: Is this just a natural endowment?

---

[*] Admiral Martin may have been referring to the Royal Air Force's Gloster Meteor, which was the first British jet fighter. It first flew in 1943 and first went into operation in the summer of 1944.
[†] The Air Force P-80 jet fighter—later F-80—came into the Navy in the late 1940s. Initially the Navy designated it as TO-1, a trainer built by Lockheed. After the Navy changed the manufacturer Lockheed's symbol from O to T, the plane became the TV-1.
[‡] On 25 August 1947, Major Marion E. Carl, USMC, set a new world speed record of 650.796 miles per hour while flying a Douglas Skystreak D-558-1 over a three-kilometer course at Muroc, California. He was earlier noted for his combat exploits during World War II. He eventually became a major general.

Admiral Martin: I believe it is. I used to fly with both of them when we would go up to the Bureau of Aeronautics. We would take off in a two-place Beechcraft plane—pilot and copilot.[*] One would fly it up to Anacostia, and the other would fly it back to Patuxent River. It just seemed to come so easy for Trapnell and Marion Carl to fly it so smoothly and their landings so perfect. I realize that I was really working on it to try to equal them; I don't think I ever did. They were recognized as the leaders.

The next jet we had was the XP-59, which was the first jet that the Navy might be able to use, and it was built by Bell.[†] It didn't work out; it was lacking in performance. On a simulated carrier approach, for example, if you got a little bit too low and slow, you would have great difficulty, because you would apply full throttle, and it would be a slow count of about five before it would take effect. It was not a successful aircraft, and it was not produced. Whereas the XP-80 became the P-80. A number of them were built, and later they were designated the T-33. There are still some of those flying.

John T. Mason: You must have had a close liaison with industry too. Were they there shepherding their product?

Admiral Martin: They had all of these aerospace companies' representatives there. They were resident; they lived there, and others would come in on a special project. When a new airplane was being tested there, the manufacturer would have a special representative on hand to make sure there would be no delay in getting parts and helping with various discrepancies that came up. They were extremely cooperative, and in an amazingly short time, when a deficiency was found, they would solve it and bring in the parts that were necessary to correct it.

Here again, the principal for the aircraft and the power plant was the flight test division. They were very, very attentive to all five test divisions and the problems that they had with their particular projects. The same is true for the manufacturers in the electronic communications area and in the ordnance area. There was a very close and a

---

[*] The SNB Kansan was a training aircraft manufactured by Beech Aircraft Company. The Navy first ordered a version of the airplane in 1941; the Army designation of the equivalent plane was AT-11.
[†] On 21 April 1943 Captain Frederick M. Trapnell, USN, became the first U.S. naval aviator to fly a jet aircraft. He flew the Bell XP-59A Airacomet at Muroc, California.

very valuable tie between the test division, the Navy, and the various manufacturers. It was a very healthy thing. I have always believed that the so-called military-industrial combination, which has had a lot of criticism—I consider it one of the nation's most valuable combinations.

John T. Mason: Did the fleet units also cooperate, in terms of carriers, landing some of these planes on carriers?

Admiral Martin: Yes, the two type commanders, Commander Naval Air Force Atlantic Fleet and Commander Naval Air Force Pacific Fleet—through them we would arrange to use the carrier flight decks for special purposes, and they were always available and very cooperative.[*]

Of course, in turn, the Chief of the Bureau of Aeronautics was very close to them. The Chief of the Bureau of Aeronautics and the Commander of Naval Air Systems Command today are very responsive to the problems of the fleet.[†] A lot of those problems would come back to Patuxent River for them to help solve, because we had the facilities there and the talent to do it. I think that was one of the reasons it was almost invariably the aspiration of pilots in the fleet to eventually become tests pilots at Patuxent River. Each year, when the Bureau of Personnel was setting up the selection board to determine the ones that were going, the Bureau of Aeronautics and the type commanders would have representation to pick the best from the fleets to go to Test Pilot School. Then the best from the Test Pilot School usually were the ones selected to remain there as test pilots and as instructors in the school. Usually from there, they would select one or two who would go to the Empire Test Pilots' School.

John T. Mason: What were some of the criteria for selection?

---

[*] A type commander is in charge of a subdivision of the fleet, primarily for administrative management purposes. The type commanders here were involved with planes, aircraft carriers, and seaplane tenders.
[†] The Bureau of Ordnance existed until 1959, when it was combined with the Bureau of Aeronautics (BuAer) to form the Bureau of Naval Weapons (BuWeps). In 1966 there was a split that separated out the former BuOrd as the Naval Ordnance Systems Command (NavOrd) and essentially the former BuAer became the Navy Air Systems Command (NavAir), which still exists. In 1974 NavOrd was merged with the Naval Ship Systems Command to form the Naval Sea Systems Command (NavSea), which still exists.

Admiral Martin: Each command in the fleet, even a squadron commander, would nominate one or more, and the air wing commander would put in an endorsement, and the commanding officer of the carrier, I am sure, would endorse it. It would come right up through the channel, each one with their endorsements. Then the selection board for that purpose would go over these endorsements. They would have many more; the pilot himself would have to put in for it. That had to be one of them. They would select them, similar to the way they would select for promotion. They were very carefully selected—how well they had done. Naval aviation has always been one to try to measure proficiency in the air. Those who were accident free and those who had been able to put an E on their plane for gunnery, for bombing, or for whatever purpose—those all, I am sure, gave them "brownie points" toward being selected for Test Pilot School.*

I think that is about all I have to say about the test pilot experience.

John T. Mason: I take it this fulfilled your expectations, and you said that as a pilot in the fleet you wanted to become a test pilot.

Admiral Martin: Yes, it did. Those three years were three very exciting and rewarding years for me. Before the test center was started and before World War II, the Bureau of Aeronautics had come up with something they wanted test data on, and they would put it out to one of the type commanders, or maybe both, and the various fleet squadrons would test that thing—like oxygen equipment and things of that sort.

John T. Mason: Was this before they had Anacostia in operation, or was it in conjunction with it?

Admiral Martin: In addition to that. Anacostia did some wonderful things, but they did it on their own initiatives and with their own ideas and concepts. There were some wonderful people who did that test work. Trapnell was one of them, Dutch Duerfeldt, a

---

* The "E" stands for "efficiency" and is awarded for superior performance in various exercises and readiness inspections.

lot of old-timers.* That was before I was of sufficient rank and position in naval aviation to know precisely what they were doing. They did a lot of it, and where they needed a lot of data they would give it to the squadrons. So much for Patuxent River.

I went from the Test Pilot Center to become the executive officer of the Fleet All-Weather Training Unit Pacific. This was continuing interest in all weather. I became Paul Ramsey's executive officer at the naval air station in Barbers Point.† The Fleet All-Weather Training Unit was called FAWTUPAC at the beginning and then FAllWeaTraPac. We opposed changing the name. It wasn't our idea, but they just didn't think that FAWTUPAC got in the weather part of it. So they called it FAllWeaTraPac, and it had the mission of training for the Pacific Fleet, their night-fighter pilots, night attack pilots, and the CIC officers who were to become fighter control for night-fighter operations.‡ We had our own radar station called Seaweed, which was just outside the acreage that contained the naval air station.

John T. Mason: Did you ask for that assignment?

Admiral Martin: Yes, I did, and Paul Ramsey asked for me. Paul Ramsey and I had been together before on the old *Idaho*, my first ship. After I left Annapolis, I went to the *Idaho*, and Ramsey was one of the junior officers on board. He asked for me, and I asked for this assignment, so that was where I went.

We did all of the training for the pilots and the air controllers that were going to deploy in the Pacific Fleet for specialized night work. We had an additional mission to assist the ComFAir Hawaii in conducting the operational readiness inspections of the deploying carriers that would come through Hawaii.§ They would spend probably two weeks there in concentrated training, and at the end of that time they would be given an operational readiness inspection to make sure they were at the proper level to deploy into the Western Pacific.

---

* Clifford H. Duerfeldt, who eventually became a rear admiral.
† Captain Paul H. Ramsey, USN. Barbers Point was the site of a naval air station at the southwest "corner" of the island of Oahu, Hawaii.
‡ CIC – combat information center.
§ ComFAir – Commander Fleet Air.

During that tour, the Fleet All-Weather Training Unit received the first jets that ever came into Hawaii. We got two of them, and they were the P-80s.

John T. Mason: You already knew about them.

Admiral Martin: Yes, and there were only two pilots in Hawaii who had flown jets before, Paul Ramsey and myself. Paul had been at the Naval Air Test Center during the war. He was there shortly after it started, and so Ramsey and I, who had both been in test work, were the only ones who had flown jets. So it became our responsibility to check the other pilots out and put them through the familiarization course.

John T. Mason: You had your own little school.

Admiral Martin: Yes, we established our own little school. That was pretty interesting. Also while I was there, Admiral Radford was the CinCPac, and he sent for me.[*] I had seen him frequently. The first time we talked he asked me, "How long would it take me to become instrument qualified?"

I said, "Admiral, if you will give it the time, it could be done in concentrated fashion in probably a couple of weeks, but it would take at least 12 flights, depending on how well you do, to get a standard instrument rating." He wanted to do it, and he came over to Barbers Point. I had a fellow named Don Issit that I thought was a better instructor than I was, so Don took him up in the Beechcraft.[†] This was a four-star admiral who hadn't done a lot of flying in recent years, but after his very first flight Don said, "He's a natural, and it's going to be easy because he has the aptitude for it."

John T. Mason: Certainly the drive.

---

[*] Admiral Arthur W. Radford, USN, served as Commander in Chief Pacific/Commander in Chief U.S. Pacific Fleet, from 30 April 1949 to 10 July 1953.
[†] Commander Donald K. Issit, USN.

Admiral Martin: Certainly the drive and determination. I don't recall how many flights he took, but he took far less time than any of us estimated that it would take for him to become a proficient instrument pilot for that particular airplane.

John T. Mason: What was his reason for this?

Admiral Martin: Radford was always this way. He wanted to know what the young fellows were up against. I think it just became a goal of his. Here he was an aviator, and he really wasn't qualified to fly at night or in bad weather, and he just took this on as a goal. Because of that he could be extremely helpful to the all-weather effort there. His understanding of the needs of naval aviation was most unusual. As you know, he came up with the integrated maintenance system. I have forgotten the short title for that, but he had a big effect on naval aviation from the time he was a captain right all the way through four stars.

During this period he was very concerned as to what was happening to naval aviation and what appeared to him to be a threat by the Air Force that had this unification thing.* He had opposed the way they were about to do it, and here again I got in on just the fringes of that until it became a matter of concern to the Congress. They decided to have an investigation of the B-36, which was supposed to take over all of the offensive air of the country.† This is when he said we shouldn't put all of our eggs in one basket, as you remember. The House Armed Services Committee was determined to have what they called a B-36 investigation. But it was actually getting into the deepest concepts and strategy of the country. So it was a misnomer to call it the B-36 investigation, but that had to be dealt with first, before they could go on to other things. During a period of 18 months, Admiral Radford sent me to Washington eight times.

---

* In 1949, the Navy and Air Force were competing for scarce defense dollars. Secretary of Defense Louis Johnson accelerated production of the Air Force's B-36 bomber and canceled the aircraft carrier *United States* (CVA-58) soon after the beginning of construction. The Navy fought back, as detailed in Jeffrey G. Barlow, *Revolt of the Admirals* (Washington, D.C.: Naval Historical Center, 1994). See also Paul Schratz, "The Admirals' Revolt," *U.S. Naval Institute Proceedings*, February 1986, pages 64-71.

† Consolidated Vultee, based in San Diego, built the Air Force's B-36 bomber, known as the Peacemaker. The B-36D model was equipped with four J-47 jet engines in under-wing nacelles and six piston engines that drove propellers. The jet engines enhanced the plane's maximum speed from 376 miles per hour to 435 miles per hour. It first flew in 1946 and subsequently was operational in the Strategic Air Command from 1948 through 1959.

John T. Mason: Your special mission being what?

Admiral Martin: My mission was to assist in picking the technical panel that would shoot down the B-36, that would deal with the airplane itself, in order that Admiral Radford and others could deal with the more important points of the nation's defensive strategy.

John T. Mason: You had to have an intimate knowledge of the B-36 yourself?

Admiral Martin: Not too intimate, just how it performed and what its general performance characteristics were. The Air Force didn't want us near it. Not that I personally tried to get near it, but I was told by others that they wouldn't let anybody fly in one of them. I don't think that was essential, though, to deal with it. We knew what its performance characteristics were. The Air Force had some really ridiculous claims that because its wings were bigger and because it had four engines that it would fly higher than anything else. That just wasn't the case. When we were test flying, we were flying above 50,000 feet, and the B-36 couldn't do any better than that. It was really a very vulnerable airplane because those four big propellers and the size of the aircraft itself would give a tremendous reflection to radars. It would be picked up over 200 miles away by that radars of that period even.

John T. Mason: Why did the Air Force select this particular plane then as a focal point?

Admiral Martin: I don't think it has ever been published, and maybe you couldn't document it, but it was the belief of some in the Navy that the Air Force and the Army had a conspiracy at a very closely held level—that the Air Force would assist the Army in taking over the Marine Corps, if the Army would help the Air Force take over all of Navy aviation and Marine aviation. I don't know if that could be documented even today, but it certainly seemed to be their aim, and Admiral Radford had expressed himself strongly enough on this—by putting such a large proportion of the defense budget into the Air Force for strategic purposes only, left the tactical side out of it, and the Air Force was neglecting their tactical air forces all the time. It was just out of balance, so the Armed Services Committee decided to have this investigation.

I think it was the eighth time I was sent to Washington by Admiral Radford, and he came over to Barbers Point to see me off. He told my family, because I had been going so frequently, "Bill will come back quickly from this, because he is going over on this plane, and he is coming back with Admiral Fiske." Fiske was then the commander of Trust Territories in the Pacific.* On the strength of that, I took an extra shirt, extra underwear, and a toothbrush. I got over there in September, and I didn't get back until November.

John T. Mason: So much for his word.

Admiral Martin: So much for his word. I hadn't even taken my winter uniforms or anything like that. But the whole thing broke while I was there. The congressional committee investigation commenced, and that took quite a while. When it was clear that it was going to happen, there was a lot of preparation that had to be made, selecting those who would testify, and I personally—

John T. Mason: That was part of your role?

Admiral Martin: That was part of my role. Commander Bill Leonard, who later became a flag officer—he was such a capable test pilot, he was with me in the tactical test division at Patuxent River—was asked to testify on the ability to shoot down the B-36 in the daytime, and I was selected to be the one to take care of the aspect of being able to deal effectively with the B-36 at night.† Others were handling various other aspects of it—ordnance and so on. This is a little amusing: at that time, Congressman Dewey Short, who had given me my appointment to the Naval Academy, was number two on

---

* Rear Admiral Leon S. Fiske, USN, Deputy High Commissioner Trust Territory of the Pacific Islands.
† Commander William N. Leonard, USN.

that committee under Carl Vinson.* I was staying with Dewey at his apartment out on Connecticut Avenue; his wife was visiting her sister in Europe. Each night during this period I would go back there with him, and Dewey and I would have our talks about it.

John T. Mason: Connivance?

Admiral Martin: It turned out that way. It wasn't planned, but it turned out to be very helpful. Dewey asked me one Friday evening, "Now, Bill, you've been above 40,000 feet?"

I said, "Well, I've got quite a bit of jet time, but I don't think I have spent much time above 40,000 feet."

He said, "Have you conducted a night intercept in this Skyknight?"† That was the Navy's first plane designed from the beginning to be a night fighter. It was a Douglas twin-engine aircraft.

I said, "Yes, I've had night interceptions in it, successfully."

He said, "Above 40,000 feet?"

I said, "No."

He said, "Don't you think you had better go down to Patuxent River? You are liable to come up before this committee next Monday. Don't you think you ought to go down and do that before you appear before the committee? You're going to be asked that, and you'll be a lot more effective if you've done it."

So I called Admiral Soucek at Patuxent River, and he said, "Come on down, and we'll work on it this weekend."

So that Saturday I got the McDonnell Phantom I and easily went above 40,000

---

* Dewey J. Short, a Republican from Missouri, served in the House of Representatives from 1929 to 1931 and from 1935 to 1957. Carl Vinson of Georgia entered the House of Representatives in 1913 and was appointed to the Naval Affairs Committee in 1917. He became the ranking Democrat in 1923 and chairman in 1931. When the Armed Services committee was formed in 1947, Vinson became chairman and held that position, except for two short periods when Republicans held the House, until his retirement from Congress in 1965. The aircraft carrier *Carl Vinson* (CVN-70) is named for him.

† The Douglas F3D Skyknight was an all-weather jet fighter used by the Marines as a night fighter and for electronic countermeasures. It was first delivered to VC-3 in 1951. The plane's two-man crew of pilot and radar operator sat side by side. The F3D-2 version was 46 feet long, wingspan of 50 feet, gross weight of 26,850 pounds, and top speed of 600 miles per hour. It had four fixed forward-firing 20-millimeter guns.

feet and conducted some intercepts above 40,000 feet in the daytime.* Then we had two Skyknights down there that were operating well, but each time I took it up at night I was having trouble of one kind or another, and it wasn't until after midnight on Sunday night that I got it above 40,000 feet with all systems working and successfully completed a number of night air intercepts against aircraft much, much smaller than the B-36. I was very happy he did that, because the next day I was before the committee, and I was asked if I had personally done those two things. I was very happy that I was much more competent.

John T. Mason: You didn't tell him it was that very day?

Admiral Martin: While I was before this committee, and I knew this was going on back at Patuxent River, Fox Turner and Hugh Tate, both of them, took Navy jet fighters above 50,000 feet and took beautiful photographs of the Capitol—50,000 feet down. This was right after Vandenberg had said the B-36 was not vulnerable, and this was a ridiculous claim.† While I was testifying, the brought an envelope in to me. That very morning Fox Turner and Hugh Tate, these young junior officers, had taken photographs above 50,000 feet of the Capitol, right where we were. These photographs were passed on to members of the committee with the announcement, "These were taken by Navy fighters this morning about 50,000 feet." It was a very interesting time and completely convincing.

John T. Mason: Tell me about the committee, the complexion and the experts they had assembled. They must have had some real experts with them.

Admiral Martin: The Air Force had had their time, and members of the committee tried to shut it off after members of the Air Force had finished their testimony. I am convinced the Navy would never have been heard had it not been for Captain John Crommelin. I am sure this is written up in detail someplace, and I am just giving it to you from

---

* The FD-1 Phantom I, soon redesignated the FH-1, was a jet fighter built by McDonnell. It first entered fleet squadrons in 1947. The FH-1 had a wingspan of 41 feet, length of 39 feet, gross weight of 12,035 pounds, and top speed of 479 miles per hour. It was armed with four .50-caliber machine guns.
† General Hoyt S. Vandenberg, USAF, was Air Force Chief of Staff from 30 April 1948 to 29 June 1953.

memory.* But John Crommelin was getting into some serious trouble because he kept talking about the uselessness of the B-36 and the bad strategy and so on. He had been told to shut up. I don't know by whom, but he was finally put on the shelf at the Western Sea Frontier, San Francisco, which is the end of the road for an aviator, and after that he got out.† John Crommelin was a wonderful pilot and a wonderful leader. He had been executive officer on the *Enterprise* during the first year of the war when I was out there, and he was the stimulus for the whole ship and the whole air wing—a very promising officer. He would have made flag rank without any doubt and would have been one of the first selected if he hadn't opened up on this particular thing, but he wouldn't be quiet on it.

John T. Mason: And this was the House Armed Services Committee, and Carl Vinson was the chairman.

Admiral Martin: Yes, House Armed Services Committee, Carl Vinson the chairman. Dewey Short was the senior Republican, the minority leader, and they had Hebert.‡

There was a very lengthy report on that, and there was a fellow named Bryce Harlow who was the chief counsel of the House Armed Services Committee. He is a brilliant fellow—lieutenant colonel in the Army Reserve—and he is still in this area.§ Bryce was so very competent and articulate, a good writer, and he was responsible for the report. He told me before I went back to Hawaii, after I testified, "If you are going through San Francisco, see John Crommelin and tell him that he will not object to any part of this report. It completely sees the Navy side of this thing, so tell him to just be quiet now until the report is out." I did see Crommelin and asked him to do that, but he

---

* For a description of the role of Captain John G. Crommelin Jr., USN, in the "revolt of the admirals," see Edward P. Stafford, "Saving Carrier Aviation—1949 Style," *U.S. Naval Institute Proceedings*, January 1990, pages 44-51.
† Crommelin retired from active duty in June 1950 with a "tombstone" promotion to rear admiral on the basis of combat awards.
‡ F. Edward Hebert (1901-1979), a Democrat from Louisiana, was elected to the U.S. House of Representatives in 1932 and came to Washington as part of the Democratic sweep that led to the New Deal legislation of 1933-1935. He retired from office in 1976 after being stripped of his chairmanship of the House Armed Services Committee.
§ Harlow served during World War II on the staff of General of the Army George C. Marshall, USA. After serving on the staff of the House Armed Services Committee, 1947-51, he was later an advisor to President Dwight D. Eisenhower and President Richard M. Nixon.

didn't think it was a time to be quiet. The report actually bore out all of the Navy's side of this. It was entirely favorable, but the after result of it was not as great as the report itself.

John T. Mason: What sort of role did Carl Vinson play during the hearings?

Admiral Martin: That of the wise counselor. Completely objective; I believe he had a leaning toward the Navy. He had been at the head of the old Naval Affairs Committee before they had the House Armed Services Committee. He appreciated the Navy and had a great understanding of the value of sea power and of all the things that we in the Navy think are great. He thought they were great too. But, in my opinion, he wasn't partial. I was able to get Dewey Short very well informed on the Navy side of this thing, and he was very helpful.

John T. Mason: Now, the Navy must have had a whole staff of experts, too, for this particular hearing.

Admiral Martin: Yes, they did. They could call on all of the services as they wished, but the services themselves—the Air Force and the Navy on their own to present their side of this thing—they had their experts. There were some very capable people like Bryce Harlow who were impartial and were experts in their own field. And if they didn't know it, they knew where to get it. That sort of thing still goes on today. On the staffs are some people who are extremely capable and knowledgeable, and I think the House Armed Services Committee has always been exceptional in having very good people that are heading up the chief counsel of those committees. I think that is one of the reasons that the report that came out was very, very fair.

Admiral Martin: You were Radford's liaison, were you not? He didn't come back, did he?

Admiral Martin: I didn't have that important a position. I had specific things to do when he sent me back here.

Admiral Martin: He himself did not come back for the hearings, did he?

Admiral Martin: Oh, yes, indeed. He appeared, and the first day he called the B-36 a "million dollar blunder." That hit the headlines, but the little people like myself dealt with the B-36 as such. Radford's presentation was at the statesmanship level. I think it was one of the most erudite things I have ever read and was very convincing. Of course, he went on from there to become the Chairman of the Joint Chiefs of Staff.[*]

John T. Mason: So he didn't really suffer from this then?

Admiral Martin: No, he didn't.

John T. Mason: How come you weren't tarred somewhat?

Admiral Martin: Well, my classmates said I would be, and some of my friends told me that I would never make flag rank because of my part in that. I was told later when I was senior aide to Arleigh Burke—there were three of us, Jack McCain, George Miller, and Martin, the three M's—that we were going to get into a lot of trouble because of what we were doing at that time.[†] Jack McCain was OP-09D; I think the name of it was Progress Analysis. It wasn't what you would call nefarious, but it did certain little OP-23-type things.[‡] He came up with a whole sea power presentation while he was in that job, and he gave it many times, still does. George Miller, an excellent writer, was one of the best minds that the Navy has ever had.

---

[*] Admiral Arthur W. Radford, USN, served as Chairman of the Joint Chiefs of Staff from 15 August 1953 to 14 August 1957.

[†] Captain John S. McCain Jr., USN, later a four-star admiral; Captain George H. Miller, USN, later a two-star admiral; Martin became a three-star admiral. The oral histories of McCain and Miller are also in the Naval Institute collection.

[‡] In 1949 Captain Arleigh A. Burke, USN, headed OP-23, officially the Organizational Research and Policy Division of the Office of the Chief of Naval Operations. Essentially, it was a group that gathered information critical of the Air Force. Burke's Naval Institute oral history covers his OP-23 experiences.

John T. Mason: George should perhaps have gone on a little higher. Was he affected by that?

Admiral Martin: No, I don't think so. As you know, all three of us did make flag rank, and we made it the same year.

To go back to this House Armed Services Committee, I thought that the report was very fair. It even brought out the views of General Omar Bradley, calling the Navy admirals a bunch of "fancy Dans."[*] You may recall that.

John T. Mason: I certainly do.

Admiral Martin: There were a lot of headline things that came out of that. The Navy was opposed not only by the Air Force but also by the Army on this. I could never understand the Army's opposition to the Navy's view, because the Navy was pushing the importance of conventional weapons, the importance of tactical things other than going along with the Air Force. They thought all we needed was the big bomber to blast everything, and that was all we were going to need. Therefore, I couldn't understand the Army taking that position—unless they were in a conspiracy in fact to do away with naval and Marine aviation and do away with the Marine Corps altogether. It may be possible some day to document that, but I don't know.

John T. Mason: You were telling me off tape about the assistance you received from OP-23 in preparation for your testimony.

Admiral Martin: Yes, each of us that were to appear before the committee prepared our own statement, and it was then submitted to OP-23, which had some extremely talented people who went over it and put it into better English than some of us had done on our

---

[*] General Omar N. Bradley, USA, served as Chairman of the Joint Chiefs of Staff from 16 August 1949 to 14 August 1953. On 22 September 1950 he was promoted to five-star rank, general of the Army. During his testimony to the House committee, Bradley said the Navy admirals were "fancy Dans who won't hit the line with all they have on every play unless they can call the signals."

own. Also, they made other suggestions for improving it, strengthening some points and perhaps expressing others in a different way. We were so impressed with the people that Admiral Burke had working for him and OP-23—their capability and their dedication and their belief in what he was trying to do. So there was sufficient help to provide the staff backup to those who were appearing, and they kept themselves up to date on everything. I was able to provide information on what seemed to be the mood of the committee through my good friend Dewey Short. Dewey died just ten days ago.[*]

John T. Mason: I saw the notice of his death, last weekend.

Admiral Martin: Yes, a great man. They took him back to Missouri to bury him.

If John Crommelin had not—now, Dewey Short told me this—delivered the document "in the dark corridor" that morning and it got in the paper—he made sure it did get into the paper, and it got headlines. The document stated that the committee was meeting, and they were going to shut the hearing off that morning. If Crommelin had not delivered that document that morning and made sure it got into the papers, they would not have continued the hearings. Dewey Short told me he was convinced he could not have kept the hearings going. The majority of the committee thought they were disturbing things too much. I don't know what all the reasons were.

John T. Mason: You mean in terms of national defense?

Admiral Martin: Yes, they thought they were getting into things that were going to get classified and that they couldn't finish it perhaps without getting into classified areas. There were a number of arguments, most of them by the Air Force, I think, that the hearings ought to be shut off. The committee had heard the Air Force, so let's quit right here. Dewey Short told me the thing that turned it around and convinced the committee, probably through public remand since it had gotten into the public domain, was the headlines in the newspapers that morning, and had it not happened that John Crommelin

---

[*] Former Representative Dewey J. Short died 19 November 1979 at the age of 81. He was buried in Galena, Missouri, the town where he was born on 7 April 1898. Following his defeat for reelection to the House in 1956, he served 1957-61 as Assistant Secretary of the Army.

delivered that document in the "dark corridor," the hearings would have stopped. They were continued, and the Navy was fully heard. That's why the report turned out so fair and so favorable.

I think there are some lessons to be learned from this, and I hope that it is explained one day just what went on and how certain influential groups, whether they are right or wrong, become—especially when wrong—too influential. They can have quite an effect on Congress and on the outcome of some very important issues. I think it would be very helpful to have that fully explained.

John T. Mason: I am sure that that has happened from time to time with other committees too.

Admiral Martin: I'm sure it has—where the truth doesn't come out fully.

John T. Mason: How much time were you able to stay with Admiral Ramsey out there in Barbers Point?

Admiral Martin: He was a captain at that point, and I was a commander. We did a very good job of producing capable night fighter pilots, night attack pilots, and night air controllers. In addition, I think we did a very good job on the operational readiness inspections of the carriers and their air wings that came through, getting the word from one back to the other that were in the beginning stages of preparing for the deployment so they would know what to do.

John T. Mason: It was an educational process then.

Admiral Martin: Exactly. We weren't trying to find deficiencies. We were trying to keep them from having them, and so the deficiency we would find with one air group or the ship, we would let the others know so they would know where to put some emphasis. And I was flying a lot, which was adding to my enjoyment.

John T. Mason: Focusing on the subject of night fighters for the moment, were there any new developments in that area at this point?

Admiral Martin: The deficiencies that we saw at that point particularly were deficiencies of radar presentations. Our recommendations resulted in those being corrected later. For example, the night fighter—the intercept radar was a simple cathode ray tube again, and as you were coming in, closing on the target, when you would get at a distance from the target that was the same as your altitude—say you were at 15,000 feet. When you get 15,000 feet from your target, the ground return would be at that same point and would blank out the target, because you were 15,000 feet from both of them, and you would lose the target at that point.

We came up with a technique, when we were approaching that point, of applying full throttle and diving through it. For example, we would go from 15,000 feet down to 500 feet, pick up speed, and come back up to it. The target would have passed through that 15,000-foot level, and we would have closed on it to bring it within the 15,000 feet, and we wouldn't lose it in the ground clutter. This is one of the techniques that we designed.

Later the whole presentation of the intercept radar became a polar plot, which is like looking at a map, and it was much easier to read, and it got easier, and easier, and easier. Right now the thing is handled automatically. The radar operator pushes the button when he is tracking the target that he wants to go in to, and it will automatically take him right in there to it. It will even compute it so he is taking a pursuit course that is going to close him. Let's say they are both changing courses. It will keep up with it and will automatically tell him where and what is the best course to intercept this target on his present course. It has become much easier, much more reliable, and certainly much more precise.

John T. Mason: Does this strain the pilot in any sense? Is the system becoming so effective that it makes it more difficult for the pilot?

Admiral Martin: Not in the case of the pilot. If he has long-range weapons that will home in on the target, I don't see that it's any big strain. Now, if he has to close so close that his short-range weapons are getting him into a possible collision situation, that can be quite a strain. For example, the F-14 with the Phoenix missile, you launch it and leave it.* You don't have to stay on the course and keep the target illuminated with your own radar. You launch this Phoenix, and it will home in on the target from over 100 miles out—how much over 100 is classified information. If you are out at night and all you have is guns, that has to be very tricky.

John T. Mason: What I was getting at, I supposed that the human factor might be outdistanced by the electronic developments—getting beyond the capability of the man himself.

Admiral Martin: A lot of these things that are done automatically are done more proficiently than can be done by the pilot. For instance, the automatic landing system that they have now. It is working beautifully on the fields, and it is working well on the carriers. It will actually give the plane, with its automatic control—its final approach is more precise than the pilot himself can do it.

John T. Mason: Yet he has to be there in case it isn't infallible.

Admiral Martin: Absolutely. I thought I would never trust an automatic pilot below 500 feet, but they have become so good—I went up to Buffalo. Bell had a Navy contract there for the all-weather automatic landing system, and I flew in a very heavy snow in the F3D Skyknight, the twin-engine jet night fighter. I just monitored it closely and let it bring me right down to a landing. It would do the approach part of it better than the pilot, better than I was. The landing itself wasn't quite as smooth as I could make it. You are

---

* Grumman F-14 Tomcat fighters first entered training squadrons in late 1972. The F-14A version was 64 feet long, wingspan of 38 feet, normal takeoff weight of 55,000 pounds, and top speed of Mach 2.34. It was equipped with a 20-millimeter cannon and was designed to carry a variety of types of missiles—Sparrow, Sidewinder, and Phoenix—and later equipped to deliver bombs as well. On 10 March 2006 the F-14 completed its last deployment when the 22 planes of the VF-31 Tomcatters and the VF-213 Black Lions flew to Naval Air Station Oceana, Virginia.

going to come in and land on your wheels with a fairly hard landing if you leave it on automatic pilot. But at night on a carrier you can't see the deck, and that's the way you do it anyway. You just hold what you've got all the way down.

In the daytime, just before you are to touch, you can flare it out, ease the nose up slightly, and you'll make a landing much softer than just holding what you have in the approach. There are many areas where the improvements in the state of the art have been so improved and so refined that a lot of this stuff is done automatically. They haven't done it to the point where a single-place night fighter can be nearly as good as a two-place night fighter, where you have the radar operator—what we call the naval flight officer who is handling the radar and closely monitoring nothing but the electronics.[*] That is all he has to look at. The pilot has to be concerned about his fuel, control, and the operation of the aircraft. If this is being done automatically, he has to be closely monitoring that. The two of them are doing different things. It's developed to a very fine art today and the great improvement in all areas of the night intercept thing, and all areas of the attack as well, of being able to match your radar to what has already been mapped by reconnaissance aircraft, so it will take you right over that same route, just like matching it up. Some of the things that they do are unbelievable.

John T. Mason: It must seem fabulous to you to have lived through these developments, to begin with them and then to see these fighter techniques and then to see it in its present stage.

Admiral Martin: They have stand-off weapons now so the pilot in the attack plane, when he has the target lined up he can launch his weapon several miles out, and he doesn't have to come in as did the previous generation of these. He could launch it that far out, but he would have to continue coming in toward the target to illuminate it with his own radar until it reached the point.

---

[*] The F-14 Tomcat was the top Navy fighter at the time of this interview and had a two-man crew, pilot and radar intercept operator. The plane has since been superseded by the F/A-18 Hornet, a jet aircraft capable of both fighter and attack roles and with only a pilot. It first entered operational service with VFA-125, a fleet readiness squadron, in May 1980. The F/A-18E and F versions are known as Super Hornets.

John T. Mason: And consequently be vulnerable himself.

Admiral Martin: Now he can come in there and launch, before he gets into the antiaircraft fire, both missiles and guns. The offense is always a step ahead of the defense, but maybe not by much, for whatever offensive capability the enemy comes up with, we are working on a defense against it, and his surprises are short-lived, because we are either already working on it or will very quickly come up with something to effectively counter.

John T. Mason: But it pretty much works in reverse, too, doesn't it? The enemy is also working to counter our weapons.

Admiral Martin: There's an interchange, back and forth.

John T. Mason: Is there ever to be any ceiling to any of this?

Admiral Martin: I don't think so. Especially in recent times—a curve on advancements especially in electronics fields has come up gradually, and now it's very, very steep. Who knows when it will level off.

Beginning in 1951, I went back to Washington, and I was in OpNav, called OP-05W, which was advanced concepts, and I had the all-weather desk there.

John T. Mason: There seems to be a great deal of consistency in the assignments that you got.

Admiral Martin: Well, I sort of planned it that way and also on some of these things there were very few who had been in this line of endeavor. All-weather flight had no emphasis on it until the end of World War II.

John T. Mason: But it doesn't always work out with a naval career that this happens. Was it because your assignments were under BuAer or BuPers?*

Admiral Martin: BuPers actually picks them, but in the case of aviators the Deputy Chief of Naval Operations for Air had the controlling influence.

John T. Mason: So that accounts for the consistency in your assignments?

Admiral Martin: I am sure it does. Some of these were my own planning. I had urged that they have a desk for all-weather flight within the Deputy Chief of Naval Operations for Air, and so they did establish that.

John T. Mason: So you came into it and set it up?

Admiral Martin: I was the second one in there. I think Captain Jim Gray, who was at the time a commander, was the first one. Jim had been with a night-fighter detachment during the war.† I would say the biggest accomplishment that I had in that period was to get an OpNav instruction which made it a requirement that every naval aviator have at least a standard instrument qualification. There were so few that had it, that that really created quite a fuss, because this became a requirement. A pilot who came up for promotion—the selection board might look askance at him because he wasn't a fully qualified naval aviator. I sort of paid for this myself, because I went from there to the Naval War College.‡ So, in addition to establishing the course, I spent more time with that across at Quonset Point as the only instrument flight instructor at the war college.§ All the naval aviation students and all of the naval aviators on the staff who had to qualify before the next year—I became their instructor.

---

* BuAer – Bureau of Aeronautics; BuPers – Bureau of Naval Personnel.
† Commander James S. Gray Jr., USN, commanded Fighter Squadron 20 (VF-20) on board the *Enterprise* (CV-6) late in World War II.
‡ Commander Martin was a student at the Naval War College from June 1950 to June 1951—before he reported to OP-05W in the Pentagon.
§ Quonset Point, Rhode Island, was the site of a naval air station until the mid-1970s.

John T. Mason: You are still at OP-05W. Tell me about any kind of cooperation you developed with the weather bureau.

Admiral Martin: I had started that kind of use of the weather bureau when I was at Patuxent River in the all-weather business. One particular project we had was on this structural icing—what is the extent of the dangers of structural ice, picking up ice day or night. We had a project on the forerunner of the P2V.[*] It was an experimental job, and the Lockheed people came over and provided a lot of services on that. The first winter that we had this project we flew up over Nova Scotia, Newfoundland, over the Atlantic beyond Newfoundland, all over the Great Lakes—looking for ice. And every time we would get a report from the weather bureau that there was icing up there—here was an airliner with severe icing conditions, and he had requested clearance at a different level to get out of it—the moment we would hear that, we would jump into a plane and go in that area to try to find it. We found just a trace but not enough to determine if the P2V had an anti-icing system (which was put into the plane after it was built) that was effective against icing.

One occasion I recall very well. This pilot we had from Lockheed—I can't remember his name, but he was killed the year after this happened in a P-80. On a P2V he was a remarkable pilot. He heard this KLM pilot on the air and recognized his voice.[†] He had checked this fellow out in the Lockheed Constellation, Super Connie, and of course the Navy had some of those with AEW radar in them.[‡] This Lockheed test pilot had checked out the KLM pilot and recognized his voice when he was calling in quite excitedly for another altitude assignment because he was picking up ice at a great rate. He talked to him, and just as soon as he had cleared the area—we were up over Maine at

---

[*] The Lockheed P2V Neptune was a land-based patrol plane that first entered an operational squadron in March 1947 in VP-ML-2. The P2V-3 was 77 feet, 10 inches long; wingspan of 100 feet; gross weight of 64,100 pounds, and top speed of 337 miles per hour. In 1962 the aircraft was redesignated the P-2.
[†] KLM – Royal Dutch Airlines, a commercial carrier.
[‡] The WV Warning Star was a military version of the Constellation commercial aircraft. Lockheed started delivery of the WV-2 model to Navy squadrons in 1954 for use as airborne early warning posts. The WV-2, powered by four propeller-driven engines, had a wingspan of 123 feet length, 116 feet, 2 inches; gross weight of 145,000 pounds; top speed of 368 miles per hour. The Army Air Forces used the Constellation as a transport in World War II. After the war it became a commercial airliner.

the time—we cleared into that area. We went back and forth through it, both sides, looking for ice at that specific altitude, and we found no icing at all.

John T. Mason: Does this say that icing conditions are highly localized?

Admiral Martin: There are different things that cause it. This was a case of what the weatherman called "super saturation," an area of clouds that were super saturated, and they were at the point of either snowing or some kind of precipitation or of remaining in that state. It was their belief that the KLM plane flying through it had disturbed it, had changed its state, and therefore it fell out in the form of snow or sleet.

John T. Mason: You get some reflection of that in driving an automobile through bad weather sometimes.

Admiral Martin: Yes, that happens sometimes.

Now, there is another icing condition that is pretty treacherous, and that's what we ran into later down in Spartanburg, South Carolina. This was on a Saturday morning, and we had been looking all over the country where icing was supposed to have been. A fellow named Witherspoon, who was up in Michigan, would call us when he knew there were perfect conditions for icing. We would go up there and not find any. On this occasion we were going over our reports on Saturday, which wasn't supposed to be a working day, and we just decided we wouldn't go out looking for it that day. We got a call from our friend in the weather bureau, who said, "I've got definite icing for you down in Spartanburg, South Carolina."

We said, "Let's don't do it." So we went down to the club and started to have a beer. Our conscience began to bother us, and we felt we just wouldn't be comfortable with it, and the Lockheed people said, "I won't either, so let's go." So we jumped in and flew down to Spartanburg, South Carolina, and we picked up ice at a great rate. The reason for that—it was a frontal condition where you have cold, moist air overriding warm air, and you will find a wedge in there, and it's always like this. It usually has a rather definite line, normally from north to south or northeast to southwest or northwest to southeast. The line is fairly precise, and the weather being reported on both sides will indicate where it is. He told us, and flew down there and flew back and forth until we got more ice than we wanted.

We wanted to land at Spartanburg as we were near the airport, and we wanted to land there so we could take pictures of this thing. We had picked up three or four inches of ice, and the plane was losing its stability. When we put down the wheels, it wasn't good at all, so we pulled them right back up. We had enough power to climb, so we climbed up to 2,000 feet. We climbed normal to the line where we were flying back and forth in this line. In a case like that if you fly 90 degrees to this line you will get out of it in a few minutes. We did both. We climbed and took a course that was 90 degrees to it, and we got out of the ice.

John T. Mason: But you lost your pictures?

Admiral Martin: No, we hadn't. We stayed at that higher level because it would be colder. When we landed at Patuxent River, we still had lots of ice on every protuberance, where the antennas were. The thing we found where the heaters were greatly deficient was on the vertical tail, about 14 inches from the base of the vertical fin up. There was no heat, and that collected huge gobs of ice, and we couldn't melt it off.

John T. Mason: I suppose the moral is when you are working on a project like that, you stay with it regardless of whether it is Saturday or Sunday or whatever.

Admiral Martin: That's true. This was in March, and we had been looking for it from November up to this time and not finding it. It is a good thing the weather bureau fellow called us. I don't know if he was the head of it or not, but he was the one we were always talking to; he was the one in the operational side of it. I doubt if the head of the weather bureau would keep track of the operational side of it from hour to hour and day to day. We were delighted, and he was delighted too.

John T. Mason: In this type of project did you have anything to do with the Coast Guard and their weather ships and that sort of thing?

Admiral Martin: No, not really. I don't think you could tell from one station on the surface at just what level you were going to find icing above.

John T. Mason: For other weather factors I think they might have been useful to you in your study.

Admiral Martin: I don't recall that we used them. Later on, when in my first job at flag rank I was in Argentia operating with the Coast Guard and other services. We worked very carefully with them but mostly on icing at the surface. We had an iceberg patrol.

John T. Mason: But that's an area where the Coast Guard does operate. What about the Navy facilities for weather forecasting in a general sense?

Admiral Martin: I think there has always been good coordination and exchange of information between all the services and the weather bureau. I think that has been excellent all along. When I tried to establish this at Patuxent River for our own purposes, everyone was so cooperative, and we were able to get not only the combined forecasts for a certain area, but specific reports from pilots and the various stations.

John T. Mason: When you were operating in the Pacific in World War II the weather facilities for forecasting were not that good, were they?

Admiral Martin: No, they were not good.

John T. Mason: It was just developing into something, and the war gave it impetus.

Admiral Martin: That's why there would frequently be a very early weather flight before they took off. Most of the naval air stations used to have that early morning weather flight to determine what it was going to be, and this was especially true in the training commands at Pensacola and Corpus Christi. Because you don't want these students going out into an area where they are liable to encounter weather they cannot handle. They just weren't that capable yet. I would have to say that the coordination and exchange of information between the services and the weather bureau has always been good.

John T. Mason: When you were in OP-05W did you have any concern at all about the hurricanes in the Caribbean?

Admiral Martin: No, that wasn't part of our concern. It was a matter of interest, and the Navy had the hurricane hunters—the Super Connies that we had used to fly that. They were nearly always the ones that would penetrate the hurricanes that were over water. I think today the Air Force has taken over that function, and they use primarily C-130s—planes that have been modified somewhat, and the equipment they carry is for those specific reasons.[*]

In addition to pilot qualifications, we were able to specify equipment that should be available to the pilot and to the crew to handle the weather things. For example, such things as the requirement that a flashlight be provided and carried; in case of electrical failure in the flight instruments you could put your flashlight on. More than once this happened to me, where I had an electrical failure, and I had to make an instrument approach landing with a flashlight carried in my teeth until I had broken out from under the clouds. I am not the first one to do that, nor the only one. There are several who have done that.

John T. Mason: A pilot has to be pretty inventive, doesn't he?

---

[*] The Lockheed C-130 Hercules is a cargo aircraft powered by four turboprops. It was developed for the Air Force in the 1950s and has since been adapted for use as well by the Navy, Marine Corps, and Coast Guard. The plane has a maximum cruising speed of 357 miles per hour and a maximum takeoff weight of 135,000 pounds.

Admiral Martin: We actually had an OpNav instruction—this was the instruction from the Chief of Naval Operations or his staff—and this was something that just couldn't be violated. We established the pilot instrument qualification, and that was the minimum, and it was enforced. We also established the equipment for the plane that was to be cleared to fly in weather or under instrument conditions. It had to have these provisions—a clock with a stopwatch capability. There must have been a dozen items on this list that had to be provided. It required that the Navy provide these things and that they be available for the pilot to take with him and not at his own expense.

John T. Mason: Did you feel it necessary to monitor this whole situation to the point that you saw that they were supplied?

Admiral Martin: Yes. You know, the Navy has always had inspections of all kinds: readiness inspections, the admiral's inspection, captain's inspection, inspections for uniform, inspections for proper maintenance. On those inspections that had to do with the condition of the aircraft, all of these various items had to be in place, so they were enforced. Putting it out as an OpNav instruction, those are taken very seriously. The Chief of Naval Operations doesn't just sign those things perfunctorily. He realizes what the costs are going to be, the difficulties of enforcing it. An OpNav instruction is to be enforced, and they are enforced.

John T. Mason: So an OpNav instruction is binding on the budgeteers, then and immediately?

Admiral Martin: Oh, yes. The logistics people and even the bureau people who are going to provide it, it goes through them first for an initial before it goes to the CNO for signature. Now, the Chief of Naval Operations himself personally doesn't sign all of these. His deputies are authorized to sign an OpNav instruction within their own limits. I am sure if it came to a point, as in the OpNav instruction requiring pilot qualifications that was going to have such a broad effect, that the CNO himself signed that. On others he authorized his deputies to sign certain things.

Well now, let me see. Where did we get to?

John T. Mason: You were at OP-05W and were about to depart after a year.

Admiral Martin: A little over a year. I went to the war college.

John T. Mason: Did you have a voice in that?

Admiral Martin: No, I didn't really care to go at that time, and I was backed up by Admiral Radford, who said it was not necessary for everybody to go to the war college. He had never been to one at all. There was another assignment that I wanted at sea; I had always been struggling for sea assignments. I think that has shown up in my performance almost every place. I have had more than one of my seniors say, "Why is it that you do so well, outstandingly, at sea, whereas ashore you are adequate?" Twice when I was a flag officer I was told that, by Admiral Eph Holmes and the other by Charlie Martell, who was three stars.[*] He said, "Bill, why is it that you are so outstanding, in fact brilliant on occasion when you are at sea, and ashore you are adequate?"

John T. Mason: Well, you do have a very interesting combination of being activist but also of being intellectual.

Admiral Martin: I don't consider myself to be an intellectual at all, but when I see a requirement I like to stay with it until something is done about it. When I see a deficiency, especially an important deficiency like this night and all-weather business, it really becomes a campaign of mine to see it through.

John T. Mason: But at the same time, don't you think you have an extra deal of imagination which you employ in focusing on any one of these projects?

Admiral Martin: Well, and maybe so in finding solutions to some of them.

---

[*] Admiral Ephraim P. Holmes, USN: Vice Admiral Charles B. Martell, USN.

John T. Mason: That's what I mean by the intellectual aspect of it.

Admiral Martin: I call that luck.

I have already told you about the war college. You know what that course is. I think it is good, though I have heard a lot of criticism about it. Admiral Richard Conolly was head of the College, and he was killed in an aviation accident.[*] His assistant was Rear Admiral Don Felt, an aviator.[†] I thought they were both fine. Felt was very, very demanding, but he was demanding of himself too.

John T. Mason: Had you run up against him before?

Admiral Martin: Oh yes, he was very difficult. My first squadron was Scouting Two in the *Lexington*. He had Bombing Two that was right next door to us in the same hangar, and we could hear him when he was raising hell in there. But our paths crossed many times, and we became very good friends. I think I have told you one of the things, if we have time for it.

When I was aide to Admiral Burke when he was CNO, Felt was Vice CNO after Duncan.[‡] On this occasion I didn't take the trip with Admiral Burke. He was going overseas, and I stayed behind. I thought I would get some rest with Burke gone, but it turned out the other way. Felt kept me busier than the dickens. A piece of correspondence had been lost, and he wanted to see it. He knew he had seen it twice, once at the start of the routing and once when had been through the routing. He called me in and said. "Find it. Nobody around here can find it; you find it." So I started looking.

---

[*] Vice Admiral Richard L. Conolly, USN, served as president of the Naval War College from 1 December 1950 to 2 November 1953. On 1 March 1962 Admiral Conolly and his wife Helen were killed in the crash of an American Airlines plane that crashed into Jamaica Bay after taking off from New York's Idlewild Airport, now John F. Kennedy Airport.
[†] Rear Admiral Harry D. Felt, USN. The oral history of Felt, who retired as a four-star admiral, is in the Naval Institute collection.
[‡] Admiral Arleigh A. Burke, USN, served as Chief of Naval Operations from 17 August 1955 to 1 August 1961. His oral history is in the Naval Institute collection. Admiral Harry D. Felt, USN, served as Vice Chief of Naval Operations from 1 September 1956 to 28 July 1958. His oral history is in the Naval Institute collection. Admiral Donald B. Duncan, USN, served as Vice Chief of Naval Operations from 10 August 1951 to 1 September 1956.

One thing that is essential to the story is that Burke had this idea of saving a lot of paperwork by having certain people that were to see this thing, having their own color. Burke's was green. All the ordinary colors were taken when he established this, because all of the deputies had a specific color of their own, and the only one left was purple, so I was purple. I had a purple-colored pencil, and I would write, small but legibly, in the margin in that color. This piece of correspondence we were looking for, I had to go back and tell him I couldn't find it.

Finally he said, "Bring in everybody that's been looking for it; bring in the whole staff." There must have been 20 or more. He said, "Now, I am going to tell you what we are looking for." He sat back and closed his eyes. He said, "It was a page and a half, and there were marginal notes on the first page, and at the third paragraph the notes were in purple. Goddamnit, Bill Martin! Where's that paper?"

We laughed and we laughed and we laughed, and he said, "Get out, get out, go on out!" Then he sent for me after he had cooled off a little bit, and he said, "What was so Goddamned funny?"

I said, "Admiral Felt, we couldn't help it. Everybody who knows you knows that you have a photographic memory, and we could just see you. You had put this right up there on your screen, and you were just reading it off. You could just see it exactly. We knew you had a photographic memory, but this is the first time we had positive proof that you photographed in color." And I walked out.

Five minutes later he called me back, and he said, "It is funny, isn't it?" But by this time we had found this piece of paper.

John T. Mason: So you are up at the war college.

Admiral Martin: Yes, and I mentioned that more than half of my time was taken as an instrument flight instructor over at Quonset Point. We had to go back and forth by boat.

John T. Mason: How did you manage that and attend the lectures also?

Admiral Martin: I think I would have had a better performance in the war college, and I would have done a lot more reading than I found time to do. I performed all the requirements, and I wrote the paper and did all the exercises, but I didn't spend as much time on any of it as I would have liked to do because my time was taken up.

John T. Mason: Did you have your family up there?

Admiral Martin: Yes. I enjoyed the war college. I thought it was very worthwhile. The so-called principles of warfare—concentration of forces, surprise, maneuverability, and all of those—have really interested me, and I believed in them, and I enjoyed the exercises that would exercise this part of the war game.

John T. Mason: Were they electronic at that point?

Admiral Martin: No, that was put in later. We did have one where manually you would move ships around. I liked it, and I thought Admiral Conolly did a wonderful job, and I thought Admiral Felt did a wonderful job. All the instructors up there, Shirley Miller—no, he was in my class, but he was older and more mature than the rest of us.[*] He was practically like an instructor. I got a lot out of that course, and I realized that I was probably wrong in not wanting to go there.

John T. Mason: What did you focus on in terms of a paper?

Admiral Martin: It was foreign policy.

John T. Mason: You were an unusual student. I don't know of any other who had the same experience where you had two jobs. You were a student, but you were also an instructor somewhere else.

---

[*] Captain Shirley S. Miller, USN.

Admiral Martin: The beginning of that was rougher than later on. I started picking the ones that were more adept, and I made instructors of them. I would never have gotten through the year had I been the only instructor there. After about a month or two, I had others like this fellow named Hoyt Mann, who was very, very good.[*] As a student he was very good on his instrument check and under actual weather conditions he was very cool, and he became a very good instructor.

John T. Mason: How many men did you have passing through there at Quonset Point?

John T. Mason: There were 40 or 50 aviators at the war college, both on the staff and in the student body. These were the ones that had to meet this requirement in the next year. So while the burden was very heavy until I got three or four instructors—Joe Ruddy was one of them—who were very good, and then they could take over a part of the load.[†] I believe in the case of Ruddy and Mann and one or two others, I was able by the end of the year to qualify them for the special instrument rating, the green card.

At the end of that course, when they were talking about ordering me someplace, they wanted to send me to Canada to McGill University to take the summer course in arctic warfare.[‡] I really didn't want to do that at the time because I didn't feel I would get too many assignments in the Arctic.

John T. Mason: That was influenced by the fact that we were currently very concerned about the Soviets and the Arctic, weren't we?

Admiral Martin: Once I had thought it out, and certainly during the course, I began to realize that we liked to fight in temperate climates. We would far rather fight in the topics than on the Arctic Circle, far rather, and we were far better at it. And there were some problems up there that we weren't finding out what they were until we did it. Yet the Russians live and they work in that environment, and what we considered to be an arduous and difficult situation in cold weather, it is nothing to them. They do it all the

---

[*] Commander Hoyt D. Mann, USN.
[†] Commander Joseph A. Ruddy, USN.
[‡] McGill University is in Montreal, Quebec.

time. I think that even today this is a very important consideration that we would do very poorly inside the Arctic Circle, certainly at the outset. Americans are adaptable enough that eventually they would catch up with it, but initially I don't think we would do well at all.

John T. Mason: Did you go to McGill?

Admiral Martin: I did. One of the things that influenced me was this—the week before they had to submit orders I came down here while I was working on my paper, the final paper. While I was here for a full week—this was in May—it was 90 degrees every day. I was in a little room over where they had some officers' quarters and enlisted quarters in those old shacks that used to be over at Fort Myer, which have since been torn down for the extension of Arlington Cemetery.* None of these spaces were air-conditioned, and in fact there wasn't even a fan. I sweltered during that time. I had to do this work, and after seven days of that I said, "Send me into the Arctic." So I went to school at McGill University. They conducted this course at Stanstead, Canada, which was just across the border from Vermont, and I lived almost on the border that summer.†

John T. Mason: Were all the students military for this course, U.S. and Canadian?

Admiral Martin: Yes, all military. U.S. and Canadian, and all the services were represented.

John T. Mason: How long a course was it?

Admiral Martin: Two and a half months. The instructors were awfully good. One man there had done a lot of work in the Arctic and some names I was well aware of at the time, though now I have forgotten them, people who had actually been on long treks.

---

* Fort Myer, an Army post, is in Northern Virginia, adjacent to Arlington National Cemetery.
† The summer course was at Stanstead College, an independent school in the border town of Stanstead, Quebec.

Amundsen was one of them.* They were still living though getting along in years, and they came to lecture, and I must say that was stimulating.

John T. Mason: What did you learn in particular?

Admiral Martin: There was a lot of it from the actual warfare side that was focused toward the Army requirements—ground warfare and some of that I didn't think was too exciting, but, on the other hand, I realized later that if we would get into a war and some of our targets were in that area, this knowledge would be very valuable. You get an awful lot of weather on it, which helped me. My first job in flag rank was at Argentia, Newfoundland, and I had all those responsibilities for the ice patrol and the replenishment of the DEW Line and that sort of thing, and the iceberg survey, and it was very helpful.†

John T. Mason: In your career all of these things just dovetailed.

Admiral Martin: Just meshed, some of it just by chance. It wasn't through my own planning in some cases, because in that case I was just sort of forced into it, but it was a good thing that I was.

John T. Mason: Was the underwater school in San Diego, or wherever it is, involved in this course? A fellow out there, Waldo Lyon, is particularly interested in submarines, in operating them up into the Bering Sea.‡

Admiral Martin: Yes, they had—I can picture them now—two from the Pacific, one was

---

* Roald Amundsen, Norwegian polar explorer, led the first expedition successful to reach the South Pole in December 1911. He died in 1928.
† DEW Line – Distant Early Warning Line, a chain of radar sites built 1,200 miles from the North Pole in the early 1950s as a means of detecting Soviet bombers approaching the United States over the Arctic.
‡ Dr. Waldo K. Lyon (1914-1998), a civilian employee of the Navy, was director of the Arctic Submarine Laboratory. He did pioneering development work that made possible submarine operations under the arctic icecap. His oral history is in the Naval Institute collection.

from MSTS.* The aviators were mostly transport types from the logistics services, and the service force types who operated in the Northern Atlantic and Northern Pacific, the people who were in the business of re-supply of the DEW Line.

John T. Mason: Did the summer course at McGill also entail a field trip of any kind?

Admiral Martin: We did go a few miles from the school on a field trip.

John T. Mason: I was thinking of a much more ambitious trip, up to the Arctic Circle perhaps?

Admiral Martin: No, nothing like that. We lived it vicariously, though, from these wonderful old gents who had spent so much time up there. I am sorry to have forgotten their names, but at that time they were well known to me.

John T. Mason: Amundsen was certainly a well-known name. Was Sir Hubert Wilkins still alive?†

Admiral Martin: I would certainly remember that, because he was the one that delayed our midshipmen's cruise.‡ I don't know whether he was still alive then or not. We took a field trip to a paper mill, where they were handling lumber, wood pulp, which as I recall really had no direct relationship to what we were studying. A picnic-type thing and for local color. As I said before, I couldn't see where this was going to apply directly to naval operations in the arctic regions, but since that time I see where it was useful. It's like a lot of other things that you learn in school and university that you see no need for, but you find as you go along that you are using them without being too aware of it.

---

* MSTS – Military Sea Transportation Service, a part of the Navy that operated ships for support functions. In some cases it chartered the ships, and it some cases it ran the ships directly with civil service mariners. In 1970 MSTS was renamed Military Sealift Command (MSC), the current title for the command.
† Sir George Hubert Wilkins attempted to reach the North Pole by submarine in 1931, a dismal failure. He died 30 November 1958. His ashes were scattered at the Pole on 17 March 1959 by the crew of the submarine *Skate* (SSN-578), which the previous year had been the first submarine to surface at the Pole.
‡ See page 8 of this oral history.

John T. Mason: And the fact that you had this course went into your dossier. Does it fit in in any way with fitness reports?

Admiral Martin: Yes, but I was very quiet about the fact, because I didn't want to be known as an arctic specialist. As to the fitness report, I couldn't answer that. None of the officers who were in the course with me, and I don't know of any other officer that took it who made flag rank, for example, so I don't think it was considered a choice stepping-stone for advancement.

I don't know that I could add anything to that summer's experience. From that I went right back into the all-weather business out at Hawaii. I had been in Hawaii before as executive officer with Ramsey, and this time I went back to command.

John T. Mason: Who was CinCPac at that time, Admiral Stump?[*]

Admiral Martin: Yes, it was Stump, but I had no close dealings with him. I had had dealings with Admiral Stump on only one other occasion when I was making these all-weather talks around at the air stations. He was then commander of the Air Technical Training at Memphis.[†] I didn't know that he was in the audience there; he wasn't when it started. He always gave a little talk on the problems that the Air Force was giving us, and I was somewhat embarrassed to find that he was there when I finished up. He asked me to come to his office, and he asked me to, "Lay that on thick. That's important to naval aviators to know where some of our opponents are, some people who don't really care to see us succeed."

My next assignment was in command of the Fleet All-Weather Training Unit Pacific at Barbers Point, Hawaii. Within weeks after I had arrived there, I was ordered to take it back to North Island and reestablish it there.

John T. Mason: What was the reason for the move back?

---

[*] Admiral Felix B. Stump, USN, served as Commander in Chief Pacific and Commander in Chief U.S. Pacific Fleet, 10 July 1953-14 January 1958. After he was relieved as CinCPacFlt on 14 January, he remained in the joint billet as CinCPac until 31 July of that year.
[†] As a rear admiral, Stump served as Chief of Naval Air Technical Training Command from May 1945 to December 1948.

Admiral Martin: Some things that were going on that I didn't know about. There were several reasons perhaps. One of them was the cost of sending people out there, all the way out from the coast, or from wherever they happened to be, and the families, too, because it was a six months' thing. Also, the Air Force had stated they could not provide air defense for that part of our coast, that they were spread too thin already. They could cover the northern part of California but not San Diego, because everything down there was Navy. The Navy agreed. Whether this was the principal pressure that moved us back I don't know, but when we moved back and had just gotten to the point where we could operate, we found we were committed to the Air Force to provide air defense for that part of the coast. For that operation we operated under their rules and regulations, subject to the same inspections and that sort of thing—the unexpected drills and so on. Those are the two reasons that I could think of that moved us back.

John T. Mason: This was unification being apparent, wasn't it?

Admiral Martin: Yes. Also, they wanted to beef up the patrol squadrons, patrol aviation at Barbers Point, and I think they needed some justification to avoid cutbacks at North Island.

John T. Mason: So there were a lot of differences?

Admiral Martin: There were, and they were mixed together, and that is what happened.

John T. Mason: Didn't this loosen your relationship somewhat with CinCPac?

Admiral Martin: You see at this time ComNavAirPac was in San Diego, and our connection with CinCPac—unless he was a personal friend, as Admiral Radford was to me, was never an essential thing. As I say, I knew Admiral Stump, but we were not such close friends that he would want to see me personally, whereas Radford and I would see each other frequently. My immediate boss was ComAirPac, Harold "Beauty" Martin, no relation.[*] He was a wonderful man, and I would like to have been related to him. We got along beautifully.

John T. Mason: He was from Tennessee?

Admiral Martin: I think so.[†] He later married Forrest Sherman's widow or the widow's sister, I've forgotten which.[‡]

We had just about completed the shakedown of getting established. I moved them back in increments in order that we wouldn't have to completely stop training. When that was just about accomplished, Arleigh Burke was selected to be the Chief of Naval Operations, and he was making his around-the-world trip that I guess they always take to get a very recent look at all the major naval commands.[§] He had done this going from west to east, and when he came through San Diego he sent for me. I was at the Naval Hospital Balboa getting a small piece of shrapnel cut out of my knee that hadn't been discovered before.

John T. Mason: You mean it was a World War II souvenir?

Admiral Martin: Yes. It had begun to bother me, and it got swollen. So I went over, and they had to do some surgery on it. I was at the point where I could move around on crutches, but it wasn't easy. He said he wanted to see me, so I went over and approached him on crutches. I sort of suspected what he wanted. I quietly thought maybe appearing on crutches might discourage him, and he would leave me alone in San Diego, California. I had just gotten there and had a wonderful flying job.

John T. Mason: And you wanted to work only 12 hours a day, not 24?

---

[*] Vice Admiral Harold M. Martin, USN, served as Commander Air Force Pacific Fleet from 1 April 1952 to 1 February 1956.
[†] Martin was born in Michigan. He lived in Memphis, Tennessee, after he retired from active duty in 1956.
[‡] Admiral Forrest P. Sherman, USN, served as Chief of Naval Operations from 2 November 1949 until his death on 22 July 1951.
[§] Admiral Arleigh A. Burke, USN, served as Chief of Naval Operations from 17 August 1955 to 1 August 1961. His oral history is in the Naval Institute collection.

Admiral Martin: So he said, "Bill, I want you to come in as my executive assistant and senior aide." There was a pause, and he said, "You don't seem to be very happy about it. Do you think I'll work you too hard?"

I said, "Admiral, I've worked with you before. I know you work us too hard, but that's not really what I dislike about it. I'm a captain now and have been that for just a short while. I came into the Navy for a full career, and from what I have observed and from what advice I get, if I don't get some ship experience soon, I'll never make flag rank, and I'd like to do that. That's in my plan and has been all along."

He said, "Why haven't you asked for a ship?"

I said, "Admiral, I have."

He said, "Well, you haven't asked recently."

I said, "Yes, I have."

"You mean you can't even get a little spitkit like a seaplane tender? We've got three of them." Maybe they had more than that at that time, but I think we still had three of those that operated tending the Middle East Force.

I said, "Yes, sir."

"Well, what did they say?"

I said, "They told me I was too junior."

Fortunately, I had the letter with me, and I brought out this letter signed by Chick Renard from BuPers.* It said to this effect, "We told you only two months ago that you are too junior, and you are still too junior to get command of a ship."

Admiral Burke said, "Where will you be early in the morning?"

I said, "I planned to go up and spend the night with my mother in Pasadena, so that's where I'll be."

He took down the phone number and said he would call me early in the morning. I thought he would call at some reasonable hour like 8:00 o'clock, but that's 11:00 o'clock in Washington, where he was going to be.

At 8:30 or 9:00 Washington time—5:30 or 6:00 Pasadena time—the telephone rang. It was Admiral Burke, and he said, "Well, it's all arranged. You are going to the *Saipan*."

---

* Captain Jack C. Renard, USN, a naval aviator.

I said, "Admiral Burke, there is a garble on this circuit here someplace. I could swear you said *Saipan*, and that's a middle-seized aircraft carrier." You know, built on a cruiser hull.

He said, "No, no garble, but you are not going to be there long, three months, maybe four at the outside."

So I said, "Aye, aye, sir."

John T. Mason: Does that short a period qualify you when the selection board comes along?"

Admiral Martin: Yes. As a matter of fact, when I was selected I had orders in my hand to put the *Independence* in commission. I didn't get to do that, and I argued with them then. I said, "I haven't really had a big carrier. Leave me a captain for at least a year so I can put the *Independence* in commission."*

I had already done the work for it. Tom Gates was the Secretary of the Navy, and his wife had agreed to be the sponsor.† I had done a lot of the work preparatory to putting the *Independence* in commission, and I really wanted to do that. But they said, "No, you have already had command of a carrier, and we are going to need you for a flag position before you can do it." So I lost that argument.

John T. Mason: As you do with most of them when you argue with BuPers.

Admiral Martin: Exactly. So I had command of the *Saipan*.‡

John T. Mason: How long did it take you to get off the crutches?

---

* Captain Rhodam Y. McElroy, Jr., USN, commanded aircraft carrier *Independence* (CVA-62) from her commissioning on 10 January 1959 to 3 October 1959. McElroy was in the Naval Academy class of 1935, one year behind Martin.
† Thomas S. Gates, Jr., served as Secretary of the Navy from 1 April 1957 to 7 June 1959.
‡ USS *Saipan* (CVL-48) was a light aircraft carrier, the first of her class. Built on a *Baltimore*-class cruiser hull, she was commissioned on 16 July 1946. The ship had a standard displacement of 14,500 tons; full-load, 20,000 tons; length, 684 feet; beam, 77 feet; maximum width 115 feet; maximum draft of 25 feet; a top speed of 33 knots; and capability of handling about 50 aircraft.

Admiral Martin: About two weeks.

With command of the *Saipan* I was able to take a refresher course in navigation, which I really needed. You see, I had flown from the time I was an ensign, but I hadn't had ship's duty as such since I was an ensign.

John T. Mason: And you needed a course in ship handling?

Admiral Martin: Exactly. Yes, the things that give you a better understanding of a ship than I had, although I must say I was a pretty good junior officer. Even when I was an aviator, I would volunteer to take watches on the *Enterprise* during the war, and I required all of the members of my squadron to do that. We had a very, very close relationship to the ship's officers. They appreciated that. A lot of the aviators that stood watches in the firerooms and the engine rooms would come back up and say, "Those are the people who deserve extra pay. We aviators don't deserve it. What we are doing is fun, and those poor devils down in those hot crew rooms do deserve it."

On the other hand, on some training flights we would take some of those officers with us in our back seat, dive bombing, and they would come back with a much better appreciation, saying, "You deserve every penny you get." We had a very close association, which I believe made the last year of the war with this night outfit—that it was really a burden for the carrier. The fact that we had been with them two years before and had this close association—17 of us—I think was a very important factor that made it work.

So I went to the *Saipan* at Pensacola. It was the carrier that was giving carrier training to the flight students, making them carrier qualified before they went out to their squadrons. Literally within hours, by that I mean ten hours after I had said, "I relieve you, sir," to this officer whose name was Jimmy Lang—Jimmy is dead now.[*] He had orders to Bermuda, and he was anxious to get there. I think he might have known there was a hurricane stirring around that was headed for the Gulf of Mexico. He wanted to get out of there, and he did. He didn't even have coffee with the guests that he had invited aboard ship. Then I began to be briefed on the messages that were coming in, and it was

---

[*] Captain James G. Lang, USN, commanded the *Saipan*. Lang died 6 February 1987.

clear to me they were going to use us for that. Before dawn the next morning we had orders to prepare to go down toward the Yucatan, because that's where this hurricane was headed.

John T. Mason: Had it hit the coast yet?

Admiral Martin: No, it hadn't hit the coast. Before dark they brought in load after load of cornmeal, beans, and the staples the Mexicans need. They had taken aboard a squadron of helicopters that are used for training and had taken every doctor that could be spared in that general area, and away we went.

John T. Mason: Under whose Aegis was this done?

Admiral Martin: Well, our orders were from OpNav—CNO. This Captain Lang that I had relieved, almost every other paragraph of advice that he would give me was his concern for hurricanes, and this was in October, the beginning of the hurricane season.

John T. Mason: Obviously he had been through one or two?

Admiral Martin: No, he actually hadn't been hit by any, but his idea was to get the heck out of there: "Don't get caught in the Gulf with a hurricane coming. Get out of here while you can. Get around the capes and get out of Gulf of Mexico early enough that it can't catch you." Here I was with orders that would take me right into the teeth of this one. I was actually headed on a collision course for it. I really had not had time to feel out the ship. I had been out with Lang only one time, out that rather treacherous channel. There is a long, narrow channel with shifting sands, and I found out the range markers that are supposed to tell you exactly where you were within the river channel were not accurate. They hadn't been corrected for quite a long time. Also, everybody who had ever had a carrier in there had been aground at least once, but with no damage because it was sand bottom, but they had a little problem getting off. I got no drill like that where you could make runs on orange crates and things like that and really get some ship handling experience before I had to do it. Also, in the Gulf of Mexico they had pilots for ships up to 10,000 tons, but none of their pilots would take on a ship above 10,000 tons.

John T. Mason: The *Saipan* was what?

Admiral Martin: The *Saipan* was just under 20,000. It was certainly up to the commanding officer to do the whole thing—the ship handling and the works.

John T. Mason: Your prospective mission of mercy could only be effective after the hurricane had passed on, after having done its damage. Why were you required to head into it?

Admiral Martin: It was the timing. We got away more quickly than they expected us to, for one thing. You can't tell. A hurricane does a lot of erratic things; you cannot really predict them. I studied hurricanes at that time, where all their paths were. There is no point in the whole of the Gulf of Mexico that hasn't been crossed by at least one hurricane. We made good speed down there.*

John T. Mason: You had no problem getting out through this long channel?

Admiral Martin: No, we had no trouble getting out of there, and I got so I really knew how to go into and out of that channel. In the next four months I really learned how to do that. In the middle of the night, before we were going to get into a blow from this thing, the hurricane had hit the coast of Mexico down around Vera Cruz. It was pretty clear, just from reading the dispatches, that the area that was really going to be in trouble was Tampico.

John T. Mason: It is very low there and very swampy.

---

* Hurricane Janet hit near the city of Chetumal, Mexico, on the Yucatan Peninsula on 28 September 1955. The following day it hit between Veracruz and Nautla.

Admiral Martin: It was quite a bit north of Yucatan where I had orders to proceed, so I changed course then and sent a message as to what I was doing and requested concurrence, though I had already done it. We headed for Tampico, and the message came back, "That is our best estimate too." So we headed into Tampico. It was a pretty exciting thing to do because I had a lot of charts, but there was no chart that had any information after 1900. If they had taken any measurements in there since 1900, they didn't show—this is now going toward Tampico Bay. They had a number of derelicts that showed up on the chart where somebody had run aground and the depths that were in there. It said that the depths that were in bold letters were known, and the others were estimates. There was also the derelict symbol at that point which meant, "The reason we know it's that deep is because a ship ran aground there."

My navigator, who was a nervous fellow anyway, told me I shouldn't go any closer, and I began to believe him when things began to come toward us, disgorged from the Tampico River—drowned livestock. And here we had to go another 15 or 20 miles in there. A funny thing—the scoreboard for baseball or soccer or whatever, but "Tampico" and "Visitors" floated by, the scoreboard from their playing field. It was getting dark, and we had gotten in there to about ten miles or so. A fellow named LeFevre who was the skipper of the of helicopters had been studying this thing, and he said, "If we don't get in there within five miles, we are not going to be able to cover the area that's been assigned." So I was determined to go within five miles.

We got closer and closer in there, and it was just beginning to get dark when I asked him to assign a couple of pilots and helicopters to go over and hover over one of the three symbols that were on the chart. The symbol looked like a water tower or a radio mast. I couldn't tell which one was which, and I asked, "Can you do it?"

He said, "I'd like to get volunteers." Of the volunteers he picked the two he thought were most capable. They did a fine job. They were in there until it was really dark. At that time the helicopters weren't qualified for night operations, and that was taking quite a bit of chance. But with them in there and hovering over what actually turned out to be the water tower, we used that as our principal navigating point. We went through these last-century-charted waters, to within four and one-half miles, and there we anchored.

I will never forget that red river that was coming out of there; everything in there looked clay colored. The very next morning, predawn, all the helicopters were up, ready to go, and so we started, and we operated in there for, I think, four days.

John T. Mason: Dropping supplies?

Admiral Martin: Mostly picking up people that were going to drown if we didn't. They figured that we got 12,000 people. In some cases we were just moving them to higher ground from what had been high and was no longer high. Some we picked up more than once, I am sure. We were just moving them because they were about to drown, and we picked them out of second stories. Half of the city of Tampico was under water, and there was just a torrent flooding through the streets. They estimated that 12,000 people would have drowned if we had not been in there. People in trees, people on high ground where the water was going to come up on them, and they would have been stranded for days, and people out of second stories where the helicopter would dangle a cable in there and hoist them out, and from rooftops. Those boys did a really heroic job.[*]

We organized a boat flotilla, really a task force, using our own boats and commandeering Mexican boats that were in there and that were big enough to do the job and looked like they were seaworthy enough to do it. We had a large group of ships that were doing that too. There were some places they couldn't go, but they picked up people that were stranded in the buildings. Some of these places you couldn't very well get a helicopter in, places where there were three stories, and these people were above the first floor on the second floor, but with masts and poles and things like that where the helicopter couldn't hover and lower a hoist.

Where we were operating there was a Rear Admiral Miles—he was called Mary Miles—of China fame, a very good friend of Arleigh Burke's.[†] He was brought up from Panama and put in charge of that operation. I had a great respect for him, because he just

---

[*] The *Saipan*'s official history in the *Dictionary of American Naval Fighting Ships* included the following: "From 1 to 9 October [1955], her helicopters evacuated survivors, flew in rescue personnel, and distributed food, water, and medical supplies, primarily in the flooded Tampico area. On 12 October she returned to Pensacola." Another source reports the dates as 3-10 October.

[†] Rear Admiral Milton E. Miles, USN, was the on-site commander for Operation Friendship, the flood-relief program at Tampico. During World War II he was deputy commander of the Sino-American Cooperative Association (SACO).

had a second sense about things. He was so very cooperative. I offered him my ship as his headquarters, and he happily took it. He had everything laid out—the highest point, the buildings, the grounds where the helicopters could operated even if the water rose as high as it would rise, that it would be above it. It turned out to be the nicest country club and golf course. The golf course naturally had lots of space for helicopters to operate. That became headquarters. The whole operation went off so well, the maintenance of the helicopters was close to 100% availability throughout the whole thing.

On the second day of the boat flotilla, and the rescue operations by the boats, we had one hell of a blow in there. The winds came up suddenly to 50-55 and up to 60 knots. We had two motor launches alongside, 40-footers, and they both broke their moors and parted the lines, and away they went. We had to use a helicopter to pull some people out of one of them as it was swamping. And I lost two 40-foot motor launches under conditions in which I was complimented instead of getting a general court-martial. It is an awfully serious thing to lose a 40-foot motor launch, terribly serious, but if you have sufficient excuse and the reasons are good and substantial—

John T. Mason: What was it, a secondary backlash from the hurricane?

Admiral Martin: I really don't know.

John T. Mason: Something weather-wise you could not anticipate?

Admiral Martin: No, you couldn't. Nobody anticipated this thing, but there it was. That didn't stop us, a lot of the sailors on that ship, and the officers too—I had boat officers with the big good-sized boats, and during the hours of darkness, predawn, and after dusk, I would have a boat officer in there too—there were many instances when they and the helicopter people risked their lives to save others.

John T. Mason: How long did this operation take?

Admiral Martin: After four days we were relieved by another carrier, the *Siboney Bay*. The skipper was Whitey Moore out of the class of '32.[*]

John T. Mason: You must have been pretty much exhausted by then.

Admiral Martin: Yes, we were. We worked together for some period, and then the water had begun to recede, so we were relieved to go back out.

Do you know that after taking that operation and what we did for the Mexicans, Mexico City didn't recognize that there was a catastrophe at all. A couple of years later, when the Secretary of the Navy, who had been the Secretary at that time, wanted to go down and make an official visit; they didn't want him.[†]

John T. Mason: So the *Saipan* then returned to Pensacola?

Admiral Martin: Yes, we did. During this time our students were all piling up back there in Pensacola because there was no carrier on which they could qualify. We had what they call a full-power run, which you are supposed to do once a year, from Mexico back to Pensacola. We got there in time to work a full day and a half of qualifications before we came back in and sort of caught up with the load. We got a very nice complimentary message from Admiral Artie Doyle, who was Chief of Naval Air Training at Pensacola.[‡]

John T. Mason: That was rather a strenuous tour of duty you had, wasn't it?

Admiral Martin: And so quickly. Now, the rest of the job seemed simple after that. I knew I wasn't going to put the ship on the rocks after that. The fact that it was on a cruiser hull gave it maneuvering characteristics that made it a lot more nimble than a battleship. (A real sailor wouldn't use the word "nimble," but I would say it.) Imagine handling a destroyer; it is much more sensitive and responsive.

---

[*] Captain Robert B. Moore, USN.
[†] Charles S. Thomas served as Secretary of the Navy from 3 May 1954 to 1 April 1957.
[‡] Vice Admiral Austin K. Doyle, USN, Chief of Naval Air Training.

John T. Mason: Better maneuverability.

Admiral Martin: Yes, maneuverability—that was the point. What experience I have had on ships had been on the old battleship *Idaho*, where you would put over to full rudder and start counting, and it was some time before it showed up.

The harbor at Pensacola was really quite confined, and I had asked Captain Lang when he was bringing the *Saipan* in alongside. And this was the only time I had observed it before I had to take over. I asked him, "What makes the ship handle so strangely in this area?"

He said, "I really don't know. It could be strange winds or something that happens." Later the operations officer, when we had gotten in and tied up, told me he thought the ship was in the mud for the last 600 yards. So I took a boat out to take some soundings, and, sure enough, the last 600 to 800 yards before coming alongside, you were in fact aground in about four feet of mud that you were pulling along with you.

John T. Mason: No court inquiry on this?

Admiral Martin: No, none. And you got so you knew how to deal with that. It was an excellent course in ship handling.

John T. Mason: Didn't Doyle and people like that at Pensacola know this?

Admiral Martin: If they did, they didn't tell me. I told Artie Doyle. I knew Artie Doyle very well. We had been shipmates on the old *Idaho*, and I had known him back at the Naval Academy. He was a baseball coach back there for the junior officers. He was a nifty guy, a good aviator and a fine naval officer.

That was a pretty short cruise. In February I was ordered to proceed to the Pentagon, and I was relieved by Captain Allen M. Shinn, who later became a vice admiral.

Interview Number 4 with Vice Admiral William I. Martin, U.S. Navy (Retired)
Place: Admiral Martin's home in Alexandria, Virginia
Date: Tuesday, 4 December 1979

John T. Mason: Well, sir, we come to a very significant point in your career, I believe when you returned to Washington to take up your job as executive assistant and senior aide to Admiral Arleigh Burke, who was then CNO, and this was in January of 1956. You'd had a very interesting and successful career in the *Saipan*, largely in the Gulf of Mexico and down at Pensacola. Afterward you came fresh from that to Washington.

Admiral Martin: Picking up the beginnings of that, I think I told you about Admiral Burke asking me to come in on the job. Before I came, while I had the *Saipan* for four months, I got quite a bit of correspondence from the man I was to succeed, Thurston Clark.[*] Thurston was Admiral Carney's executive assistant and had been promoted to rear admiral in the job.[†] He sent me some notes and files and publications, rather a large stack of them, and said, "You just peruse them." And then he said, and he underscored this: "And then memorize them!" That was the preparation for the job.

John T. Mason: Was this material that you'd be called upon to bring up to Burke?

Admiral Martin: These were sort of dos and don'ts and background. Although I'd had Pentagon duty before, I hadn't had it in the hub of operations like I was going to. Back then I was a junior commander in almost an obscure branch of the DCNO for Air. So moving into the middle of the arena was something new to me.

Admiral Martin: Like moving into the eye of the hurricane?

Admiral Martin: The eye of the hurricane, exactly!

---

[*] Captain Thurston B. Clark, USN.
[†] Admiral Robert B. Carney, USN, was Chief of Naval Operations 17 August 1953 to 17 August 1955.

Thurston Clark wrote me a letter after he had sent me the stuff he was going to send me, and he said, "I just realized that everything I've told you about this job is not good news to you and could be discouraging. There are two very good things about this assignment. One is that you have a parking space out on the mall, right along with the three-stars, and the other one is that this Washington traffic never bothers you. You come to work before it gets congested, and you leave long after it's cleared out." Those were the two nice things about the job.

John T. Mason: He might have said one other too. He might have said, "I just got promoted to rear admiral."

Admiral Martin: Yes, he might have said that too. I don't think anybody ever had that assignment that wasn't later selected for flag rank.

As you might imagine, being on the fringes of such a busy man, the fringes were very, very busy. Part of my job was, of course, to relieve the strain as much as I could from Admiral Burke, to take care of as many details as I could at my level, or to condense the things that had to go in to him.

John T. Mason: Perhaps you should begin by telling me about what your duties involved in a typical day.

Admiral Martin: Most of my day was spent on the telephone. Almost every minute there was something coming in. The highlights of that time, and this gets around to a typical day, that I recall were the telephone calls that I would get from Admiral Rickover.[*] They were not usually lengthy. But the calls I got from Red Raborn, who was director of the Polaris project at that time, were lengthy, giving me some details of the progress that they were making, which I would condense and put into a memorandum to go in to Admiral

---

[*] Then-Rear Admiral Hyman G. Rickover, USN, was considered the father of the nuclear Navy. He ran the Navy's nuclear-power program for many years, eventually leaving active duty in 1982 with the rank of four-star admiral on the retired list.

Burke.* This didn't mean that Red didn't see Admiral Burke frequently, because he did, and so did Admiral Rickover.

Also, many calls were from Richard Evelyn Byrd, who was quite ill at the time, very nervous and easily upset over things, sometimes details that weren't or didn't appear to be in his field of interest, but he had some comment to make on them.†

John T. Mason: Was he in the hospital?

Admiral Martin: No, but he had spent a lot of time in the corridors of the Pentagon. He passed away a little over a year after I went in there, so he was ill.

This brings up something that I should have started out with, I guess. I had already learned many things from Admiral Burke when he was a commodore and chief of staff to Admiral Mitscher.‡ He set an example that I tried to emulate, because I thought that was the best. I still think it was the best. The time that I spent with him as his executive assistant and senior aide, watching the details of how the man thought and how he operated and just the faultless integrity, was a tremendous example to me. This brings up one of them.

Admiral Rickover and Admiral Byrd were very difficult at that time, both of them. I heard many of their complaints, and the complaints by the OpNav officers, even down to the commanders and captains, but certainly in the flag ranks that they were being—what's the word for it?—almost hazed by Admiral Rickover.

John T. Mason: Maybe "bullied" would be a better word?

Admiral Martin: Well, that would apply in many cases.

---

* Rear Admiral William F. Raborn, Jr., USN, was director of the Special Projects Office, which developed the Polaris submarine-launched ballistic missile system. He held the post from 1955 to 1962, being promoted to vice admiral in 1960. His Polaris oral history is in the Naval Institute collection.
† Commander Richard E. Byrd, Jr., USN (Ret.), explored Antarctica in 1928, 1933, 1939, 1947, 1955. He was retired for physical disability in 1916 but continued to be promoted, eventually becoming a rear admiral in 1929. Byrd died 11 March 1957.
‡ Vice Admiral Marc A. Mitscher, USN, served as Commander Task Force 58, the fast carrier task force, in 1944-45.

The word finally got around to Admiral Burke, and he asked me about it. There were many cases when I tried to keep bothersome things from him, but he knew it. He always had an extra sense. He knew things were going on that I didn't know he knew were going on. Things that I tried to keep from him I found out later that he knew about them. So he asked me the size of the problem, and I told him it was considerable. Also, that in some cases the responses that some officers were giving to Admiral Rickover and Admiral Byrd were not too favorable and in some cases weren't very friendly.

Admiral Burke called all the four-stripers and flag officers together in the Army's auditorium on the fifth deck of the Pentagon, that would accommodate more people than any other space in the building, I guess. It was very short and, in essence, it was this: "Admiral Byrd and Admiral Rickover are distinguished Americans, and they will go down in history as such. We are going to treat them as distinguished Americans, and whatever patience it takes and whatever time it takes to deal with them as distinguished Americans should be dealt with." I thought that set a very fine example and, in fact, it began to—just that commonsense approach to it seemed to level off not only the complaints from Admiral Rickover and Byrd but also the complaints that we had been getting from the people who were dealing with them.

Another lesson of looking realistically at the problem, especially the development of it and the future of it, how it is going to be looked upon later. And so that eased things considerably.

John T. Mason: You did say that Burke himself saw these gentlemen frequently, so he did confront them personally, and he knew the problems that they presented?

Admiral Martin: Yes, and also we knew that they had carved out their niches in history. They were distinguished people. I thought one of the big problems—and continues to be one, I think—with Admiral Rickover is that he gets into areas that he really has no responsibility for whatsoever and in some cases where he may not be the expert in that particular field.

John T. Mason: That is a common complaint.

Admiral Martin: Yes, and I'll tell you a little story about that later, after I was a flag officer. My flag was in a nuclear-powered ship, the *Enterprise*, in which I saw him frequently.

As I said before, my dealings with Admiral Burke—someone had to be outside at all times, and there were times when meetings were going on in the inner sanctum of Admiral Burke's office which I could have sat in on, but I didn't have time. Therefore, I didn't get into the depths of a lot of things.

John T. Mason: Did you sit in on a lot of his conversations with people?

Admiral Martin: Some of them, much less than half, though, I would say, because many of them were lengthy, like the JCS sessions, which were very lengthy, and I had to be out manning the store on the outside.[*]

John T. Mason: I wondered if he had laid upon you a responsibility for checking on some of the decisions that were made to see whether they were implemented by the men in question.

Admiral Martin: Yes. Even if I didn't sit in on them, sometimes I'd be called in and be given notes, the various sides. We had some wonderful aides at that time. Tom Weschler was the personal aide on the other side.[†] His Marine aide was a lieutenant colonel whose name escapes me, but a very high type. This made my job lots easier.

John T. Mason: What sort of record did you keep of decisions that were made and had to be implemented?

Admiral Martin: I'd just keep rough notes on them until I had time to write them up into a memorandum. Then they would go to the deputy involved or sometimes, if it was at a lower level, to the actual division or branch involved.

---

[*] JCS – Joint Chiefs of Staff, of which Admiral Burke was a member.
[†] Commander Thomas R. Weschler, USN, served as aide to Admiral Arleigh Burke from 1955 to 1958. The oral history of Weschler, who retired as a vice admiral, is in the Naval Institute collection.

Admiral Burke dictated like a machine gun, though, and if it was on something that was going to be really involved and complex, he would very quickly ring for his writer. That's another story. His writer was a chief yeoman named Bob White, and he was a superb man. He later became a limited duty officer. I thought that he was more overloaded than anybody else on the staff, and I determined that a week or so after I got in there. So I began to look for another Bob White to put in there to spell him so that he could take a day off occasionally and so he wouldn't be around there at the late hours.

John T. Mason: This was dictation he had?

Admiral Martin: Yes, dictation. A man who could take dictation running alongside Admiral Burke on his way down to a JCS meeting or his way up to the SecNav's office. They weren't close together at that time; they were several offices apart. Wherever he was going, almost always his chief yeoman—his second yeoman was Chief Yeoman Blue.

John T. Mason: White and Blue!

Admiral Martin: White and Blue. They were both very good, and it was very frequently that Admiral Burke would be dictating, and they'd be taking it down on the run. Sometimes, when he was going someplace in his car, he'd take one or the other with him, going over to the Hill, or wherever he was going, it wasn't unusual for him to take his yeoman with him and dictate to him.[*]

John T. Mason: Did he have a sheaf of papers with him when he did that sort of thing?

Admiral Martin: No, Admiral Burke never needed any notes. He never spoke from notes, and I've seen him speak many times. He may have had some rough notes that he'd made out for himself. On some occasions he'd have a speech he'd really worked on. His speechwriter had so much guidance, a lot of it while Burke was getting his hair cut in the

---

[*] "The Hill" refers to Capitol Hill in Washington, D.C., that is, the U.S. Congress.

back room, which was just beyond his head. That used to disturb him, because he couldn't get anything done while he was having his hair cut, because he'd have his glasses off. I looked all over Washington try to find some pince-nez glasses so that he could get his hair cut and still read. I never did find a pair.

John T. Mason: I can't imagine him wearing them either.

Admiral Martin: George Miller will tell you this too. He was assisting Admiral Burke on his speeches and in many other things. George Miller is a remarkable man, and he would frequently be with the admiral while he was getting his hair cut.

John T. Mason: George wrote speeches for him, did he?

Admiral Martin: Yes, he did. There was a fellow named Ralph Williams who helped with speeches and Frank Manson.* Do you know Frank Manson?

John T. Mason: No.

Admiral Martin: You'll have to get to know him, because he's a good writer, very knowledgeable, and he retired as a captain. I'll be happy to put you in touch with him, because he has a good memory. Frank was a lieutenant commander when he went into the public relations specialty. When I first knew him, he was already in a pubic relations code, 1650, and he retired as a captain.† A very trustworthy, very capable man.

A typical day would start about 7:15, because the admiral came in at 7:30.

John T. Mason: He was then living where, up on Massachusetts Avenue?

---

* Commander Ralph E. Williams Jr., SC, USN. Williams was also a prolific author for the *U.S. Naval Institute Proceedings*. Lieutenant Commander Frank A. Manson, USN, a public affairs specialist. Manson was the coauthor, with Malcolm W. Cagle of the book *The Sea War in Korea* (Annapolis: U.S. Naval Institute, 1957).
† Each naval officer has a four-digit code called a designator that identifies his or her specialty; 1650 is the designator for a public relations specialist in the regular Navy.

Admiral Martin: Where the Vice President is now living. They still call it Admiral's House. It's in the Naval Observatory area off Massachusetts Avenue.

He would come in at 7:30. After I had his briefers selected and briefed on what we expected them to do, they would come in at exactly ten minutes of 8:00 and, if it was just a routine day, they could be out by 8:00 o'clock.

John T. Mason: Now, they briefed him on dispatches?

Admiral Martin: Yes. They would come in around 4:00 or 4:30. Stansfield Turner was one of these briefers. He was just a bright lieutenant at the time, but outstanding, a Rhodes Scholar, and, of course, he's the head of the CIA now.[*] Then there was a Marine named Robinson who, I believe, made general rank. I just haven't kept up with him, but they were both very capable, and it worked out fine because they'd go through the dispatches. The CNO and the Vice Chief would keep up to the moment on everything that was going on through the day, so the briefings were actually needed to bridge the gap from late in the evening until early in the morning, the developments that went on.[†] Something that was a continuing thing got more tense or less tense, but the developments of that from the previous day, the briefers would bridge the gap.

John T. Mason: Did you have something comparable to what we called a war room in World War II?

Admiral Martin: No, that came later. Admiral Burke asked for that. He wanted a flag bridge, so to speak.

John T. Mason: Charts and all that.

---

[*] Admiral Stansfield Turner, USN (Ret.), served as Director of Central Intelligence/Director of the Central Intelligence Agency from 9 March 1977 to 20 January 1981. The first part of his tenure was on active duty, prior to his Navy retirement on 1 January 1979. His oral history is in the Naval Institute collection.
[†] Admiral Donald B. Duncan, USN, served as Vice Chief of Naval Operations from 10 August 1951 to 1 September 1956. Admiral Harry D. Felt, USN, served as Vice Chief of Naval Operations from 1 September 1956 to 28 July 1958. His oral history is in the Naval Institute collection.

Admiral Martin: Yes, all the charts could be kept. It was called flag plot at the beginning. I don't know whether that's the name they give it now. When I left, it was working well, but there were continuous changes. For example, there was a space that was designated as the top secret area in which only the Chief of Naval Operations and the Vice Chief would sit in on a briefing. They would meet with the deputies and others. Then they would go into the top secret space, and sometimes there would be nobody but the CNO and the Vice Chief, because it got into these cosmic and other clearances that were limited to those who needed to know. In some cases the appropriate DCNO would be with him, but that was a limited top secret thing where they could keep the classified charts and things like that, classified displays at that level, and nobody else was permitted in that space.

John T. Mason: The briefing in the morning.

Admiral Martin: So the briefing. As I say, on a routine day with no big developments, what you might call a no-news day, that briefing would go off very fast, and they were to be prepared to make it within 10 or 15 minutes. If it ran beyond that, then the CNO was asking some questions that kept them beyond that time. But it wasn't unusual or them to come in at exactly ten minutes of 8:00 and leave at exactly 8:00 o'clock.

John T. Mason: So the word was, "Be succinct."

Admiral Martin: That's right. Be succinct, but that was fine, and I think that saved Admiral Burke a lot of time. I felt that that was my number-one mission, to conserve the time of that very busy and very important man as much as I could.

John T. Mason: How did he seem to absorb best, by listening to a briefing or by perusing a document himself?

Admiral Martin: It depended on what it was. I think that, for example, on the JCS matters that were really voluminous, I think he got more out of reading them. It was unusual that he didn't take briefcases home with him at night. But he absorbed very, very fast—faster than the briefer could talk, of course. The days before the JCS days—there were specific days on which the JCS met—and I think that was a good thing, because it could be put on the Joint Chiefs' schedule and prepared for accordingly. He wouldn't be out of town if something came up.

There was always a JCS briefing for the CNO prior to those meetings, and a lot of things were hammered out there: details that needed emphasis, details where the admiral wanted to ask somebody who was loaded with details for more information on one particular subject. I got into very little of the JCS business, except to try to conserve his time for him.

During that period, as you know, the admiral was selected—he was two stars as Commander Destroyer Force, and he was selected overnight over other flag officers, not only from two stars to four stars but from two stars to the Chief of Naval Operations, which was rather a shocker at the time.*

John T. Mason: Which he admitted in retrospect was really a difficult thing.

Admiral Martin: Yes.

John T. Mason: It had its built-in problems.

Admiral Martin: It could have had, and one of them would be—and here's where he was absolutely marvelous. All of the flag officers who had previously been senior to him before his selection, he never failed to meet with them, and sometimes this would take until late at night. Usually it was a two-star who would come in and take his time until 11:00 at night, but he stayed until it was over. He'd give particular attention and seek out the counsel of those who had commanded fleets and those who had had experiences at the three-star and the four-star levels. He would seek their counsel, and he set an

---

* Rear Admiral Arleigh A. Burke, USN, commanded Destroyer Force Atlantic Fleet from 20 January 1955 to 17 June 1955.

excellent example that maybe hasn't been followed too closely since then, not mentioning any names!*

As a consequence, I believe that he got 100% support. There may have been those who thought that he had made it too fast, until his first commanders' conference and, as I recall, this was almost exactly a year after he had come in. He held the major commanders' conference at the Naval Postgraduate School at Monterey. I went out with him on that session, and he laid out this period of two days or two and a half—I don't recall—starting early in the morning and going until late in the afternoon for each one of those who were there to talk as much as he wanted. I sat in on all of those, and I think I was the only officer there who wasn't a flag officer. I took some notes.

He reserved for himself the last two hours of the period there. He got up in front of them and, referring to no notes, he talked for the full two hours on the highest level of the nation's concerns and where he considered the Navy best fitted into that and what the Navy should be doing in planning the future. When he had completed that, at the end of two hours, I believe that the most senior four-star people in there had the same impression of that that I had, that here was *the* man to be Chief of Naval Operations. He was the most knowledgeable of anybody there. His grasp, his scope, of the most difficult of the nation's problems was, to me, just—I don't know what the word is to express the impression I had of it—that he could have such a broad understanding of even the economic situation affecting the country, not just the military but outside the military, that they were going to have an impact, directly or indirectly, on the defense establishment and the Navy. His view, as he saw it, of the status of the country at the time and his predictions of the future were to me phenomenal. If there had been any foot-dragging in support of him prior to that, it was certainly gone when that was over.

John T. Mason: And this was in the year '56?

Admiral Martin: Yes. As you say, he came in in '55, so I guess that's right—August 17 of 1955, and I think it was in August of '56 that this took place.

---

* Though Admiral Martin did not mention any names, one can surmise that he was referring to Admiral Elmo R. Zumwalt Jr., USN, CNO from 1970 to 1974. He also became CNO by being promoted over a number of flag officers who were senior to him.

John T. Mason: Well, reverting to your day.

Admiral Martin: Yes, to my day.

John T. Mason: The briefing and then—

Admiral Martin: Then, as I say, there were notes that were being brought to me. When I was on the phone, somebody else took the message, and I was to call, or they were to call me back. I spent so much time on the telephone that I couldn't get through my "incoming" basket.

    I remember Admiral Burke passing my desk. Coming from his office he'd pass my desk to get into the head or the barbershop. He came by one time when I'd been on the phone all day long, and my "incoming" basket was stacked high. He looked at me and said, "Don't bottleneck it!" I didn't read as fast as he did, and I couldn't shift gears like he could. He could shift gears from the Bureau of Ships, where there were some very difficult shipbuilding problems, into electronics, into JCS. I thought he was a genius. I still think he was a genius. He could shift gears and totally concentrate on something else, yet not forget something else he had to do, and he'd excuse himself to do so.

John T. Mason: Part of that, I suppose, was the wealth of background he had.

Admiral Martin: Exactly. The pigeonholes in which he put things that came out in very orderly fashion. I was never able to do that. I think that's why some of my seniors said I was pretty good at sea, but not so good ashore.

    A typical day had me on the telephone, except when I was sent for, and in the planning of the admiral's trips, when he'd have Tom Weschler and Lumpkin, he'd frequently call me in, so I could see what the details were for trip planning.[*] He would also ask me to come in with George Miller, with Jack McCain, who was then OP-09 Dog,

---

[*] Commander Pickett Lumpkin, USN, was a public affairs specialist assigned to the staff at that time.

which I guess was progress analysis.* He was actually shaping the sea power presentations that began with him. McCain, Miller, and Martin frequently would be in there with the admiral on current matters and some future plans that were not written up anyplace.

John T. Mason: Was Ramage around there at that time?†

Admiral Martin: Yes, Red Ramage was doing some things that were in the R&D area.‡ I didn't spend much time with Red in there. I never knew exactly what he was doing.

John T. Mason: It had to do with missiles and so forth, didn't it?

Admiral Martin: Yes. Red was considerably senior to me, but he was always so very, very helpful and nice to talk with.

Some of the time that I would spend—and this was almost every day too—was responding to requests for Admiral Burke's time, in which he was going to get a briefing that was going to be lengthy from the various bureaus, especially the Bureau of Ships, because theirs were the most lengthy of all. They'd want an hour of the admiral's time, and it just couldn't be done. So I would sit in on these and try to give them some guidance on where they might condense it.

I recall one time especially when Admiral Mumma was the Chief of the Bureau of Ships, and he had this presentation.§ He said to me, "This just can't be given to the admiral in less than 45 minutes." He had asked for an hour and had cut it down as much as he could, he thought, and it was going to take 45 minutes. So I saw it a second time and said, "Admiral Mumma, this just has to be cut down to 20 minutes because Admiral Burke knows a lot of these details. Tell him things he doesn't know about this." So it was finally cut down to 20 or 25 minutes, and Admiral Mumma told me himself after it

---

* "Dog" was the word for the letter D in the phonetic alphabet of the time.
† Rear Admiral Lawson P. Ramage, USN, was special assistant to the Chief of Naval Operations and headed the Antisubmarine Warfare/Submarine Warfare Division. Ramage, who retired as a vice admiral, is the subject of a Naval Institute oral history.
‡ R&D – research and development.
§ Rear Admiral Albert G. Mumma, USN, served as Chief of the Bureau of Ships from 1955 to 1959. His oral history is in the Naval Institute collection.

was all over that it was a better presentation, more appropriate to give to the Chief of Naval Operations in 20 minutes than it was in 45.

John T. Mason: Because he crystallized it.

Admiral Martin: Yes, and there were several cases I had to contend with, to remind them that Admiral Burke was so well informed that they simply had to deal very briefly with the things that he already was informed of and give him information he didn't have before.

On another occasion there was a young chaplain along with Chaplain James Woodrow Kelly, who was a commander at the time, and this other young fellow was John O'Connor, who was just a lieutenant.[*] They were working on what we called moral guidance, which later became leadership.

John T. Mason: It was first under the aegis of the chaplains, wasn't it?

Admiral Martin: Yes. Jim Kelly was gone at this time, but he had been on the very beginnings of this moral guidance and then the leadership program. O'Connor had been in almost from the very beginning himself, and he had a presentation that he wanted to get to Admiral Burke and wanted 45 minutes.

Finally it was scheduled, and it had the blessing of the Chief of the Bureau of Personnel. It wasn't supposed to go to 45 minutes, but at the end of his 20 minutes he'd barely gotten into his subject, so Admiral Burke shut that one off himself. He said, "I can't stay any longer."

I worked with John O'Connor and with others to get this down to where the full thing could be presented in 20 or 25 minutes, and it came back to Admiral Burke, and it was very, very good. It gave the whole picture.

That was one of our principles—that we just wouldn't permit any presentation to run over 20 minutes.

---

[*] Rear Admiral James W. Kelly, CHC, USN, served as the Navy's Chief of Chaplains from July 1965 to June 1970. Rear Admiral John J. O'Connor, CHC, USN, served as the Navy's Chief of Chaplains from July 1975 to June 1979.

John T. Mason: That was a very difficult assignment you had, to insist upon this and to achieve it.

Admiral Martin: Yes, it was. I was dealing continuously with people who were senior to me; some of them were flag officers.

John T. Mason: But with the full authority of the CNO behind you.

Admiral Martin: Yes, especially if you don't get into too much trouble. I found that out all along. You can do a lot of things. You can do things without permission, as long as you don't make a mistake—if you're right. As a fleet commander, I moved the fleet without asking anybody, but I had to be right, and it turned out that I was, luckily.

I learned a lot of things about Burke then by taking the initiative and, as he said when I was selected for flag rank and got my first assignment, "One of the reasons and the most important perhaps that we have flag officers is to expand responsibility. Every flag officer must observe, and he's responsible for everything of naval interest, large or small, as far as he can see, plus three miles."

John T. Mason: Yes, he's supposed to have a pretty broad vision, plus three miles.

Admiral Martin: I learned that. My first assignment was in Canada, where there were very few Navy flag officers around, so I had the responsibility for everything that was going on there. But it was a real lesson to me, and it makes you observe a lot of things that you might say, "Well, that's somebody else's responsibility." But if you're the flag officer there, it's part of yours, too, and ultimately you're held responsible for it. That's a good thing, because there aren't enough flag officers to cover the whole blooming thing. But as a principle I think it's good, and it turns out to be workable.

John T. Mason: How did Burke get along with Wu Duncan? I know both of them.

Admiral Martin: Very good.

John T. Mason: Wu was a deliberate kind of man.

Admiral Martin: Yes, and a procrastinator. I know that because I'm one myself; I was one myself. I greatly admired Admiral Duncan, and I don't intend for this to be disparaging at all, but if there was a difficult piece of paper that he just wasn't ready to deal with, he'd put it in his bottom right drawer, and it would stay there. That solved a lot of problems, because something that seemed to be so heated and so necessary, and he just had to deal with it at that moment, whether he was ready to or not—he'd put it in his drawer.

John T. Mason: I wondered how that stacked up with such a gung-ho person as Burke.

Admiral Martin: Here again, I think Admiral Duncan knew that things were ultimately going to solve themselves. I don't mean that he'd put down something that was extremely important that should have been dealt with at the time. He just had a knack for knowing the things that did not have a suitable or a possible explanation at the time or a solution at the time, and that things probably should have cooled for a week or two. But we used to go into his right lower drawer when he was gone, and we'd find a lot of correspondence that time had solved usually. But Admiral Duncan had been a four-star admiral for some time, and Burke was a brand-new four-star.[*] Burke treated him with great respect, leaving him out of nothing that he should have been in.

I think the way Admiral Burke handled that situation, which would have been extremely difficult for anyone who didn't have his great capacity for patience and good judgment, which was really the way he dealt with that. Coming into a job without having all the experiences that a four-star admiral usually has, he made up for it by getting the total support of all the flag officers.

John T. Mason: Well, your day went along, and then you had this in basket that you had to deal with after the telephone calls subsided, which meant you were into the evening.

---

[*] Duncan's date of rank as a four-star admiral was 9 August 1951, four years earlier than Burke made it.

Admiral Martin: Yes, but I wasn't alone. There were many officers, especially down in 06 in plans and in operations too.* If there were reasons for people to stay late, they did, but it was very often that Admiral Burke, as Chief of Naval Operations—his offices were the last ones to turn out the lights. I used to hear it said by some of my contemporaries that Admiral Burke was setting a very bad example. That here he was, the most senior officer in the Navy and in a position that every officer should aspire to, but he was setting an example that wasn't a good incentive because he was working longer hours than anybody else in the Navy. I said, "Now, hold it. There's somebody who works a little longer than Admiral Burke. There are some of us who are there when he comes in and some of us who are there when he leaves. So it's not quite the longest day."

What I would call his normal day was 7:30 in the morning to 7:30 in the evening.

John T. Mason: How did he manage his social life, which devolved upon the CNO?

Admiral Martin: Sometimes he just didn't go. If they were important enough—here was where that wonderful, sweet, little wife of his would come into it.† She would come by for him, and when the word got to him that his wife was there, he'd shut up shop. He might take an extra briefcase home with him that night, but he'd never keep her waiting. They had a wonderful relation ship and still do. That little Bobbie was as quiet and even-tempered as she was a sweet, wonderful, little lady. She could be very astute.

Tom Weschler will tell you this and the Marine. There were frequent trips that I wouldn't go on, but they were always happy when Mrs. Burke was on the trip, because if the hour was getting late at night, she could very graciously get the admiral to leave, and the host would understand. She could help keep him on schedule and do it in such a quiet, wonderful way.

We wondered how this was going to happen, because we noticed that when it would get near midnight, he'd pick up his briefcase and leave. And the chauffeur—I wish I could remember his name; Admiral Burke would remember it so well—an awfully

---

* Vice Admiral Ruthven E. Libby, USN, served as Deputy Chief of Naval Operations (Plans and Policy), OP-96, from August 1956 to June 1958. Libby's oral history is in the Naval Institute collection.
† Burke had married Roberta Gorsuch on 7 June 1923, the day he graduated from the Naval Academy. She stood about a foot shorter than her husband.

good man, a chief petty officer in his later years, would help the admiral carry the briefcases down. He'd always get out around 11:00 or 11:15, but on this one night and all the people who were there, eight or ten, would be watching this, you see, to see if we were looking forward to working into the next day. We'd come so close to it, and on that evening, at exactly 11:59 he came out, and he knew that we were looking forward to this thing. I don't know how he sensed it, because our offices there looked out on Arlington Cemetery, and he said, "What are you doing? What are you looking at?"

I said, "Admiral, I'm looking out there. Some of our predecessors might be there because they worked too late."

He didn't think that was funny.

John T. Mason: Tell me about this. Did you observe this? Admiral Burke told me one time that when he had Don Felt there, because Don Felt was not a yes man, he was a no man, and if he disagreed he said so, and that's what he encouraged. He also told me that in connection with Whizzer White, who had been with him down in the South Pacific.[*]

Admiral Martin: Yes, Whizzer White, Byron White.

John T. Mason: Did you observe this about Felt or any of the others? I mean, did he appreciate somebody disagreeing with him and telling him why?

Admiral Martin: I don't recall that there were very many yes men around Admiral Burke, because his understanding of things and his introspection made him find out very quickly if they were agreeing with something that they really didn't believe. So I don't think it frequently happened that they were yes men. Certainly Don Felt was not a yes man, and one of the reasons that I think Admiral Burke wanted him in there was because they had worked together before when Admiral Burke was OP-33, I guess it was.

John T. Mason: OP-30, which became OP-60 after a while, but not under him.

---

[*] Byron R. White was appointed an Associate Justice of the U.S. Supreme Court in 1962.

Admiral Martin: Yes, and Don Felt was in there with him. Don was very able, very bright, and also called them exactly as he saw them. I'm sure that that was one of the qualities that Admiral Burke was looking for.

John T. Mason: Well, I think it served to give him another dimension to a picture.

Admiral Martin: No question about it, yes. Now, to say that Don Felt was a no man, he didn't say no to everything. He could be very strong for the things that he believed in.

John T. Mason: But with the capacity of being—

Admiral Martin: Exactly. The things that he would say no on were the things that were things on which all the information wasn't in yet, or else he had good reason to disagree with them. He could be very difficult, or have we talked about that before?

John T. Mason: Yes.

We touched momentarily on the social aspect of the CNO's job, but you, as senior aide, must have been involved in some of these things as well, were you not? Did you have to go to dinners with him occasionally?

Admiral Martin: Not frequently, no. This was where I could stay behind and work on that "incoming" basket. He could take Tom Weschler with him. The admiral was very good about separating out the personal aide's things from the professional side, but he had such terrific aides. Tom Weschler was so capable that he was capable of taking over all the professional things, but he handled all of the personal things, and he did them so competently. Tom Weschler was the perfect aide, knowledgeable and, as I say, he didn't confine his interest to just the personal side. He knew the professional as well.

John T. Mason: Now, I wonder if you would focus on the Polaris subject.* You said you were on the periphery, but you do have things to contribute to the story.

Admiral Martin: I really don't have much. It was interesting to me and, so far as I know, Red Raborn was the one who developed this line-of-balance technique for handling a major project.† It was a very interesting one in which you laid out the things that had to be done, even to the smallest details, and made sure that they were laid out in proper order of accomplishment when it can possibly be accomplished and at what stage it must be accomplished. That was called the line-of-balance technique, and it had another term—

John T. Mason: PERT.‡

Admiral Martin: Right. There was a fellow over in BuAer named Hugh Hanson who had something to do with that. Hugh was also a very good writer, a civilian, one who was a close friend of Arleigh Burke.

Red asked me to come over and see his planning room. It was over in the old Munitions Building on Constitution Avenue.§ In this rather large room he had all the charts laid out exactly where every aspect of the development was. And he always had in red up there the thing that was either behind or it looked like it was going to be behind, so that he could immediately put priority on that area. And it wasn't an easy thing, because

---

* Polaris was the name for the U.S. Navy's first submarine-launched ballistic missile, which became operational in the early 1960s. Its more-capable follow-on was the Poseidon missile, which entered the fleet in 1970.
† Rear Admiral William F. Raborn, Jr., USN, was director of the Special Projects Office, which developed the Polaris submarine-launched ballistic missile system. He held the post from 1955 to 1962, being promoted to vice admiral in 1960. His Polaris oral history is in the Naval Institute collection.
‡ PERT – Program Evaluation Review Technique, a system of milestones for tracking the progress of a program against its schedule.
§ Main Navy was the popular name for the old Navy Department building at 17th Street and Constitution Avenue in Washington, D.C. The building remained in use from its opening in 1918 until the early 1970s, when President Richard Nixon directed that it be demolished. The adjacent Munitions Building was long occupied by the War Department. In 1943, with the opening of the Pentagon, the Army moved out and transferred the Munitions Building to the Navy.

while I guess Lockheed had the primary responsibility for Polaris and I guess they still have it for Trident, they were keeping track of things, I'm sure, as Raborn's office was.*

John T. Mason: Did you ever attend any of those Saturday morning sessions that Raborn held with great regularity?

Admiral Martin: I think only one, because I was in Raborn's space on two occasions. One when I went over, and he and Levering Smith, who had been a friend of mine, took me through, and then I did go over one Saturday morning.†

John T. Mason: That was when they pulled everything together.

Admiral Martin: Yes. They had some highly capable people working with them. Each of them was outstanding in his particular field. So far as I know, that was the beginning of that technique of having a major project, and that continues to be it now.

John T. Mason: The SP, yes.

Admiral Martin: Yes, it was the first Special Project.

John T. Mason: Whose concept was this? Was it Raborn's or was it Burke's?

Admiral Martin: I don't know whose concept that was. I've always given Raborn credit for it. He was the first I ever heard speak about it, and it was through his office that they were developing it and refining it as it went along. My knowledge of it after or even before I got my briefing—that's why I was invited to go over there, because I was getting these long telephone calls from Raborn, who didn't have the time to come over, or possibly thought it would take less time by him giving me his reading of the day on

---

* The Trident I (C-4) submarine-launched ballistic missile, with a range of about 4,600 miles, was deployed in 1979 and phased out in the 1990s and early 2000s. The Trident II (D-5), with a range of about 7,500 miles, was deployed in 1990.
† Captain Levering Smith, USN, was the second technical director in the Special Projects Office. He succeeded Captain Grayson Merrill, USN, when Merrill retired in 1957.

Polaris, rather than coming over and spending possibly more time with Admiral Burke. By giving it to me, I could get it to Admiral Burke at some period in his program in which it would fit without taking him from something else.

John T. Mason: How much time did Burke spend on the whole Polaris thing? I mean, he kept abreast of it all the time.

Admiral Martin: It was a daily thing, absolutely, either from Admiral Raborn, or I think Red Ramage was involved as well.

John T. Mason: J. B. Colwell was there, too, for the first year.[*]

Admiral Martin: Yes, I know J. B. well, but I didn't have very much connection with him at the time. He was just an extremely fine officer.

John T. Mason: He was deputy for the first year.

Admiral Martin: Yes. He and Raborn had worked together before. In World War II they had come out to the fleet in the combat area on ordnance problems to try to straighten out some problems that we had like bomb launchers, gunsights, and things of that kind.

That's about as much as I can tell you about Polaris.

John T. Mason: All right, fine. Now let's shift to Richard Evelyn Byrd.

Admiral Martin: As I say, Rear Admiral Byrd and Admiral Rickover—sometimes their concerns were really outside of their fields.

John T. Mason: Byrd's program at that point had been developed fully, had it not, and someone else had taken over?

---

[*] Captain John B. Colwell, USN, later vice admiral, was deputy director of the Fleet Ballistic Missile Project Office, and is the subject of a Naval Institute oral history.

Admiral Martin: Well, yes. I don't know just what his status was on this, because he'd reached the stage of retirement, and he wasn't well. Whether he had a consultant's relationship with the program or just what it was, but his interest in everything arctic and antarctic continued, the Deep Freeze program and that sort of thing.* But frequently his complaints weren't in that area at all.

John T. Mason: What sort of complaints would they be?

Admiral Martin: Things that had appeared in the newspaper, for example, or some periodical with which he didn't agree, or in some cases where they hadn't given him credit. I think Admiral Byrd looked out for credit that was rightfully his. I just can't remember any of the details that he was unhappy about. Most of them, I think, were on what was appearing in the press, but he was very nervous and vociferous about the things that bothered him, the things he disliked. I can't give you a specific example.

John T. Mason: Well, it was something much more specific with Rickover?

Admiral Martin: Yes. Rickover was then, as he is today, I guess, interested in every detail of a ship that was nuclear powered, even surface ships that were nuclear powered, getting into the operational areas and so on. I can give you an example of that.

They put a sort of a modified Polaris capability, or long-range missile capability, in the *Bainbridge*, and Admiral Rickover took great interest in that area.† He was always getting out of the nuclear-propulsion system, which was really his only responsibility, and getting into the operational aspects. The skipper of the *Bainbridge* told me that Admiral Rickover had been very helpful to him in getting certain layouts or

---

* Operation Deep Freeze is the Navy's program of providing logistic support to scientific study in Antarctica.
† USS *Bainbridge* (DLGN-25), a nuclear-powered frigate, was the only ship of her class. She was commissioned 6 October 1962. She had a standard displacement of 7,600 tons, was 565 feet long, 58 feet in the beam, and had a maximum draft of 29 feet. Her top speed was 30-plus knots. She was armed with two twin launchers for Terrier missiles, two 3-inch guns, ASROC, and six torpedo tubes. She was redesignated a cruiser, CGN-25, on 1 July 1975 and eventually decommissioned 13 September 1996.

configurations changed as the skipper wanted them changed, that would improve the functions of the ship.*

I've heard the same thing from the commanding officer of the *Enterprise*. My flag was in the *Enterprise* for a year and a half, and Admiral Rickover was extremely demanding on the nuclear side. But he also took interest in other aspects of the ship, which the commanding officer of the ship, which was Captain Vince de Poix, who put the ship in commission, and later Captain Mike Michaelis, who took it over when the ship was fully operational.† De Poix became a vice admiral, and, of course, Mike Michaelis just recently retired with four staffs from Chief of Naval Material.

As you know, Admiral Rickover got some criticism because he thought the educational system of the whole country was wrong, and he wrote a lot of things on that.

John T. Mason: Especially the Naval Academy.

Admiral Martin: Well, yes, particularly that, but he didn't think that any of the educational institutions were being run right. He wrote some articles on it that got a lot of flak because they just said that he should stay in his field of nuclear propulsion and stay out of the educational sector.

I guess Admiral Rickover's desire to have things done exactly the way he wanted them done would get him into other people's areas because it wasn't just the Bureau of Ships that he was dealing with. He'd get into other bureaus as well. In some cases, I think this was good, and in some cases I believe it had the effect of obstruction. He was very, very possessive, especially in the areas for which he was responsible. That had to be done precisely the way he wanted it done, and I think the result is that we've never had a nuclear accident in the areas for which he was responsible. At least I don't know of them.

---

* Captain Raymond E. Peet, USN, commanded the guided missile frigate *Bainbridge* (DLGN-25) from her commissioning on 6 October 1962 until 17 July 1964. He was assigned to the ship well before completion. The oral history of Peet, who retired as a vice admiral, is in the Naval Institute collection.
† Captain Vincent P. de Poix, USN, commanded the aircraft carrier *Enterprise* (CVAN-65) from the ship's commissioning on 25 November 1961 until 20 June 1963. Captain Frederick H. Michaelis, USN, commanded the aircraft carrier *Enterprise* (CVAN-65) from 20 June 1963 to 17 July 1965. The oral history of Michaelis, who became a four-star admiral, is in the Naval Institute collection.

John T. Mason: He insisted that there couldn't be because it would destroy the program.

Admiral Martin: Yes, and his demand for very, very tight control and his quality control of things, I think perhaps, was the result. You know they built a merchant ship—*Savannah,* wasn't it?*

John T. Mason: The *Savannah*, yes.

Admiral Martin: And it turned out to be a very unhappy result.

John T. Mason: In what sense?

Admiral Martin: Maybe because they didn't insist on quality control and very rigid rules and regulations for its construction as well as for its operation and maintenance.

I continue to look upon Admiral Rickover with the respect that you'd give a distinguished American. I think he deserves it, but he's not somebody I'd want to go camping with.

John T. Mason: Did he attempt ever to throw any monkey wrenches into the office of the CNO while you were there?

Admiral Martin: I believe that those would be the times when Admiral Rickover would talk to the admiral in person, and I wasn't ever present on those. I really don't know what went on there. Only Admiral Burke could tell you if he had headaches with Admiral Rickover, although I've known a number of other flag officers who were very vocal on the problems that they were having with Admiral Rickover.

---

* NS *Savannah* was the world's first nuclear-powered passenger-cargo ship as a joint venture of the U.S. Maritime Administration and the Atomic Energy Commission. She was nearly 600 feet long, displaced 22,000 tons, and had a top speed of 24 knots. She was launched 23 March 1962. She carried cargo from 1964 to 1970 after several years of at-sea testing. She was retired in 1971 and later spent several years as a museum at Patriots Point, South Carolina.

John T. Mason: Admiral Burke has always been interested, and he certainly is even today, in cooperation with foreign navies and in his personal relationship with foreign CNOs.

Admiral Martin: Yes, the counterparts.

John T. Mason: This must have cropped up in your time there too.

Admiral Martin: Yes, it began, and it remained under way as long as he was Chief of Naval Operations. I think the program continues even today. The admiral had correspondence with the Chief of Naval Operations of every country that was of particular interest to the United States. I feel sure that he was establishing the program in which the Chiefs of Naval Operations of foreign countries would come here to visit began with the navies of most interest to us, either where those nations were of interest to our Navy as allies, or with countries with which we actually did operate or wanted to operate with units of their navies. This extended, of course, to all of the NATO navies but also to South American countries that were of most interest to us.[*] I think he attempted to get—of course, every country doesn't have a navy or doesn't have one of sufficient size to operate with us.

When I was in the Med, we tried to operate even with those that had nothing but a few minesweepers. I thought this was a very good thing for the nation as a whole, to develop friendships and to have at least a few trusted friends and countries that weren't traditionally close friends. They weren't allies, but if we had some friends in those countries they could be very helpful. I think he did this at the international level because on their visits here the admiral would have a schedule of introducing them to other services and to the Office of the Secretary of Defense. In some cases, their visits here would not be entirely to naval establishments, but maybe to the Army or Air Force, but it was a very valuable program.

---

[*] NATO – North Atlantic Treaty Organization, which was established in 1949 as a means of coordinating defense against a potential attack from the Soviet Union.

Along with that, he established the exchange system where we would send officers to their naval schools, and they would send officers to ours. That continues today, I'm quite sure.

John T. Mason: He's very proud of UNITAS, the South American combined fleet operation.*

Admiral Martin: Yes.

John T. Mason: Did that happen in your time?

Admiral Martin: It began at that time. Yes, that was a very helpful thing, because the admiral believed that—and this is something that I carried out when I had the Sixth Fleet—to try to get our ambassadors with their heads of state out for visits. Sometimes that would be the only time the ambassador would have a moment alone, and if you could get them alone aboard ship together, he could have several hours together with the head of state, and that was very helpful.

John T. Mason: He had during the Eisenhower years a very intimate relationship with the general as well and went to the White House quite frequently.† Were you knowledgeable of that?

Admiral Martin: Yes, I was. Of course, through the Eisenhower period the National Security Council meetings would be attended by any of the military, the Chiefs of Staff of the Army and the Air Force, the Chief of Naval Operations, along with the Chairman, would sit in on them. Today, I guess starting with Kennedy—I'm not sure of this—only the Chairman of the Joint Chiefs of Staff, which is too bad, I think, because I believe the

---

* UNITAS is the name given to a series of annual exercises that began in 1959 and continue to this day. U.S. Navy ships operate with those of South American navies during at-sea exercises and in-port training.
† Dwight D. Eisenhower served as President of the United States from 20 January 1953 to 20 January 1961. During World War II he had been Supreme Commander of the Allied Expeditionary Force for the invasion of Europe. In the early 1950s, as a five-star general, he served as Supreme Allied Commander in Europe when the military portion of the North Atlantic Treaty Organization (NATO) was established.

President should have access to—well, he has access—but I think he should routinely see the Chiefs of the other services. I don't see how he can get a balanced view of the armed forces by seeing only one person.

John T. Mason: Well, Eisenhower had an appreciation of that fact because he was a military man. But I was referring in particular to Burke's relationship with Eisenhower and becoming something of a confidant.

Admiral Martin: I believe that's true. As I understand it, Admiral Burke was very quiet for the first six months or so on the National Security Council. One day a subject came up on how to put some pressure on somebody, and, if my memory is correct, it was Egypt. Everybody had run out of anything to say and, as I understand it, the President turned to Admiral Burke and said, "Admiral Burke, you're very quiet. Do you have some idea on what might be done in this case that hasn't been mentioned?"

So Admiral Burke said, "Yes, I do," and he went over some economic things that really impressed Eisenhower on the admiral's grasp of international economic aspects. I think he was speaking about long-staple cotton, as I recall it. It's been a long time ago now. But from that point on President Eisenhower almost invariably would ask Admiral Burke for his views, because he really valued them, and this is in areas that were outside the military.

I think that's all I have to say on that.

John T. Mason: You were there during the Suez Crisis?[*]

Admiral Martin: Yes.

John T. Mason: Do you have any reflections on that?

---

[*] On 26 July 1956 President Gamal Nasser of Egypt announced that his country was nationalizing the Suez Canal Company. Israeli forces invaded Egypt's Sinai Peninsula on 29 October 1956. Britain and France then intervened militarily on behalf of Israel in an unsuccessful attempt to secure the Suez Canal, which was damaged and closed to traffic. Rather than support the British and French, the United States asked for a United Nations resolution to end the fighting. A cease-fire took effect on 6 November.

Admiral Martin: Well, I sat in on some of those briefings, and I know that Admiral Burke took some actions in moving the fleet that I don't believe he could do today. He said that he was the last of the Chiefs of Naval Operations, and I don't think the CNO since that time has been truly on the operational side of directing operations.

John T. Mason: Since 1958 when they changed the National Defense Act.*

Admiral Martin: Yes.

John T. Mason: But up to that time and during the Suez crisis he certainly had legal control, operational control of the fleet?

Admiral Martin: Yes, particularly.

John T. Mason: But I was thinking particularly of the fact that he apparently did disagree with the policy that the President and the Secretary of State were pursuing in terms of the Suez crisis.

Admiral Martin: I didn't get into it at that depth. I just knew that he was taking initiatives then that you couldn't take later. I know that he would tell the other Chiefs on the Joint Chiefs that "We have to settle this among ourselves, because if we don't, it's going to be settled by the Office of the Secretary of Defense, and it won't be nearly as good as we can settle it ourselves."

There were matters that the Joint Chiefs could handle, and their expertise should be in the decision-making process on that, because to give a military matter to the civilian level to solve themselves and make a decision isn't the way to do it. It takes it completely out of the judgment of the people who know most about it. I think the Chiefs of Staff of the Army and Air Force tended to agree with this, because, later, the SecDef's

---

* The Department of Defense Reorganization Act of 1958 contained a number of provisions, including removal of the service secretaries from the chain of command; removal of the service chiefs' operational command authority over their forces; establishment of the principle that the Joint Chiefs of Staff could act only under the authority of the Secretary of Defense; and transfer of control of the Joint Staff from the JCS as a whole to the Chairman.

office kept taking over more and more and more of the decision stuff. They have been doing it in recent years of determining what weapon system will be procured and getting right down into the details of every aspect of all the services. I think that's an undesirable thing, believe, as we all do, in "civilian control," but not to a point where they are ignoring the best judgment of the military commanders.

John T. Mason: And directing the military operations?

Admiral Martin: This has been done in some detail.

John T. Mason: You must have needed a period of rest after this very strenuous, around-the-clock assignment with Admiral Burke before you took on your next tour of duty. Did you manage something of that sort?

Admiral Martin: Maybe a few days but not very much. I recall I was going to join ComCarDiv 5 as chief of staff to Admiral Fitzhugh Lee, and he was deployed at that time, so I don't think I got more than a week or so before I had to report in to my new job.[*] As a matter of act, I never have had much time between changing jobs. Again, I was something like Admiral Burke. He was always wanted so much at his next assignment that he never got much time.

John T. Mason: Was this job something that you had a voice in getting?

Admiral Martin: No, I had such good assignments, such favorable assignments, assignments that I wanted, that it wasn't necessary for me to request any special assignments. I was very happy I got the ones that I had, especially those that kept me in night and all-weather aviation, but I took the assignments pretty much as they came. I do recall requesting one assignment, and I got it.

---

[*] Rear Admiral Fitzhugh Lee, USN, Commander Carrier Division Five. The oral history of Lee, who retired as a vice admiral, is in the Naval Institute collection.

No, I was very happy to go as chief of staff to an attack carrier division and very happy to go to work with Admiral Fitzhugh Lee. I'd known him before. He was my very best flight instructor when I was going through Pensacola. I had an extremely high regard for him. It was an extremely interesting and valuable assignment.

At the time I reported, and they had just deployed, so I got the full deployment of six months. It was during that period that I was selected for flag rank, which was a very big surprise for me. As a matter of fact, the message came in during the night. Admiral Fitzhugh Lee saw the message that gave the names of those who were selected. He saw it before I did. I was taking my shower, and he sent his orderly down to bring me a copy of the message. The orderly knocked at the shower, and I said, "What is it?"

He said, "The admiral has sent down a message for you to see."

"Is it important?"

"The admiral says it is."

So I dried one hand, took the message, and I saw my name. It was the last name on the list, you see, and I said, "You go tell the admiral that I'm not really impressed with his form of practical jokes."

He said, "I can't do it."

I said, "You do it, or you're in trouble with me."

John T. Mason: Put the poor orderly on the spot.

Admiral Martin: Yes, and he went back. Fitzhugh Lee had a really fine sense of humor, and I really thought he was pulling me leg on this for quite a while. I didn't really believe it until we were coming into Yokohama, and I flew in to call the Bureau of Personnel, which I did. I talked to Bud Needham, who was detailing at that time in the Bureau of Personnel.* But just died a couple of months ago, you know.

John T. Mason: Yes, I saw the name, but I didn't know him.

Admiral Martin: I said, "Bud, this dispatch that I've got a copy of, I hear it is true."

---

* Captain Ray C. Needham, USN.

He said, "Yes, it is true."

I said, "Well, I've had in my hand now for four months orders to put the USS *Independence* in commission, and I've made a lot of arrangements for that. I've gotten the wife of Secretary Gates to be the sponsor, and I've got my own PERT system lined up on what has to be done to put that ship in commission. So, please, leave me a captain for at least a year so I can commission this ship and take her to sea and shake her down."

He said, "No, can't do it. This has been discussed. You've already had your carrier."

I said, "I know, but I haven't had a big carrier."

"Well, no, it's already been decided. You're going to be frocked and sent to . . . "*

John T. Mason: You did have to come back for a briefing with all the other newly caught admirals?

Admiral Martin: Yes, what we called among ourselves the plebe admirals' course. It ran for about ten days with extensive briefings in the Pentagon, and we took a trip down to Cape Canaveral and other trips. All in all, it took about ten days.

This was the first time they had selected anybody from my class, and they selected three officers. They selected a destroyer man, who was B. J. Semmes; a submariner, who was Chick Clarey; and an aviator, who was myself.† We were selected early from our class. We weren't really to be in the zone for another two or three years.

John T. Mason: Oh, it was deep selection then?

Admiral Martin: Yes, it was, one of the first times they deep-selected. They've done it a lot since then. I think that was written into the precept by the Secretary of the Navy to

---

* "Frocking" a naval officer refers to the practice of allowing him to wear the insignia and assume the title for which he was recently selected. The officer does not receive the pay for the higher rank until a vacancy appears on the lineal list so he can be officially promoted.
† Captain Benedict J. Semmes, USN Jr., later vice admiral; Captain Bernard A. Clarey, USN, later four-star admiral. Both have been interviewed for the Naval Institute's oral history program.

deep-select, and whether they were directed to do this, to try to take a surface-warfare man, a subsurface man, and an aviator, I wouldn't know.

John T. Mason: Was Gates Secretary then?*

Admiral Martin: Yes.

I was really disappointed that I didn't get to carry out the commissioning of the *Independence*.

John T. Mason: Your stay with the Seventh Fleet was a very brief one, just a sort of a temporary assignment, wasn't it?

Admiral Martin: Well, as I say, I completed one deployment, and we were on our way back, near the end of the deployment, when I was selected. I came back with the ship and, as I recall, I left ComCarDiv 5 before my relief came in order to get to the plebe admirals' course.

Then I went to Argentia, Newfoundland, where the major assignment was Commander Atlantic Barrier.†

John T. Mason: And just what was that?

Admiral Martin: It consisted of manning four stations, extending from Argentia down toward the Azores—1,200 miles. They had a destroyer ever 300 miles, so there were four of them that were rotated every two months. They were positioned at those points, and they were relieved on station. We kept three of them down toward the Azores and one, position Charlie, was up toward Greenland, and that was always manned by a Coast Guard ship.

John T. Mason: Because of the icebergs and that sort of thing.

---

* Thomas S. Gates, Jr., served as Secretary of the Navy from 1 April 1957 to 7 June 1959.
† Rear Admiral Martin served from July 1958 to December 1959 as Commander Airborne Early Warning Wing Atlantic.

Admiral Martin: Maybe. I often wondered how they talked the Coast Guard into taking that station, because it was the least desirable of all of them. Of course, the most desirable one was the one nearest the Azores, because they were in much better weather down there.

I don't think I had been there two weeks until I began to doubt the value of it. In addition to the four DERs plus the Coast Guard ship, we had three squadrons of Super Connies.* We called them the Willie Victors; they had a big radar dome on them.

John T. Mason: Willie Victors?

Admiral Martin: Willie Victors, WVs.† The "W" was for airborne early warning, and the "V" was for Lockheed, so that was a Lockheed early-warning plane. They were Super Connies that had a huge dome on top, a 14-foot dome, and several radar positions. There were 23 people in the crew.

John T. Mason: And they'd fly back and forth?

Admiral Martin: They'd fly back and forth, and there was always one on the surface, always.

It was an extremely expensive operation, and the only thing we were capable of doing was pick up an aircraft of the size that could carry out the mission of Soviet Russia to the United States. I just didn't see that as a threat.

John T. Mason: Could you give me the background to this?

Admiral Martin: Why was it started in the first place?

---

* In the 1950s, the operate the barrier patrols, the Navy converted a number of destroyer escorts to radar picket destroyer escorts (DERs) with by adding more radar capability.
† The WV Warning Star was a military version of the Constellation commercial aircraft. Lockheed started delivery of the WV-2 model to Navy squadrons in 1954 for use as airborne early warning posts. The WV-2, powered by four propeller-driven engines, had a wingspan of 123 feet length, 116 feet, 2 inches; gross weight of 145,000 pounds; top speed of 368 miles per hour.

John T. Mason: Yes.

Admiral Martin: I rather suspect that the Air Force got us into this thing because they wanted to keep us in it, and it was a terrible drain on other things. It took up, as I recall, 900 electronics ratings, and they had to be awfully good. It was just a terrible drain on the Navy, and I just can't believe the Navy accepted it willingly. It had been there for at least four years, because Joe Clifton had it at one time and I think maybe Wes Byng.* They were both became flag officers. I relieved Paul Masterton, and Johnny Hyland relieved me.†

John T. Mason: What occasioned it? Was it the potential Russian threat?

Admiral Martin: The question, as I understand it, came up with regard to continental air defense. The Air Force had appropriations for the Air Defense Command, and they, together with the Canadians, had the DEW Line. That covered our frontier to the north, but there was nothing equivalent to it from the Atlantic side, from the northeast, which was really the most direct route to our industrial Middle West and industrial New England.

John T. Mason: The Azores constituted the anchor at the end?

Admiral Martin: No, the Azores just happened to be there. I think it would have fanned out in that direction anyway. There was a detachment in the Azores at Tenerife. This was one of the issues. The Air Force, for example—and this happened not long after I arrived there—had a paper in that would have frozen these positions for the DERs and the Coast Guard ship and would have made those compulsory reporting points for aircraft, commercial even, going and coming. Had that happened, we would never have been able to get rid of them.

---

* Rear Admiral Joseph C. Clifton, USN; Rear Admiral John Weston Byng, USN.
† Rear Admiral Paul Masterton, USN; Rear Admiral John J. Hyland, USN. The oral history of Hyland, who retired as a four-star admiral, is in the Naval Institute collection. Hyland commanded the Atlantic Barrier Patrol from December 1959 to September 1960. See "Barrier Patrol," *Naval History*, Fall 1989, pages 58-59. This is an excerpt from his Naval Institute oral history.

So I made a trip to Washington and then on out to Colorado Springs.[*] That's where the Air Defense Command was and still is. It doesn't have nearly the importance that it used to have, but before I left Argentia on that trip I started fanning them. I said, "We don't want people to know where we are. There are lots of arguments, so far as the barrier is concerned, for them not knowing where we are."

And so I started moving this around. It was still pivoted from Argentia, but we'd move them around on a line that was to the east and to the west of the Azores extended, so that they could not make them compulsory reporting points for air navigation purposes. That kept us from getting into concrete on that. Then I kept bringing up, "Just what is the importance? Is it worth the cost to air defense against the big bomber? Is that sufficient threat to warrant all this expenditure?"

I think it was while Johnny Hyland was up there, who succeeded me after I'd been there for a year, that they did away with it.[†] We had other responsibilities. One of the commands was commander of ASW in that area.[‡] We had an ice patrol; we had the resupply of that end of the DEW Line. We had Dewey West Eight and Thule and Frobisher. The northern station was Alert. It was well up into the Arctic. And we supported the Coast Guard in their mission of the iceberg patrol.

John T. Mason: Why would the Navy take over the ice patrol when you had the Coast Guard?

Admiral Martin: They only had one aircraft there, and you really needed to predict the icebergs that were going to come down into the sea-lanes. We needed more information than that.

There were five titles altogether, none of them important, including what was supposed to be the most important, the barrier, which I didn't think had any importance.

---

[*] The North American Air Defense Command (NORAD), an Air Force command based in Colorado Springs, was responsible for detecting and attacking Soviet bombers headed toward the United States.
[†] The final flight of the Atlantic Barrier Force (BarLant) was on 26 August 1965. Airborne Early Warning Squadron 11 (VW-11) was decommissioned 7 October 1965. The last commander of BarLant was Rear Admiral Ralph Weymouth, USN.
[‡] ASW – antisubmarine warfare.

John T. Mason: It must have been a very dull assignment for the men on the destroyers, to be anchored out there.

Admiral Martin: Terrible, and that's another thing I did shortly after I took over. I rotated them. They'd go to the worst station first, then to the second worst, and then to the third, which was down almost to the Azores and wasn't too bad.

John T. Mason: Did they get into Ponta Delgada?

Admiral Martin: Not very often, no.

John T. Mason: At least there's civilization there.

Admiral Martin: Well, they were down where the weather wasn't too bad.

    The aircraft, the Willie Victors, that operated out of Argentia would go down to the Azores. If they were having any kind of trouble, they'd go in there. I'd had the job less than 24 hours when an aircraft was missing. The last report we had on him was the last time he was to report before he got to the end of the line, nearest to the Azores, and we never did find him. He disappeared.

John T. Mason: Fell into the ocean?

Admiral Martin: We don't know. We don't have any idea. We did come up with some ideas later. We had another plane that almost went in, but he was able to control it and land in the Azores. His problem was runaway trim control, the control that they have to trim up the little tabs on the elevator to keep neutral stick forces in the aircraft. Every airplane has them. The little motor that ran that had run away and was locking it into a maximum position so that both the pilot and the copilot had to keep on the steering column to control it until they could let down at the Azores, but they did it without damage. There's where we found the trouble. I rather suspect that that's what might have happened to the plane that disappeared, because if it runs to a full control, you may not catch it in time. I just have a feeling that they dove into the water, with the loss of 23 men and a Super Connie aircraft.

John T. Mason: Pretty deep ocean around there too.

Admiral Martin: Yes, very deep. We lost two other aircraft when I was up there. One of them was serious, with fatalities. The weather at Argentia, Newfoundland, has a worldwide reputation as the worst flying weather in the whole world. I used to make trips up into the Arctic Circle, to Thule and Alert. I would ask them up there, "How can your weather be this good up here, visibility and everything?" They always had better weather than Argentia, Newfoundland, because when you get that far north these frontal systems that we have that march across, those inverted beams that march across the country. Weather comes from west to east; they don't occur in the Arctic Circle.

John T. Mason: I suppose the Gulf Stream has some impact, doesn't it, up there?

Admiral Martin: An adverse impact. It brings in moisture off the sea, and visibility is bad. Visibility above the Arctic Circle is always good except when you get blowing snow, but they don't have frontal systems. There are not many storms up there like the ones we have in the temperate zone, because they just don't have—it's cold, it's dry. The only problem you have in landing, finding the runway, is blowing snow. Sometimes that will completely obscure the runway. They said, "Everybody knows that Newfoundland has the worst flying weather in the world and that Argentia has the worst in Newfoundland."

The Air Force had a base at the other end, on the west end, at Newfoundland.

John T. Mason: This seemed to be a project in reverse in terms of the Air Force, which is always wanting to get more and more, but this time they wanted to shuck off to the Navy.

Admiral Martin: If you're trying to do somebody in, you get them real busy at something that's not important and start funneling their funds into something that doesn't compete with anything else. It didn't compete with anybody else, and how could they justify big funds for the Air Defense Command, a very expensive thing, when here's the most important sector of the defense of the United States against bombers from Europe not covered at all? Well, maybe they're not all schemers.

John T. Mason: I'm surprised that Admiral Burke acquiesced in this kind of new project.

Admiral Martin: I don't think it started under him.

John T. Mason: Oh, it began before him?

Admiral Martin: Oh, yes, because I went up there in '58, and it had started at least five years prior to that.[*] I don't know this for sure, but I feel quite sure that he went along with one of my early recommendations that they disestablish it, but it took a while to do that. You had to go through the arrangements we had with the Canadians and so on.

John T. Mason: Yes. What role did the Canadians have in it? Did the Canadian Navy help you?

Admiral Martin: They had nothing to do with my command except that we were at a base in Newfoundland, and Newfoundland is part of Canada. We cooperated on such things as submarine contacts. We had a very close relationship there. My command center was in touch with their command center for flag officers. The Canadian admiral was the Canadian Flag Officer Atlantic, and his headquarters were in Halifax, Nova Scotia. So we had good coordination on that aspect of it, and in some of the rescue work and so on there was good. Where there should have been helpful coordination we had it, both ways. It was a very friendly arrangement, but they didn't supply any forces for the barrier. They were helpful in providing alternate airports like Goose Bay, and the field at St. John's was available to us as an alternate.

---

[*] The Atlantic Barrier Patrol began on 1 July 1956, while Admiral Burke was CNO. See Captain Joseph Bouchard, USN, "Guarding the Cold War Ramparts," *Naval War College Review*, Summer. 1999.

At one time, snow got so bad—this was between Christmas and New Year—conditions got so bad that we couldn't keep the field at Argentia clear of snow, and visibility was down to zero. So it was a matter of moving our aircraft over to the western end of the island and operating the barrier from there. We had about four days of that before we could move them back to Argentia, but we kept the barrier manned. We never had a holiday in manning the barrier.* We thought we were going to have one when one of the DERs wasn't able to go out, but they repaired it in time.

John T. Mason: You must have had a morale problem with your personnel.

Admiral Martin: There was. One of the first complaints I heard up there was that if anybody is going to be sent up here to this barrier, when they finally leave it, they should be sending them south. They'd been sending too many of our people to naval air stations in Minneapolis, Seattle—

John T. Mason: Cold country.

Admiral Martin: Cold country. Send them south. So the next time I was in Washington, I went over to BuPers, to the assignment desk, and I said, "When our people have been up there for over two and a half years, send them south."

I was emphatic about that, so when I got back, one of my best commanders, a fellow named Newcomer, who'd been on the barrier for three or four years, had orders south—to the South Pole.†

John T. Mason: South Pole!

Admiral Martin: He'd been ordered to Deep Freeze. They said, "You said, 'Send him south.'" So they sent him south, to the Antarctic." So I'd stretched it too far somehow.

---

* In Navy terminology, a "holiday" is an unpainted section of a deck or bulkhead, thus a gap.
† Commander Lloyd E. Newcomer, USN.

This fellow Newcomer was the one who flew a rescue mission to bring out a Russian scientist during their winter season. It had never been done before, and when I found out what they were going to do, I sent a message: "If you want to send a really competent pilot, send Newcomer out there." So Newcomer was the command pilot to go in there and bring this Russian out, and he did it. The Russian said, "Thank you," and that's all he did say.[*]

John T. Mason: Not very loquacious.

John T. Mason: I guess the most stimulating thing that happened up there, through a little other than normal situation, was when all of the transatlantic cables went off at the same time. AT&T, by means still a mystery to me, knew within a mile or two of where they were cut.[†] We all immediately suspected that a Soviet trawler had done it. There was a big hullabaloo, and CinCLantFlt called me on the hotline. I was dealing mostly with Corky Ward.[‡] Do you know Corky?

John T. Mason: Oh, yes. I remember Corky was involved with the DEW Line, yes.

Admiral Martin: They called me, and they said, "Go up and see if there's a Russian ship at this location," which they'd gotten from AT&T, because AT&T had an old Catalina that was rigged with sensors and things like that, things they needed.[§]

We didn't waste any time getting up there. We went right away, and found out that this Russian trawler, the *R-99*, was in that position. It was the only one that was there, and it was not in a position where they normally would fish. It was not in the Grand Banks. There were two big locations up there that were fishing grounds, but they weren't near any fishing ground. Flemish Cap was the other place. It wasn't near either

---

[*] On 10 April 1961, a ski-equipped LC-130F from Air Development Squadron Six (VX-6) made a medical evacuation of Russian scientist Leonid Kuperov from Byrd Station at McMurdo, Antarctica, to Christchurch, New Zealand.
[†] AT&T – American Telephone and Telegraph.
[‡] Rear Admiral Alfred G. Ward, USN, later admiral, is the subject of a Naval Institute oral history.
[§] Catalina was the name of the PBY Navy flying boat used throughout World War II.

of those, so we came back with a report that, yes, there was a Soviet trawler near that location.

Then I was instructed to go up and find out what we could find as to whether that was the ship that had cut the cables. I said I'd do that with a DER, and I asked, "How do I go about boarding that ship?" I never got a reply.

John T. Mason: That was your discretion.

Admiral Martin: That was my discretion. They didn't want to know from me that that's what I was going to do.

I sent a DER up there, and I was very concerned that they didn't have anybody aboard that could speak Russian. I had on my staff a lieutenant commander, Supply Corps, who was very good in Russian. So I recalled him from leave, and he got there after the DER was already 75 miles away from land on this trip. At that time you weren't allowed to send a helicopter that far from land, and you couldn't send one on instrument conditions. They just weren't qualified to do it. They weren't rigged for it, and with him 75 miles out there when I recalled this fellow to get him back, they were 90 miles out when I had to send him out there. I thought a little bit about doing that because I was concerned about safety. But I sent another Willie Victor to go out with the helicopter, to keep him in sight and to track him for his own safety, and took this lieutenant commander out there. His name escapes me, but we got him aboard—

John T. Mason: Got him aboard the Russian ship?

Admiral Martin: No, no, aboard the DER, which was 90 miles on its way out, and got the helicopter back safely.*

Sure enough, when they got there, I ordered them to go aboard. I'd call them in, and we'd gone over the whole thing with this skipper and exec. Those crews were pretty

---

* The incident was in late February 1959, as reported in "Visit and Search," *Time*, 9 March 1959, pages 14-15. The Soviets had cut five of 12 U.S.-owned cables. The investigating ship was the radar picket destroyer escort *Roy O. Hale* (DER-336). The commanding officer of the DER was Lieutenant Commander Ernest J. Korte, USN. The executive officer, who led the three-man unarmed boarding party was Lieutenant Donald M. Sheely, USN. The Soviet ship was the trawler *Novorossisk*.

young, you see. The skipper was a lieutenant commandeer, and the exec was a lieutenant. I decided, though, that the exec should lead the group that was to go aboard the ship. We went over what they would look at and so on, the condition of fishing gear, and all that sort of thing, who was aboard, and so on: "It will take you at least 45 minutes to find out the things that you're going to have to find out about that ship, and don't send me a preliminary report. I don't want it, because that's what will hit all the newspapers. You may go in there and look for 20 or 35 minutes, and people are pinging on me every five minutes, but I'm not going to ping on you until 45 minutes later. I want you to report in 45 minutes. If it's going to take more than that to go through the log books and that sort of thing, take it, but you take as much time as necessary before you send me the first report."

I could just see the first report coming back and saying that they had found nothing. That would hit all the headlines, and a subsequent report would have gotten no place at all, you see.

John T. Mason: What action was to be taken if he met with opposition?

Admiral Martin: Well, it was a chance we had to take.

They went aboard, eight in the party, and they went about it very methodically. This lieutenant, who was very slight of build, was a giant in courage and character, and he did a tremendous job. They found out that all the gear they had on that ship—first, there was not the slightest odor of fishing, nor was there any evidence that they had done any fishing whatsoever. All of their deep gear was new, brand new. They looked at the cutting blades and everything, and they were new. They looked like they might have been used once but no more than that. But the thing that really confirmed, to the point that even the Soviets didn't refute it, was their own logs, which our lieutenant commander, Supply Corps, could read. They showed that at the exact time—we knew the exact time the cables were cut to the second—the entries in their log showed that they were at that exact place at that exact time. So it was conclusive proof.*

John T. Mason: At what depth were the cables actually cut?

Admiral Martin: I think there were four or five transatlantic cables, but they were all together, and they cut them all. They cut the thing clean.

John T. Mason: At what depth would that be?

Admiral Martin: I don't remember the depth, but I know that it was considerably deeper than they ever fish, you see. That was another thing; they had deeper gear than anyplace else. I wish I could remember, but I just don't recall how deep it was. But they never fish that deep, you see—never.

John T. Mason: Did you ascertain the reason why? What was the purpose in cutting the cables?

Admiral Martin: We came up with a number of reasons. They were all in my report. We figured that, first, it couldn't have been an accident, because they wouldn't have been fishing at that depth.

John T. Mason: They wouldn't cut four cables anyway, would they?

Admiral Martin: No, but if they cut one accidentally, it's conceivable that they might, if they were just cutting, have cut all four of them, but not likely. We figured that they might like to see how long it would actually take to do it, because it really disrupted communications between this country and Europe.

---

* According to the article in *Time* magazine, the *Novorossisk* had inadvertently cut the cables while raising her fishing nets. The magazine quoted a message from the *Roy O. Hale* skipper Korte, who said, "There were no intentions other than fishing."

John T. Mason: Now we have satellites.

Admiral Martin: Now we have them, right.

Also, it would considerably confuse things. There were some political reasons that were going on at the time. Khrushchev, as I recall it, was the head man over there.*

John T. Mason: This was after Sputnik, was it not?†

Admiral Martin: Yes. This was in early '59. This whole thing got a very big write-up, lots of photographs, in *Time* magazine at that time.

That was an exciting time. It was the first time that this country had ever boarded another nation's ship in over 50 years.

John T. Mason: What was the reaction on the part of the Russian Government?

Admiral Martin: I think the fact that we had conclusive proof kept them from reacting, or they didn't refute. You see, we had absolutely proof positive that this was the ship that had done it. I think that if you're confronting them with concrete evidence, they're not so vocal. It's where there's some doubt. I think there was a mild apology for the unintentional error or mistake that they had made.

John T. Mason: Was there any reaction on the part of the Russian crew of the trawler?

Admiral Martin: No. Of course, they couldn't really, because here was a DER that had enough firepower to sink them with one blast, and the fact that this crew was entirely businesslike. I thought that they might have taken steps to destroy their log or at least conceal it, but they didn't because there was a quartermaster rating who was with them

---

* Nikita S. Khrushchev served as First Secretary of the Communist Party, 1953-64, and Premier of the Soviet Union, 1958-64.
† On 4 October 1957, the Soviet Union launched Sputnik I, the first artificial earth satellite. It caused great uproar in the United States, which had expected to be first in space.

who went to that point first. It seems to me if they were really trying to get away with something they would have disposed of the log. Don't you think so?

John T. Mason: I would think so, yes. Destruct.

Admiral Martin: Destruct.

Well, it was an interesting time. If it hadn't gone off well, we would have all been in trouble, because I ordered them to board the ship, but the fact that they did an excellent job—that little lieutenant was a good executor. He knew exactly how to turn it on.

John T. Mason: Well, conversely, did you get a commendation for this?

Admiral Martin: Oh, I got a beautiful message back from Admiral Wright.* We've been fast friends since then.

John T. Mason: He was CinCLant?

Admiral Martin: He was CinCLant, SACLant, and CinCLantFlt. We became very good friends. SACLant frequently has to fly to Europe on these NATO matters, and after that he would call the tower or have his aircraft get me up there where I could talk with him. The problem was that this was usually between midnight at 5:00 in the morning. I'd have to leave my quarters, drive through the snow to wherever they were, and, in order to talk to him, I'd have to climb up four or five levels of stairs up to the tower.

John T. Mason: He wanted to keep you in trim.

Admiral Martin: But I guess I enjoyed doing it. He'd talk to me until the radio was so faded that we couldn't hear each other, and that's when we'd quit.

---

* Admiral Jerauld Wright, USN, served as Supreme Allied Commander Atlantic, Commander in Chief Atlantic Command, and Commander in Chief Atlantic Fleet from 12 April 1954 to 28 February 1960.

This was back when you could do things on your own initiative. I think today that somebody in the White House would tell them every step of the way to go, or at least somebody in the Office of the Secretary of Defense would be giving explicit instructions.

John T. Mason: One can imagine it wouldn't be handled quite so neatly.

Admiral Martin: Well, they'd tell them to find out without going aboard.

I was in the barrier when I got my very first letter to flag officers that Admiral Burke would put out to keep in touch with all of his flag officers. He had a flag letter that went to all the flag officers.

John T. Mason: He also gave you a flag, didn't he, when you became a flag officer?

Admiral Martin: You mean he gave all the new flag officers a flag?

John T. Mason: Yes.

Admiral Martin: I don't think so. I think I'd remember that.

But the thing that he wanted to get out to all flag officers, sometimes giving them information, sometimes asking for information, I guess, but this was the first one I received from him, and he asked all the flag officers to give him any suggestions or recommendations that they could think of for improving fleet readiness without additional personnel, without additional funds.

John T. Mason: Some limitations!

Admiral Martin: Yes. I wrote back right away in longhand and said, "I believe that the answer to this question is pretty obvious. If you can't have more people or more money, the most important people should remain in the fleets long enough—I'm talking about the flag officers who are in operating units—to learn their job, to come up with improvement programs, and to see these programs along far enough that their successors can't turn them around, such that they're going on to completion. This would take, in most cases two years."

At this time they were moving people every year or every year and a half, and he came back with a response to mine. He said, ""It is pretty obvious, isn't it? All right, we're going to try it in your case. When you leave Argentia, we'll send you to a carrier division." And he asked me to let him know if I'd rather go to an ASW division or an attack carrier division. And he said, "We'll leave you there for two years or not less than a year and a half."

So I wrote back and said I thought I knew the attack carrier business so well because I'd been in it so long that I would like to go into an ASW division. And so I got orders to CarDiv 19.

Interview Number 5 with Vice Admiral William I. Martin, U.S. Navy (Retired)
Place: Admiral Martin's home in Alexandria, Virginia
Date: Thursday, 20 December 1979

John T. Mason: All right, sir, we come today to your command of CarDiv 19.[*]

Admiral Martin: Yes, I think I mentioned that Admiral Arleigh Burke was having something to do with my assignments at that time.

John T. Mason: Yes, he had a particular interest in you, didn't he?

Admiral Martin: And he had agreed with me that the obvious way to increase fleet readiness was to leave the key people, the commanders themselves particularly, in key positions so that they could spend as much time as necessary, really learn it, and then to develop improvement programs and to see them far enough along that his successor could not undo them. That would take a year and a half to two years, depending on the complexity of the assignment.

And so he asked what I wanted to do, and I told him I wanted a cardiv command. He asked if I wanted an ASW division, which we had at that time—we no longer have ASW carrier divisions—or an attack carrier division.[†] I asked for ASW because I thought I knew the attack carrier business very well, and I thought also that the antisubmarine warfare programs were the ones that were most in need of improvement.

John T. Mason: Now, the ASW units were the older units, were they not?

Admiral Martin: Yes, many of them were straight-deck carriers, instead of angled decks. Most of them were of the *Essex* class and had not had a lot of improvements. There was

---

[*] Rear Admiral Martin commanded Carrier Division 19 from December 1959 to August 1960.
[†] In the 1950s a number of *Essex*-class attack carriers were converted to specialize in antisubmarine warfare and were redesignated from CVA to CVS. The last of the CVSs were phased out in the early 1970s, and the ASW function was passed on to the attack carriers.

not a great demand for updated catapults and arresting gear, because they were operating comparatively light aircraft, the Grumman S2F Tracker and Sikorsky helicopters, which are much lighter than more modern aircraft.[*] The ASW carrier divisions had a different composition of escorts. Of course, their mission was very different from the primary mission of the attack carrier divisions.

Having agreed with me on that, Admiral Burke told me that I would be in that ASW carrier division for maybe two years but at least a year and a half. So I went to the West Coast, home-ported in Long Beach.[†] I had been relieved of the barrier by Johnny Hyland. In Carrier Division 19 the flagship was the *Hornet*.[‡] I relieved Admiral Lou Kirn.[§] Something that could have been tedious was that the commanding officer of the *Hornet*, my flagship, was a classmate, Ernie Christensen, whom I sure you know.[**] He lives down in Annapolis.

John T. Mason: Yes, I do.

Admiral Martin: A wonderful man. My chief of staff was another classmate, Bob Ovrom.[††]

We worked together so well, so harmoniously, that there was no conflict or discomfort for any of us. I think both of them had stood ahead of me at the Naval Academy. Therefore, prior to my selection I was junior to them. But there was no discomfort on any of our parts, and they were both such capable and wonderful men, and that added to the harmony.

---

[*] Grumman S2F Tracker propeller-driven, carrier-based antisubmarine planes first entered fleet squadrons in early 1954. In 1962 the Tracker was redesignated S-2. The S-2E version was 44 feet long, wingspan of 72 feet, gross weight of 26,867 pounds, and top speed of 253 miles per hour.
The Sikorsky HSS-1 Seabat was an antisubmarine helicopter. Deliveries to the fleet began in August 1955. The helo has a rotor diameter of 56 feet; length, 46 feet, 9 inches; gross weight, 14,000 pounds; top speed, 123 miles per hour.
[†] Admiral Martin commanded Carrier Division 19 from December 1959 to August 1960.
[‡] USS *Hornet* (CV-12) was originally commissioned 29 November 1943 as an attack carrier, decommissioned in 1947. In the early 1950s she was modernized and recommissioned 11 September 1953 as CVA-12. In 1958 she was converted to an antisubmarine warfare carrier (CVS-12). In that role she had the following characteristics: standard displacement: 33,100 tons; length, 899 feet; beam, 101 feet; maximum width, 192 feet; top speed, 33 knots.
[§] Rear Admiral Louis J. Kirn, USN.
[**] Captain Ernest E. Christensen, USN, commanded the USS *Hornet* (CVS-12) from 20 November 1959 to 2 November 1960.
[††] Captain Robert J. Ovrom, USN.

John T. Mason: I imagine that your personality was a factor along the way?

Admiral Martin: Well, I've always been able to get along with people.

After a few weeks in Long Beach and a couple of exercises under the commander of the First Fleet, we deployed and were on our way to the Western Pacific.*

John T. Mason: May I ask at this point, did you have any particular objectives that you wanted to pursue in this new effort? Did you, in conjunction with Admiral Burke, have any new angles that you wanted to develop?

Admiral Martin: Only one, and that was that I would emphasize the night operations of the ASW people, but they were doing it. This was one of the things that I would look at and put emphasis on, this mobility at night.

My new boss was going to be Jimmy Thach, who was the commander of ASW Forces Pacific.† He was in Hawaii.

John T. Mason: He had been in the Atlantic, hadn't he?

Admiral Martin: Yes, he had been the commander of the first what they call HUK group, hunter-killer group, ASW.‡ He had that in the Atlantic and, because we had known each other before—I really admired him—I was looking forward to pursuing any ideas that he had, any of the emphases he had that he wanted placed on certain things. I was also anxious to try out any new detection and classification systems that might be coming along.

In Hawaii we were given our operational readiness inspection by Admiral Thach and his staff, and it was a very interesting time. Admiral Thach came down to work with us on two different occasions. Then we deployed to the Western Pacific and had some

---

* The *Hornet* was deployed from May to December of 1960.
† On 1 March 1960, Vice Admiral John S. Thach, USN, became Commander Anti-Submarine Defense Force Pacific. It was later redesignated Anti-Submarine Force Pacific and still later as Anti-Submarine Warfare Force Pacific. He served in the billet until April 1963.
‡ As a rear admiral, Thach commanded Carrier Division 16 in the Atlantic from November 1957 to December 1959. In March 1958 it became the basis for Task Group Alfa, a dedicated antisubmarine task group. Thach eventually retired as a four-star admiral; his oral history is in the Naval Institute collection.

very interesting operations there, some with a couple of British ships. While we were in Hawaii, we operated with some Canadian ships, which was a very interesting operation, and they were very good. The reason that they were very good was because they had continuity of their crews. It wasn't unusual to find officers and enlisted in Canadian ships who had been there as long as seven or eight years, and it made quite a difference.

John T. Mason: That's a thesis that's been stressed occasionally for our system.

Admiral Martin: But it's awfully hard to do.

John T. Mason: Why is it that the Canadians can accomplish it?

Admiral Martin: I don't know. I don't think they do it like the Russians. The Russians do accomplish this, but they operate under an edict, "It has been decided that you will remain at sea for a certain number of years." Also, I don't think they have the same pleasures when they get back home that we have. They have no freedom when they get back home. The Russians have more freedom at sea.

John T. Mason: Maybe better food too.

Admiral Martin: Probably better food and maybe better pay. I don't know. But they don't have any trouble with people jumping ship. They don't have many desertions, because they can't go back home and be free, and they can't bring their families out of there. So they don't have desertions, people going over the hill, like others do.

John T. Mason: Well, it's interesting that you did have that experience with the Canadians.

Admiral Martin: Yes, and we learned some things from them.

John T. Mason: Always employing our submarines for your exercises?

Admiral Martin: Yes.

John T. Mason: There must have been opportunities, however, for exercises that involved the real potential enemy.

Admiral Martin: We didn't run into very many of those. Later, when I got into the Med, we ran into them frequently, but in the Pacific there weren't very many of them.

John T. Mason: I guess you were a decade too soon.

Admiral Martin: Yes, they just weren't deploying that far out, not very often. I'm not sure whether they had the nuclears then or not.

John T. Mason: I rather think they didn't.

Admiral Martin: I don't think so.

John T. Mason: We were just getting them.

Admiral Martin: We were just getting them about that time.
  There isn't a great deal to say about CarDiv 19, because, instead of staying there for "two years or at least a year and a half," quoting Arleigh Burke, I got a dispatch that asked me to call Washington the first time I could get ashore. In a few days it was possible to go ashore, into Yokohama, and was told that I was to go to Germany. That was quite a shock to me, because I really looked forward to at least a year and a half. By this time I had some things that I really wanted to do, and I thought it would take a year and a half to work these programs out.

John T. Mason: How long was this after you'd taken command?

Admiral Martin: About seven months.

John T. Mason: Had Burke retired then?

Admiral Martin: No, he was still there. It was in 1960 that I had that, and he was there until '61.

I go to Bonn.

John T. Mason: Before you do, let me ask was there any activity in CarDiv 19 that involved the situation that was rapidly developing in Vietnam?

Admiral Martin: No. It was a very unsettled situation, as I recall.

John T. Mason: Yes, it was unsettled, but the portents were not very promising.

Admiral Martin: No, but that didn't take up a lot of our time, except to move around to places to be seen in much of that area.

John T. Mason: Who was Seventh Fleet at that point, Griffin?[*]

Admiral Martin: No. Beakley had been there two years before.[†] I'll add that later. I wasn't there long enough to have very much to do with him.

John T. Mason: That's the reason I asked, in the hope that you did have something that you recalled.

Admiral Martin: No, but, moving on after six or seven months—this is what I figured would take the time to learn the job and start thinking about improvement programs, develop them. I was really disappointed to leave that ASW division, because I was actually learning a lot about ASW I hadn't known before. You learn a lot from the

---

[*] Vice Admiral Charles D. Griffin, USN, served as Commander Seventh Fleet from 7 March 1960 to 28 October 1961. That encompassed the period that Martin was deployed with the carrier division.
[†] Vice Admiral Wallace M. Beakley, USN, served as Commander Seventh Fleet from 28 January 1957 to 30 September 1958.

submariners themselves, and it's one of the few times that a captain or a young admiral has a chance to work closely with the submariners. That's when you're doing ASW work. I did make sure there was a lot of coordinated effort between the ASW and the submarine people, and they were extremely helpful. A lot of the improvements that we might have come up with were coordination of that kind, as well as coordination within the task group itself.

John T. Mason: What about the night angle?

Admiral Martin: We increased the night work, and we got good enough that we were very happy to get a live one, an unknown submarine, to work on so that we could go right on through the night, and we did that. They became very competent at night work, and they became more comfortable with it. Although, let's face it, that ASW operation for the fliers, where they're operating at low altitude all the time is—daytime operation can be a lot more comfortable. Let's put it that way. If you were to have a complete engine failure—let's say you lost suction, although the Tracker, the S2F, was a twin-engine plane, you could lose both engines, and you wouldn't have much time to do any in-flight troubleshooting before you'd have to make a crash landing, you'd have to ditch, in the water.

There were times when they were working at those low altitudes when they'd be on the other side of the horizon from the surface ship. There might not be much time to even get out a Mayday, which is the distress call for aircraft that are really in trouble. They'd have to bail out or ditch or crash. That's the distress signal, and I guess it's an international distress signal. You might not have much time to even get that out.

Also—I found this out myself when I went out to fly that pattern—we were making patterns that barely allowed you to keep the contact alive. The MAD gear, as they call it—magnetic anomaly detector—that was a long extended shaft from the tail of the airplane that would pick up the magnetic flux from a submarine. You had to be almost over it to detect it, and you had to do it at low altitude. Those patterns were patterns that had to be done with precision with regard to turns and altitudes. To do that constantly at night, until you've done enough of it to know you're very good at it, you can't relax for a second, because at that altitude if you get your nose over for even a few seconds, you'll very likely crash, and it wasn't unusual that it happened.

John T. Mason: How large a number of planes were you dealing with in this?

Admiral Martin: There was one large fixed-wing squadron and one large helicopter squadron. I should remember those numbers. I think they were 24 fixed wing and 16 helicopters, rotary wing. We could operate more than those, but it wasn't very comfortable to have the ship too loaded for your night operations. You just need more room on the deck, more room moving them through the hangar deck. The margin for error is increased.

John T. Mason: What about the sonobuoys?* Were they the very modern types at that point?

Admiral Martin: At the beginning there were some troubles with them, but they were troubles that were well known. I think it was at Johnsville or Willow Grove where they were working on these things so that they could take the impact of throwing them out and continue to be viable and operate for the number of hours that was specified.†

John T. Mason: What kind of radius would one have?

Admiral Martin: I'd have to guess at that, Jack. I just don't recall. It wasn't enough, though, to expand the pattern of the aircraft that were working on it. It didn't expend it out to where you'd like to do it. We were doing fairly tight turns. If they had given you a great deal of range, you could make easy, comfortable turns, but the range was not that good then. You'd have to come back in and put another one down closer to it, or you might lose it entirely, and you weren't able to get the MAD detection until you were quite

---

* A sonobuoy is an electronic device that picks up sounds in the water for the purpose of detecting submarines. It is normally dropped from an aircraft and then transmits sounds back to the plane.
† Naval Air Development Center, Johnsville, Pennsylvania; Willow Grove Naval Air Station, Pennsylvania.

close. You had to have it fairly localized with the sonobuoys before the MAD detector was effective.

Let me see, I was relieved by Rear Admiral Stuart, who was flown out there, of course.[*] He had to pack pretty quickly. The problem was that the Navy flag officer who was on the military assistance advisory group, the so-called MAAG, in the capital of West Germany, had been detached because his relief had been named, and his relief was persona non grata with General Norstad, who at the time was SACEur.[†] He was a controversial fellow, and I greatly admired him. It was Dan Gallery.[‡]

John T. Mason: Oh. And Norstad knew him?

Admiral Martin: I couldn't give you the details, but I think his name hadn't cleared all of the NATO countries, but I rather suspected the reason he hadn't cleared was because Norstad and company had prevailed upon them to delay his approval.

John T. Mason: Dan is a lovable man, but—

Admiral Martin: Very, but he could be difficult for some people. I know a lot of easygoing flag officers who were impatient around people who weren't doing anything that resembled their best. Blackjack Reeves was one of them.[§] If you really did your job with Blackjack and you didn't goof off on something, you'd get along very well with him, especially if you talked back to him. If there's a conflict, an argument, and you know very well that you're right, then you'd better stand up for it, or you'll get in worse trouble with Blackjack Reeves, because he didn't like people who agreed with him, or appeared to agree with him, when they really didn't. I learned that very early. I learned

---

[*] Rear Admiral William A. Stuart, USN.
[†] General Lauris Norstad, USAF, was NATO's Supreme Allied Commander Europe from 1956 to 1962.
[‡] Rear Admiral Daniel V. Gallery Jr., USN, was known for having captured and delivered to port the German submarine *U-505* while he was commanding officer of the escort carrier *Guadalcanal* (CVE-60) in 1944. He is the subject of a Naval Institute oral history.
[§] Rear Admiral John W. Reeves Jr., who commanded the aircraft carrier *Wasp* (CV-7) and a carrier task group in World War II, was known to be impatient and demanding. The *Enterprise* (CV-6), with Martin on board, was Reeves's flagship for part of the war.

it from a fellow named Walter Newton, who was on his staff.* He was a class ahead of me at the Naval Academy, a very fine aviator, a fine officer, a wonderful personality, not afraid of anything. When he'd lose an argument and Reeves would tell him what to do, he'd say "Aye, aye, sir. Goddamnit, sir," and leave the room.

So I think Dan was maybe a little bit like that, but a man with ideas and a very, very interesting man. I later was able to invite him to come to visit me in the Med, and I arranged for him to visit any ships that he wanted to visit.† I asked my boss in London about it, and he said, "By all means." So we gave Dan the red-carpet treatment, and he wrote another book.‡ He was terrific for morale. He'd go right down to the engine room. You've read his books? They're a joy to read for a Navy man. I don't know how much fun a landlubber would have with them, but Navy men really loved those books.

John T. Mason: I knew him very well as a person.

Admiral Martin: Uh-huh. So they had to get somebody on this Germany job, and that's where I went. Admiral Burke told me that I would be—he said, "You've spent all your time in the Pacific. You haven't been in Europe since you were a midshipman, so I'm going to send you to this job in Europe, and I think you're going to be in Europe for about three years."

John T. Mason: Had he forgotten his plan for you to stay in the Pacific for two years?

Admiral Martin: I don't think he cared to discuss that at the time. He had to come up with somebody to clear Norstad and NATO. I wasn't exactly non-controversial. I'd had this B-36 controversy with Burke and company, and I was pleased and a little surprised that I cleared so quickly.

After spending a little time in Washington here, I took a course in German at Berlitz. I didn't take the complete course; I took their fast one.

---

* Lieutenant Commander Walter H. Newton Jr., USN.
† This was when Martin commanded the Sixth Fleet, 1967-68.
‡ Gallery wrote a number of humorous Navy novels.

John T. Mason: How did you fare?

Admiral Martin: Oh, not well enough certainly to converse very well, but enough to get the gist of what was being said, and I continued to study when I was in Bonn, so I knew some German. I knew German well enough to carry on a simple conversation with a patient German friend who didn't mind my mistakes.

One of the things I thought of doing while I was there was what a couple of my German friends were doing. One was a very high-type German naval captain who would speak in the present tense. For example, he would say, "Bill, I'm reading a very good English book last week," or "I'm reading a very good book next month," you see.

John T. Mason: Concentrate on the present tense.

Admiral Martin: So he wouldn't have to go through all these tenses and things. I knew exactly what he was saying, and I wrote a letter recommending that we do that. You could do that with everybody but the French. The French won't speak to you unless you're speaking perfect French. At least this is Paris. Out in the outlands, maybe they're more friendly, but a taxi driver in Paris, at least at that time, knew exactly what you were saying, but if you didn't say it in perfect French, he'd ignore you, take you someplace you didn't want to go.

When I got my orders, I was to be the deputy chief of the MAAG. The chief of the MAAG had just made two stars for the job, and he wasn't very helpful because he thought I was there to steal his job, and I really did not want that job. I didn't aspire to be the chief of the MAAG at all. I hoped that I wouldn't stay there longer than a year. Admiral Burke said I might be in Europe for three years but on that job no longer than year, and I'd get another assignment in Europe for a year, and maybe another one, in order to learn the problems in Europe.

I could have done a great deal more good on that job if I'd had a more cooperative chief of the MAAG. And there was another complication. The Air Force had kept a colonel as chief of the Air Force section of the MAAG. Then they made it a brigadier's job, and they predated his commission so that he was one month senior to me.

John T. Mason: They predated the commission so that you were outranked by this Air Force man. Would you tell me the scope of this MAAG job. Was this over all the MAAGs in the various countries?

Admiral Martin: No, it was just for West Germany, and the title describes it pretty well. The military assistance advisory group advised them on all aspects of each of the services, of their people, and being responsive to all the requests that they gave to you.

John T. Mason: That was one of the major MAAGs then, was it?

Admiral Martin: Well, I think every NATO country had an advisory group of some kind. They didn't all call them MAAGs. The one in Turkey wasn't called a military advisory group; it had another title, but that's really what its function was.

The heads of sections in all the MAAGs, the head of the Army section, the head of the Navy section, and the head of the Air Force section under the chief of the MAAG, who was rotated in some countries and was not rotated between the services in others. It was supposed to be rotated between the services if the services were fairly well balanced like ours are. Some of them would have a very small Navy section, I guess.

In Germany the Army section was much larger than the others. The Air Force was larger than the Navy.

Its objectives were very good, and the friendships that you would make became friends of the United States. It was to tie the NATO countries closer to the United States and their concepts, their tactics, and that sort of thing, to be mutually helpful. Of course, something we weren't supposed to do, but the other countries did this—we weren't supposed to be agents to sell U.S. products. But I felt that we should advise them, and if we had products that were as good as anybody else's or better, to advise them and help them to do it. I think that later became a part of their objective, to be helpful to our industry that came over there, to help them and to support them where they were deserving of that support. I just thought that made sense. It was certainly in the best interest of our country, the balance of payments, the flow of gold, and so on. It could make a big difference. The British were doing it openly, the French even more so. So it had its interesting aspects.

Something I failed to mention, just to go back to the job I had in Canada. The nearest Air Force officer was in St. John's. He had been a colonel when they sent me up there. I was the first flag officer to be in Newfoundland.

John T. Mason: For the barrier force.

Admiral Martin: Yes, the barrier force. They made their colonel at St. John's, the Pepperrell Air Force Base, a brigadier, and they predated him by a month or two so that he was senior to me in the area.

John T. Mason: That isn't guaranteed to gain friends in another service, is it?

Admiral Martin: No. They gained nothing by it. They gained nothing by it either place. The man at Pepperrell Air Force Base was a good friend, and he gained nothing by it. I don't know why they did it. The brigadier that they sent to be senior to me at Bonn, we became very good friends, and I couldn't see that they accomplished anything by it except that I was ordered there as a deputy, and he was ordered there as head of a section. But, since he was senior to me, if there had been a conflict between the two of us, why, he would have been senior to me, and I couldn't have acted as the deputy. We had a captain there who was head of the Air Force section, a fellow named Medley, a very good man, so I just don't know what they gained, except I think this was just part of their modus operandi.

John T. Mason: Has that sort of thing lessened in the present time?

Admiral Martin: I really don't know. I really don't want to indict the Air force, because there are so many of them who are my good friends, but I don't think they operated on the same high principles that the Navy does. I don't think so. I think they'll run with a program that is in competition with us. We're good friends every place except Washington.

John T. Mason: Well, tell me about the scope of your business there with other persons.

Admiral Martin: I wasn't there very long. The first few weeks or months were familiarizing myself with the German Navy and making the contacts with their headquarters. They had a headquarters that was patterned very closely with ours. Their organizations were patterned very closely with ours, especially, here again, the Air Force. They had what would correspond to our Pentagon, and its name was Hardtheuhohe. I spent a lot of time there. I tried to make myself available always to the key positions in the German Navy. If I had been able to operate as a deputy, I would have made more of an effort to learn the other services, but I was a deputy in name only. I was told that by the chief of the MAAG, who pointed out to me that I couldn't really operate as a deputy because one of the section heads was senior to me. That bothered me, in that I couldn't do as good a job as I would like to have done as deputy, and so I didn't do much operating with the Air Force and the Army.

John T. Mason: You concentrated on the Navy.

Admiral Martin: Yes, I concentrated on the Navy and the Navy contacts with headquarters. Frequently the day would be filled with appointments that they asked to come and see me and others, and I'd ask to go and see them at headquarters. I spent quite a bit of time at places like Kiel, Bremerhaven, and Wilhelmshaven, which were the Norfolks and San Diegos corresponding with our service. I developed some very strong friendships, some of which continued.

John T. Mason: Did you have anything to do with Ruge?[*]

---

[*] Vice Admiral Friedrich O. Ruge was Inspector of the Federal Republic of Germany Navy, a position comparable to the U.S. Chief of Naval Operations.

Admiral Martin: Yes, I did. I'd met Admiral Ruge before and had seen a lot of the correspondence that went back and forth between Friedrich Ruge and Arleigh Burke. They were very close friends, and Ruge was a wonderful man. He was highly regarded by his navy, highly regarded by all his countrymen, an exceptional man, and I enjoyed that relationship very much.

John T. Mason: What was the status of the Germany Navy at that point?

Admiral Martin: They were a low third behind the Army and the Air Force. The Navy had to struggle for its funds. There was a real struggle for the German Navy to exist with the significance they should have had. The advisors that were closest to the Minister of Defense, who was Strauss—I pointed out to him the first time we met, when I first called on him, that he was supposed to be knowledgeable of naval forces the same as Army and Air Force, and yet he didn't have a single naval officer on his staff as advisor.* I made a point of that because after that, when Franz Josef Strauss would see me coming, he would start this little speech that I had given him the first time. As soon as I'd walk up, why, he'd start giving it back to me and tell me that he was going to put somebody on his staff, and he did. He put a very able commander on his staff, who was able to give him the word about some of the naval interests.

John T. Mason: I would think that that would have been an internal problem in the German defense system, that the Navy would have exerted itself to the point of getting somebody on his staff.

Admiral Martin: As I said, Germany and most of the NATO nations—I got this from other Navy people who were on their MAAGs—had a landlubber mentality. They thought that the Army was by far the most important service and the Air Force a close second. They didn't see where the Navy had very much to do. One of my arguments was that they expected the U.S. to provide all of the convoys and to provide all the support, actually to provide naval forces. My argument with them was that they should

---

*Franz Josef Strauss served as Germany's Defense Minister from 1956 to 1962.

have been the force that they needed to protect their own coastlines and to provide their escort for convoys that were bringing supplies into the NATO country and support, they should provide them at least halfway. Yet most Germans, not the Navy but the members of their congress or parliament, the Bundesrat, didn't think the Navy needed anything except what they called Schnellboots, which were fast boats, small boats. They didn't think that they should have anything of destroyer size. Yet, in talking with their Navy, they thought that they should have the forces to do their part of the Navy mission that was to support the NATO interests.

John T. Mason: Was the prevailing attitude among Germans perhaps influenced by the fact that in World War II the overwhelming naval effort had been the submarines?

Admiral Martin: Yes, well, right, and their submarines had excellent support with the country, better than the other part of their Navy. They had some top submarine officers—I'm trying to think of the name of one of them.

John T. Mason: Dönitz?

Admiral Martin: Well, Dönitz, yes, but there was another one who was a prisoner of war in Canada and continued to operate.*

John T. Mason: But after World War II the submarine aspect of things fell into disuse.

Admiral Martin: Yes.

John T. Mason: And I wondered if that wasn't some influence on their prevailing attitude in the '60s.

---

* Admiral Karl Dönitz served successively as commander of the Germany Navy's U-boat force in World War II and then as commander in chief of the entire German Navy. He became head of the German Government following Hitler's death on 30 April 1945.

Admiral Martin: Every aspect of the Navy was considered by the General Staff, and the Office of the Minister of Defense—certainly Strauss would listen, but he didn't have enough Navy people advising him, and they just didn't believe in, and they didn't support, the Navy as they should have.

John T. Mason: As I recall, Burke had some role in seeing that they got some destroyers.

Admiral Martin: Yes. It seems to me that they were getting them about the time I left there. I think they were getting some of ours that we were willing to make available to them. We've done that with a lot of countries.

John T. Mason: I also remember that part of the story was that the Royal Navy people were not very favorable to this whole business.

John T. Mason: Yes, they organized a force that consisted of ships participating together in a task force, and the name of it has slipped my mind, but the Germans had some craft in it, the British, the U.S., and frequently they would have an exercise that included a Navy carrier task group, with the others providing escorts.[*] It was a very valuable exercise, but there was so little support from the civilian side, the legislative body—they just didn't have any champions in there, as we have had here, like Uncle Carl Vinson, Mendel Rivers, Dewey Short, and Hebert, who believed in a strong Navy and frequently would give us programs that the Secretary of Defense didn't have anything in his budget for.[†] That happened again this year, as a matter of fact.

I was in that job 11 months, I think, and I was ordered rather suddenly to my next assignment, which was Chief of the Naval Air Reserve.[‡] The reason I got sudden orders there was because Admiral McKechnie, who was the Chief of the Naval Air Reserve in

---

[*] StaNavForLant—Standing Naval Force Atlantic, a multi-national group of ships that operated together under the auspices of NATO.
[†] L. Mendel Rivers, a Democrat from South Carolina, served in the U.S. House of Representatives from 1940 until he died in 1970. He was chairman of the House Armed Services Committee from 1965 until his death and was credited with getting a great deal of military money funneled into his district in Charleston.
[‡] Rear Admiral Martin served as Chief of Naval Air Reserve Training from October 1961 to May 1963.

Glenview, just outside of Chicago, had a heart attack.* They called him Doc McKechnie. They needed to replace him quickly, and everyone knew that I was ready to leave that MAAG job.

John T. Mason: So you fitted into that slot. This is near Great Lakes, is it?

Admiral Martin: Yes. Well, it's northwest of Chicago. Great Lakes is directly north on the lake.† Glenview is not on the lake.

I didn't want that job either. It didn't appeal to me, because it was pretty far from what I thought to be the active Navy.

John T. Mason: Indeed, the reserve.

Admiral Martin: And I knew nothing about it. I knew very little about it. You find very few active-duty people who do know very much about the reserve organization and its value, unless they've had something to do with it. Not many flag officers had ever moved up from that job.

John T. Mason: That was also a deterrent, was it not?

Admiral Martin: That was also a deterrent, but the reserves had been very vociferous with the CNO and the Secretary of the Navy to send them somebody who was sent as a flag officer who had some possibility of moving up—send us a live one who's not going to retire from here.

I was told that that figured into my assignment, and while I didn't really care for that assignment—I mean, I didn't want to go there when I went, there were several places I'd rather go than go to be Chief of the Naval Air Reserves. But I must say that it was one of the most challenging and one of the most rewarding assignments that I had. Wonderful friends, and I found lots of room for improvement there.

---

* Rear Admiral Arnold W. McKechnie, USN.
† Great Lakes, Illinois, a town on the shore of Lake Michigan, about 30 miles north of downtown Chicago, is the site of a large naval training center that includes recruit training and a number of specialized schools.

John T. Mason: Would you lay the foundation for me by telling me the scope of the Naval Reserve system.

Admiral Martin: Yes. At that time there were 18 Naval Air Reserve stations or Naval Air Reserve units as tenants of other air stations. There were 18 of these.

John T. Mason: And they were all part of your empire?

Admiral Martin: Yes, they were, and they covered the whole country. The most northeast one was at Squantum, Massachusetts. In Florida we had one at Jacksonville. In the California corner it was in Long Beach—Los Alamitos, it was called—and in Washington state it was at Seattle Naval Air Station, Sand Point. Those were the four corners, and there were 14 others around the country, some of them on the coast and some of them in, as we were at Chicago. One at Grosse Ile, Michigan, outside of Detroit; one at Memphis; one at Olathe, Kansas; one in Dallas; one in New Orleans; one in Atlanta; New York at Floyd Bennett Field; Norfolk, where it was a tenant activity on the Naval Air Station Norfolk. Then, on the West Coast, in addition to Long Beach there was one at Alameda. I don't think I've named all 18 of them.

John T. Mason: I think you've named about 11.

Admiral Martin: Well, there was a total of 18 that were either naval air stations staffed by the reserves, and all of them were commanded by active duty people. We were Naval Air Reserve Training Units, NARTUs. Those were tenant activities on the regular naval air stations. Then there were others that were called naval air stations, but their primary mission was the Naval Air Reserves that were there. That was true at Glenview; it was true at Los Alamitos in California, Seattle, where the primary mission of the naval air stations was to support the reserves.

The operations were rather unusual. Their big days were Saturdays and Sundays, so they were known as "weekend warriors."

John T. Mason: Naturally.

Admiral Martin: The Naval Reserves other than aviation had a drill once a week.

John T. Mason: They'd have that in the evening, wouldn't they?

Admiral Martin: In the evening, yes, whereas ours in the Naval Air Reserve were concentrated on those two days, Saturday and Sunday. Most of them would assemble on Friday evening, and sometimes it was permitted for them to fly if they got there and wanted to fly, but the big concentration of operations was on Saturdays and Sundays. We had sufficient air transports that were operated by the reserves to bring many of the reservists who lived too far to drive to the stations, to airlift them into the stations so that they could drill. They'd bring them in on Friday evenings and take them back Sunday evenings.

John T. Mason: Quite an operation. In terms of people, how many reservists were you training, so to speak, at one time?

Admiral Martin: I would have to get that figure. You could work it out, because I would say that each of the stations would average about 1,000, so we'd have 18,000 to 20,000 altogether.

One of the first things I did was not very popular with some people, but it had to be done. They didn't have a firm retirement cutoff for the reserves, and this caused indigestion and constipation of the system, because some of those who still had command of squadrons and air wings but were not actively flying sort of retired for a second time, without telling people. So, as soon as I felt I could do that, and justify the action without being unfair to anybody, I laid off several hundred, just retired them.

John T. Mason: How did you so quickly catch up with this problem?

Admiral Martin: I heard a lot about it. By the time I did this, I'd been through all 18 of those naval air stations and their reserve training units. This came up so frequently that after I'd finished the round of going to all of them, I knew that that was a real problem.

Then I began to really concentrate on that problem, working very closely with the regular Navy captain at each one of those places. Each of these stations had just a skeleton of regular officers. In addition to the commanding officer at Glenview, for example, I think he had five other regular officers. The operations officer would be a regular officer, and certain heads of departments were regular naval officers. And they had another program that they still have today called TAR, training and administration of reserves. These were reserve officers who wished to come on full-time active duty, and that was a rather large contingent of reserves, enough to provide the continuity of effort at each of these stations.

There were some excellent officers there, but we retired a number of them as well, not very many because most of them were just as dedicated as any regular I've ever seen, and they were just as capable. Some of them had not gone regular Navy for good reasons—some of them family reasons, illness in the family so they couldn't move from where they were, a number of cases like that. And there were many cases where the Bureau of Personnel would not accept them past a certain age and rank. They'd gotten to a point where they could and still wanted to come into the regular Navy, but they had passed the age limit. Many of them had passed it by just months.

I had a healthy regard for the TAR officers that we had, the TAR enlisted as well.

John T. Mason: In the process of retiring some of these reservists, did you run into the perennial problem with the reserves, and that is that they do have political clout?

Admiral Martin: Occasionally, although I must say that I came out of this without making any enemies. They agreed with me, you see, and it was pretty clear that the reserves were a much better outfit. There were some hurt feelings, one or two I can remember at the beginning. Then I believe what happened was that they began to see that some of their best friends, the younger people in the reserves, thought it was a good thing, too, to move out some of the older ones and some of those who were not contributing. There were a few cases where it seemed that the only reason they were connected with the reserves—these were very few—was to just get away from home for a weekend, and usually their work during the weekend would show.

This made the reserves more active. It provided places for junior people to take on more responsible jobs. It was just a general tonic.

I remember developing a seven-point improvement program and taking it down to OP-05. At that time it was Admiral Bill Schoech.[*] I first presented it, I think, to Bob Pirie and then Bill Schoech later.[†] I had an excellent staff who had really done the work on these seven points of improvement that were needed.

John T. Mason: And this again was initiated after you had made your whole survey?

Admiral Martin: Yes, but I think I'd only been there three months or so when this happened. Some of them we were not completely successful in, but we were partially successful in all seven of them. I don't remember which they were.

John T. Mason: Will you list the seven points?

Admiral Martin: No, I couldn't list those now. I've got a good friend here who's got an important position on the Hill now who could, because he was one of those training and reserve officers who was on full-time active duty and was one of the brains who developed them.

John T. Mason: Can you give me the general gist of these points?

Admiral Martin: The biggest thing that had been neglected in the Naval Air Reserve was the condition of their buildings. Their buildings and grounds had been ignored for so long that they were in pretty terrible shape. There were some leaky hangars, and there

---

[*] Vice Admiral William A. Schoech, USN, served as Deputy Chief of Naval Operations (Air) from 14 November 1962 to 1 July 1963.
[†] Vice Admiral Robert B. Pirie, Jr., USN, served as Deputy Chief of Naval Operations (Air) from 26 May 1958 to 1 November 1962. His oral history is in the Naval Institute collection.

were some airstrips that hadn't had the care that they needed. They were just generally rundown because, let's face it, the reserves got the hand-me-downs.

John T. Mason: They were low on the totem pole.

Admiral Martin: They were low on the totem pole. They would take airplanes that the regulars had finished with. When we phase out even today, we still do this. That's one of the reasons that you get to develop so much admiration for these reserves, because they were operating so low on the priorities and operating aircraft that were handed down as no longer first-line by the regular Navy, and they operate them and do well with them. That's why I say it was one of the most rewarding jobs I had, because I felt that there was a degree of patriotism there that matched the regulars, and in some cases it seemed to go beyond what you would occasionally find in the regular Navy. They were just dedicated people who wanted to serve their country and wanted to serve the Navy. They were willing to do it even though they were that low on the totem pole. Their barracks were not kept as well, their grounds were not kept as well, the total facilities weren't as well kept as the regular Navy's. Sometimes the only funds that you could get were for things that were obviously inadequate, just totally inadequate.

John T. Mason: Why was it that they didn't have a voice in the budget-making process of the Navy?

Admiral Martin: I would say that Congress has a similar feeling. The reserve programs were not as strongly supported as the regular Navy's. On some occasions the reserves did have a strong voice.

John T. Mason: I've always heard that with Congress it was, "Don't touch the reserve, because that's our province, and we have an interest there."

Admiral Martin: Sometimes that is true. Sometimes you have, as we do today—I can name a number of members of Congress on the House Armed Services Committee, for example, and in the Senate who are very strong for the reserves. If you've got a champion like that, then they could build their case, so they frequently got enough clout. Of course, they can do a lot of things that the regulars can't do. The reserves can work in political campaigns. They can make statements that a regular Navy man can't make.

John T. Mason: Also, they are in general leading citizens in their communities.

Admiral Martin: Exactly. For example, in the Chicago area there were half a dozen, exactly six, well-known millionaires who were drilling every time they were supposed to drill. Very strong. They'd go out and make speeches and things like that, successful people. I think all of those except two were in a composite reserve outfit for public relations. They would work closely with the Chief of Information, for example, Chinfo.

I've never thought that our Navy has used our reserves as much as we should, because they can do a lot of things for us that the regular Navy cannot do for itself. They can make speeches that the regular Navy cannot make without getting into trouble. They're got some real patriots in there. Churchill said that to be a reserve was to be twice a citizen—an American as well as a man in uniform.*

John T. Mason: Well, improvements, reforms, and so forth, there were seven on the list, and you talked about some of the things that needed doing.

Admiral Martin: Some of them were specific aircraft that were inadequate. The reasons for which an aircraft could get phased out of the regulars and retired, either go to the reserves or go to Davis-Monthan Field out in the desert of Arizona where they preserve them.† It was an Air Force Base at one time, but that's the bone yard for aircraft that are obsolescent and some of them that aren't obsolescent. Sometimes they've got aircraft out there that are in excess at the moment, and that's where they sit. Some of them stay there until the reserves need them, and then they bring them out of that and make them active

---

* Winston L. S. Churchill (1874-1965), who fought in the Boer War, was Great Britain's First Lord of the Admiralty in World War I, Prime Minister during World War II, and again Prime Minister from 1951 to 1955. Afterward he remained as a member of Parliament. He was also a prolific author.
† Davis-Monthan Air Force Base, Tucson, Arizona, is the storage site for old military aircraft because of its dry climate.

again. But aircraft that are being phased out of the active services, the improvement program stopped with them. They may not have an improved navigational system, or they may not have the improved communication system or the radar. It's usually in electronics that they're behind. When they get so far out of date that they're not effective, then there comes a priority program to get those updated with these effective systems, and I'm sure that of these seven points there might have been three or four of them right there.

John T. Mason: If the reservists are using the obsolescent type planes, electronic equipment, how can they be expected, once called to active duty, to function with the regulars, if they haven't had the training necessary?

Admiral Martin: The effort is to keep them with aircraft that would fit in. For example, they're getting older models of the same patrol planes that our active-duty squadrons are operating. They usually get jet aircraft that are capable of going aboard a carrier, you see. They won't do the job as well as fighters. They don't have the same performance, but they can still do a suitable job. If they're called up, you try to give them as many up-to-date aircraft as you can afford. It's just one of these things to keep their hand in. It doesn't take very long.

Let's say that you've got a squadron that's flying the last hand-me-downs of fighters. These would be the F-4s, the Phantoms.* That's a supersonic aircraft, and we've still got a lot of them working with the regulars; they're still flying the F-4s. When they're called up, it wouldn't take very long to move them into the latest of them, the F-14s and the F-18s. The transition is not very difficult once they've gotten familiar with the jets. There was a time when we had primarily jets, and they were still flying prop jobs. That was a pretty big transition, to take them from a propeller aircraft into a jet. It took a few years to do that, but now all of their attack aircraft are jets. The only propeller aircraft they have now are patrol type, which we still have. We still have prop aircraft and the transports, though some of them are jets now.

---

* The McDonnell Douglas F-4 Phantom II was the Navy's primary carrier-based jet fighter until replaced by the F-14 Tomcat in the mid-1970s.

Then, of course, with the helicopters, the rotary wing, although they're operating hand-me-downs, there's not as big a difference from model to model in helicopters as there is in the high-performance aircraft.

John T. Mason: How did you adjust the situation at a given station where they were training exclusively, the reservists, when they were weekend warriors? How did you adjust the situation to accommodate this, when during the week, what occupation did that station have?

Admiral Martin: Very few operations. It was not unusual, though, for the reserves to want more flying that they could get on a weekend. Let's say you had a station where the weather was really socked in all weekend. Then the pilots and the crews who weren't able to fly on that weekend would try to make it up during the week.

At the naval air station at Glenview, for example, which was a reserve station, there was very little operation. Transient air traffic and those who were working on the makeup program. You would spend Saturday and Sunday on maximum operations. Monday, Tuesday, and Wednesday would be very slack. Then you'd start getting everything back up, depending really on what went down. If it were a big check, for example, you might have to work Monday and Tuesday a little bit, but usually Monday and Tuesday were the Saturdays and Sundays for the reserves.

John T. Mason: Of course, there would have to be that transfer, that time off.

Admiral Martin: They were awfully good at providing maximum availability of aircraft when the reserves came in to fly. A lot of the buildings and grounds maintenance was done by the reserves themselves entirely on these odd days.

We tried to get a coordinated effort to operate them when they could come on for their two weeks' active duty. In addition to weekends, they'd come in for two weeks' active duty once a year.

John T. Mason: In the summertime?

Admiral Martin: Yes, during the summertime usually, and for that period we would try to get them operating alongside a regular active-duty squadron. We started that effort, and it's continued and increased. I think the reserves, the selected reserves, now are operating closer to fleet units on the aviation side than they ever have before. Tom Hayward is very strong for the reserves today.[*]

We figured that you could train seven reserves for the price of training and maintaining one active-duty man in the enlisted ranks. So, dollar-wise, it was a bargain.

That's about as much as I have on the reserves.

John T. Mason: Well, now, you said at the outset that this was one of the most challenging assignments you had.

Admiral Martin: Yes. There was so much to be done, and a lot of my effort was to acquaint the regular Navy with the reserve program.

John T. Mason: How did you go about doing that?

Admiral Martin: I'd go to them, visit them, speak to them, and I had some of my more articulate captains and commanders speak to them. In the summertime, when they were on their two weeks' active duty, we made sure that the regulars understood how important they were and how much more capable they would be as reserves when they were recalled if they worked as closely as possible with the active-duty Navy.

As I mentioned before, the reserves can do a lot in public relations.

John T. Mason: Yes, and how did you tie in with Chinfo on this whole thing?

Admiral Martin: To offer support, and he would provide the materials for the speeches, and the reserve officers who wanted to do that sort of thing, and were capable of doing it, would keep themselves abreast of all the material that Chinfo would send out. They

---

[*] Admiral Thomas B. Hayward, USN, served as Chief of Naval Operations from 1 July 1978 to 30 June 1982. His oral history is in the Naval Institute collection.

would either get the schedules themselves, or sometimes the Chinfo himself would send the schedule out, that he'd like speakers at certain places. It was a matter of education.

John T. Mason: Was there any cooperation in making films, for instance, using he reservists?

Admiral Martin: Yes. I had some excellent talent.

John T. Mason: You had Hollywood types, didn't you, involved in it?

Admiral Martin: Yes, we did. At Los Alamitos we had Glenn Ford and several of them who contributed time.[*]

One of our overall jobs was to provide aviation cadets for flight training, actually recruiting officers, the total recruiting job but really with emphasis on officers, aviation cadets who, once they'd finished training, would get their commissions as ensigns. That's still taking place.

John T. Mason: Was that a new program in your regime?

Admiral Martin: No, that had been going on for a long, long time. As a matter of fact, the aviation cadet program in some form was going on before I got my wings. When I first reported to the fleet there were eight or ten aviation cadets there who had been flying for at least a year or two before I got there. They were much better than I was and, instead of them flying wing on me the first year, I flew wing on them. They didn't think you should be a flight leader if you were leading somebody who was a more capable aviator than you were. So the aviation cadet program is one that's been going on for a long, long time.

---

[*] Glenn Ford, a popular movie actor of the era, was a captain in the Naval Reserve and participated in recruiting and training films for the Navy.

I spent a lot of time at various NROTCs.* There were many of them, and I visited every one of them and spoke to all of them. I spoke at their graduation ceremonies when they were getting out of college and things like that.

John T. Mason: This was approaching the middle '60s when you were doing this?

Admiral Martin: Well, 1962-1963.

John T. Mason: This was before the trouble on the campuses?

Admiral Martin: Yes, before that. There was some trouble. I remember at Madison, Wisconsin, they had some real nuts up there. It was violent. They were leading the dissenters, it seemed to me. Yes, we had other places like Marquette where they were so proud to wear their uniforms on the assigned days, because it was a policy that they wear their uniforms to class once a week. At Marquette and a lot of other places, they were really proud to wear their uniforms. In this NESEP program, which was an enlisted program to train them to be officers, they were so proud that they looked forward to the days when they were supposed to wear uniforms.† I think it was usually Wednesday, and some of them preferred to war uniform more often.

John T. Mason: What was the attitude, as you found it, in the Ivy League colleges?

Admiral Martin: Good and bad. I don't know too much about this, because I did not have any NROTC responsibilities as such. I wanted to support them, and I wanted naval aviation to get the kind of people they should have, get their share from those programs. But, not having responsibility for them, I don't know personally all the problems they had. I'm told some of those NROTCs had trouble getting enough candidates, that it just wasn't a popular thing to do at some places.

---

* NROTC – Naval Reserve Officers' Training Corps, a program that provides training leading to officer commissions at selected universities.
† NESEP—Navy Enlisted Scientific Education Program, which is no longer in existence. Under its provisions the Navy paid for the college education of promising enlisted personnel, then sent them through the Officer Candidate School for training and commissioning as officers.

John T. Mason: No, even at that point. What about the reservists and the Vietnam struggle? Were some of them going on active duty for assignment abroad?

Admiral Martin: The reserves were called up for the Berlin Airlift.* When the reserves are called up, that affects the total reserve system. At other times, they will—BuPers, I think, does this when they determine they need more people—offer the reserves who want to come back on full-time active duty a contract for a year or two or maybe more. Sometimes, if they're young enough, they'll have an augmenting program that will bring people back, even if they've been out for a while. So the reserves provide talent that keeps its hand in and keeps itself reasonably trained so that if they are called up they can fit into the active system with a minimum of refresher effort.

John T. Mason: That has its other side of the coin, too, as we saw with the call-up for the Berlin crisis. Than, if it's a general call of the reserves it's a dislocation of our economy.

Admiral Martin: Yes.

John T. Mason: And certainly a dislocation of their private lives.

Admiral Martin: Yes, very much so. This is the risk they take, but they don't become a part of the selected reserves if they're not willing to commit themselves to that. Then they've got to do it. At other times, on the Cuban thing, it wasn't a wholesale recall of the reserves.†

John T. Mason: No, because of the lesson learned with the Berlin crisis, was it not?

---

* On 1 April 1948 the Soviet Union began a land blockade of the Allied sectors of Berlin, preventing overland transport from West Germany. U.S. and British airplanes then began an airlift that flew food and coal into the city until the blockade was lifted on 30 September 1949.
† The Cuban Missile Crisis was triggered in mid-October 1962, when a U.S. reconnaissance plane photographed a Soviet nuclear missile site in Cuba and the presence of Soviet bombers. On 22 October President John F. Kennedy went on national television to announce a naval quarantine of Cuba, to be implemented on 24 October. On 28 October Premier Nikita Khrushchev of the Soviet Union notified President Kennedy that he was ordering the withdrawal of Soviet bombers and missiles from Cuba.

Admiral Martin: You get a number of them who are eager to come back for a year or two, as long as they're going to be needed. Usually, they figure out that it will be no more than one or two years, and many of the employers are sufficiently patriotic that they give them a leave of absence to do that. In some cases, they actually gain from doing it. In other firms they might lose out and lose a place in promotion.

John T. Mason: But the call has to be an obvious one and a bona fide one in order to produce this effect.

Admiral Martin: Yes. Sometimes they'll call for volunteers with certain qualifications, and there only those who can get away, although I've known of some of them who knew that they were going to lose their position on the promotion ladder but came back anyway and took their chances. Wonderful people they are.

John T. Mason: As director of the whole outfit, what were your opportunities to really get to know the men as individuals?

Admiral Martin: I'd go out of my way to develop friendships with the ones I thought had a greater influence in their communities and who I knew were going to be active, who were really going to contribute. The ones who were willing to go beyond what was expected of them, demanded of them, in the reserve programs, I became very close friends with them. They'd come to Glenview and visit me frequently. I'd go to their places. I would accept a speaking engagement at places like Philadelphia, out on Long Island, and in places where I knew it would do the Navy some good. You become a sort of public relations guy and have such capability of doing that. I offered more than the Chinfo organization took, actually. They just hadn't organized for that. If they give Chinfo adequate staff to handle it, I think we would use our reserves a lot more, and you'd find all sorts of volunteers and highly capable people who could do it.

One of the things I did that hadn't been done by my predecessors, and I talked with some of them who had the job before, and they said one of the things they liked about that job was that they had their own little Navy up there. They could operate independently with a minimum of directions and a minimum of contact really with either Washington or with the immediate boss. The immediate boss was the Chief of Naval Air Training, a three-star, at Pensacola. I elected not to do it that way. Maybe one reason was because I knew the Chief of Naval Air Training at Pensacola, Fitzhugh Lee. He was a good friend and a highly capable man. I just couldn't believe that the reserve could lose at all by dealing with him and putting him squarely in the chain of command, and it worked out that way.

I had two stars. I'd make a recommendation for the reserves, send it through CNATRA, and he'd forward it to OpNav with a three-star endorsement. Many of our programs became stronger by working very closely with him. I'd go to see him frequently, and he would come to see me frequently. He would accept speaking engagements in the reserve program. Nothing but good came of that, and it became some protection for me, protection through the support of programs that were more vital to the reserves' organization. It worked out fine, and I think it continued after that.

There have been a number of changes in the reserve organization. There is a Chief of Naval Reserves now, as I understand it, and under him is a Chief of Naval Air Reserves, who is also a rear admiral. He, in turn, I believe, remains under the Chief of Naval Training, who can be a non-aviator, and I believe usually is, since Cagle, who's a three-star man in training and education at Pensacola. But I don't know enough firsthand about the organization to comment on it.[*]

John T. Mason: One other thing before you go on to the next job, which you really wanted. They had asked for a flag officer who was going places, and obviously you were.

Admiral Martin: At least younger, young enough—

John T. Mason: Was your successor also of that type? Was this maintained as a tradition?

---

[*] Vice Admiral Malcolm W. Cagle, USN, served as Chief of Naval Education and Training, 1971 to 1974.

Admiral Martin: I really wouldn't know. He was a good man. His name was George Koch, who died a few years ago.[*] I thought highly of him. He died a few years ago on active duty. Whether he would have gone on up, had he survived, I don't know, but they've had some very good people in that reserve program. As I say, the reserves have enough clout. They can't move in on the selection boards, of course. Nobody has any influence on the selection boards. But they can ask for someone for whom it is not going to be his last tour of duty. They were asking for this from the stations as well, and I helped do that.

We had a lot of commanding officers of Naval Air Reserve stations and commanding officers of Naval Air Reserve training units, NARTUs, who were captains, and it was obviously their last assignment. That gets to be very obvious to the reserves as well.

John T. Mason: Puts it in the category of a naval district, which is usually the last assignment.

John T. Mason: Yes. So in order that it wouldn't be a one-man selection thing, I got the approval of the Deputy Chief of Naval Operations for Air and BuPers to form a board that would select these captains. They weren't always available, but the board would be told who was available. In so doing, I got officers who were going there, and certainly that was not going to be their last assignment. They were not going to have one foot in the door and one out during the period they were there. They were going to have a least one other assignment after that. I got some extremely capable people as commanding officers of all 18 of these places—very vigorous, interested, and still interested in their careers.

John T. Mason: Well, that certainly was one of the major accomplishments of your time.

---

[*] Rear Admiral George P. Koch, USN, served as Chief of Naval Air Reserve Training from 1963 to 1965. He subsequently commanded Carrier Division Six and the Fifteenth Naval District. He died in 1972.

Admiral Martin: It might have been the major accomplishment, with two goals on personnel. One, to get the deadwood out, the ones who had outlived their usefulness, and, two, to get young people who still had a naval career to concern themselves with, as commanding officers of the reserve air stations and NARTUs.

John T. Mason: I think we're going to your command of Carrier Division Two, with your flag in the *Enterprise*, an atomic-powered carrier?[*]

Admiral Martin: Exactly. That was one assignment that I really asked for.[†] Carrier Division Two had a nuclear task force, the first surface ships that were nuclear powered. It had the *Enterprise*, the *Long Beach*, and the *Bainbridge*. They were to operate together, and they were already deployed to the Med. Chick Hayward took them over there.[‡] That was a job I really wanted. It seemed to be an extension of the test work that I had done over the years, and getting into new developments, and to work out the tactics of this nuclear task force. I already was such a strong believer in the performance superiority and the tactical gains from nuclear power that I was eager to work out some of the tactics and really help prove the desirability of having nuclear-powered ships, and how it is worth the initial cost.

John T. Mason: In preparation did you have to have a special course?

Admiral Martin: Maybe I should have, but I didn't. I think in later years they did require, before going to a nuclear task force, Admiral Rickover's course.[§] It wasn't entirely foreign to me, however; I had studied the predicted advantages. Some of them are so obvious, of course, and, in fact, one of the things that used to irritate me a bit in the war games that we played at the war college and elsewhere, this thing that the tactical

---

[*] USS *Enterprise* (CVAN-65) was commissioned 25 November 1961 as the world's first nuclear-powered aircraft carrier. She was the only ship of her class. She was later modernized and refueled a number of times and remained in the active fleet until 1 December 2012. She had a standard displacement of 61,000 tons, full-load displacement of 81,500 tons, was 1,052 feet long, 130 feet in the beam, and had an extreme width of 250 feet. Her top speed was 33 knots. She could accommodate approximately 90 aircraft.
[†] Rear Admiral Martin commanded Carrier Division Two from May 1963 to April 1964.
[‡] Rear Admiral John T. Hayward, USN.
[§] Vice Admiral Hyman G. Rickover, USN, was then head of the Navy's nuclear-power program.

commander always seemed to be burdened with black-oil logistics, which this freed him from. Even before he could really get serious about what he was going to do, he had to consider where and when he could refuel.

John T. Mason: What his capabilities were.

Admiral Martin: Exactly. How long could he stay there until he was out? What would happen if this tanker sank before it got to him? Was he going to run out of fuel where the enemy has the advantage of geography, and so on?

John T. Mason: Or his destroyers need refueling before he.

Admiral Martin: Precisely. This was an extremely interesting thing, and I fortunately got it.

John T. Mason: Did Rickover have any voice in your selection?

Admiral Martin: I really don't know whether he did or not. I know that he has on all commanding officers of ships that are nuclear powered. I just don't know. I'd expect, though, that if he had, he would have insisted that I get some kind of a course before I went to it.

That turned out to be as interesting as I thought it would, and we did have a number of exercises, the kind where you're faced with some big surprise that required that you get under way and proceed someplace at maximum speed. It was just a joy under conditions like that to get these three nuclears on their way. Under a lot of circumstances, that might be all you needed, especially when it's new.

If you have a conflict breaking out, it's like Arleigh Burke used to say, "If you get there immediately, you only need a small force. If you are delayed a day, you need a larger force. If you're delayed a week, why, instead of needing a few ships, you may need half or all of the fleet." The longer you delay, he used to say, it was like his wastebasket. If the fire starts in that wastebasket, you can put it out with the coffee you have left, or you can use another, more earthy way of putting it out. If you don't observe it, or if you're slow in reacting or slow on the decision as to what you're going to do about it, pretty soon you may burn down the house. I had a number of exercises like that.

John T. Mason: These were all in the Mediterranean?

Admiral Martin: All in the Med.

John T. Mason: Why was the Mediterranean, a closed sea, chosen as the area for operations?

Admiral Martin: Carrier Division Two deployed just like any other carrier division would deploy, you see. There were always two attack carrier divisions in the Mediterranean, and they would always relieve in the Mediterranean, not outside the Mediterranean but inside. These were the ships that were ready to go on the deployment. I think it was intentional that they tried to time it so that they would deploy together in order that these tactics could be worked out.

It was a good place to do it. You had the full length of the Med, which is like the full breadth of this country, almost exactly. Actually, from Gibraltar to Lebanon is about the same distance as from San Diego to—

John T. Mason: Three thousand miles.

Admiral Martin: Yes, and other distances that have been studied for a while. These things are passed along from one carrier division commander and one group commander to another. You have the identical distances that would most closely simulate the distances on particular exercises that might be the sort of thing that you would most likely be confronted with.

To be able to just say, "Get under way," and those three ships would get under way without the long business of lighting off boilers. They were under way immediately, and they could sustain over 30 knots the full time and not have the slightest concern for themselves about fuel. To go in there and be able to operate at maximum effort for 11 days, which we figured a carrier could do, until it began to have difficulty. The first difficulty you had was selection of the most appropriate ordnance for those circumstances. You would have to substitute other ordnance or combination of ordnance if you start running low on one. If you're gong to drop something that explodes, or you're going to shoot something that explodes and you can do that for another day and a half or two, then you've got to meet up with an ordnance ship.

John T. Mason: This called for a certain amount of adjustment, didn't it, on the part of the commanding officer accustomed to more conventional types?

Admiral Martin: Yes. Your timing works like that. You get this first task force into position. Then the slower ones that are coming along, you next carrier task group, would get into position for leap-frogging, so to speak, to staging through other aircraft that you're trying to get in there. The second carrier task group is not wasted, because they can do some operating at greater distances or, as I say, they can stage on through. They could easily fly from where they were to the *Enterprise* and bring in replacements and things of that kind.

Then you figure out your black-oil requirements, where they're going to meet you, and so on. Where can they be in the least vulnerable areas and still take part in the exercise

John T. Mason: All the way down the line, didn't it call for a reorganization and readjustment?

Admiral Martin: Exactly.

John T. Mason: The skippers of all the conventional types had things to learn?

Admiral Martin: Yes, they did, but to have both of these—they called them attack carrier battle groups today, which I think is a good name for them, it indicates really what they're doing. They were their principal escorts, the ones that are essential to augment their defensive systems, if they are all nuclear powered then you could move this large, versatile force at maximum speeds without the burden of having all your tactics attenuated by the consideration of black oil. Black oil is not only bad for more frequent refueling, which takes you out of the line of battle during that period, but the refueling at sea business itself puts that carrier and the whole carrier task group into a very vulnerable situation. They're steaming along on a steady course at relatively low speeds, and there are just absolutely scores of disadvantages. Likewise, there are scores of advantages over black oil.

These have all been written down, and they've been repeated time and time again. It's a matter really of trying to take it out of the predicted advantages and putting it into an exercise that proves that this can be done, which was another reason that I so strongly supported the idea of taking the three of them around the world.[*] I don't think I could take credit for the concept. My staff and I had discussed it.

John T. Mason: Where did Ricketts get the idea?[†]

Admiral Martin: I don't know. Do you think he might have been the one who started this thing? I'm not sure, but it was a concept and no more than a concept when we started working on it. We were strongly for it.

John T. Mason: You were in the Mediterranean when you began dealing with this idea?

---

[*] Operation Sea Orbit was an around-the-world cruise by the world's first nuclear-powered task force, which comprised the aircraft carrier *Enterprise* (CVAN-65), the cruiser *Long Beach* (CGN-9), and the frigate *Bainbridge* (DLGN-25). The cruise began 31 July 1964 when the ships transited through the Strait of Gibraltar from the Mediterranean into the Atlantic. The ships then proceeded around Africa and visited numerous ports. The cruise ended 3 October 1964, when the *Enterprise* and *Long Beach* arrived in Norfolk and the *Bainbridge* in Charleston. The commander of Nuclear Task Force One was Rear Admiral Bernard M. Strean, USN. See the Naval Institute oral history of Strean, who retired as a vice admiral.
[†] Admiral Claude V. Ricketts, USN, served as Vice Chief of Naval Operations from 1 November 1961 until his death on 6 July 1964.

Admiral Martin: We were in the Med and presented all the advantages of doing this, and not just the principal ones. The principal objective was to prove without a doubt, under as typical conditions as we could, the distances to be covered. The strictly naval objectives were many on this. The primary one, of course, was to work out a number of tactical problems. Every segment of the trip was a tactical problem that you could relate to a situation that was a real test for the distances we traveled—what you must do when you get there, and so on.

John T. Mason: This was to be without accompanying ships?

Admiral Martin: Just the three ships, because that's all we had.

John T. Mason: Yes, but I mean you didn't have an escort of oil-burning ships?

Admiral Martin: No, we didn't. We worked it out so that we could go within 300 miles of as many national capitals as possible. We weren't going to stop, but we could fly out by COD our ambassadors.[*] We would give him enough time to work this out, to invite the head of state, and with COD it works like that.

It was a new thing and an interesting thing, and every situation where the head of state could come and the distances were such that we could fly him out, they accepted. This was a terrific thing for our ambassadors who were never even in a small group with the head of state, and in many cases had seen him only for a few moments in a large crowd, if at all.

John T. Mason: How did you make the transition from testing the ships under different circumstances, all imaginable circumstances—how did you make the jump from that to the indoctrination of heads of state?

---

[*] COD – carrier on-board delivery, an aircraft configured for carrier takeoffs and landings, dedicated to transporting personnel and cargo between ship and shore.

Admiral Martin: That was easy, because we didn't allow anything to interfere with a tactical problem, and it didn't matter, because we'd just carry on with the tactical problem and let them have a piece of it. There was very little in the problems that was classified.

John T. Mason: But I mean your idea, how did you leap from—?

Admiral Martin: We did the tactical things first. The first objective was to prove this thing tactically.

John T. Mason: Yes, and then to include the heads of state for what—?

Admiral Martin: Then to include as many heads of state as our ambassadors for indoctrination, PR purposes. We're always looking for friends.

John T. Mason: Did you have also in the back of your mind the idea that there was a certain amount of opposition to Polaris submarines going into ports? I mean, this was a very difficult thing to achieve.

Admiral Martin: I don't know whether this would have enhanced that, except to show how safe it was aboard these nuclear-powered surface craft. It gave us a chance to answer their questions, you see, while we were briefing them. The program that we had with them was a part of that, of course, to acquaint them, to introduce them to nuclear-powered ships, so they could see how reliable and safe they were. It might have had some effect on this thing of certain countries not wanting them in port. It might have had some effect; I don't know.

John T. Mason: As you thought about this in the planning stages, did you schedule the various countries that you were going to pass by?

Admiral Martin: Yes, but we did leave some of those out. We did go through the Med, of course, you see. I didn't do it all, because a friend of mine stole my job just before we started the rounds.

John T. Mason: Yes, Smoke Strean got it.

Admiral Martin: Smoke Strean got my job.*

John T. Mason: What I was leading up to was the tour began in the Mediterranean, and I think the first head of state was the Kind of Morocco, was it not, who came out? But, as the tour developed, one snag developed when you went by Cape Town.

Admiral Martin: Yes.

John T. Mason: Was this on your original plan?

Admiral Martin: Yes, it was. I think every Navy man who looks at it seriously sees how important South Africa is to us, and it continues to be extremely important to us.

John T. Mason: The enemy knows that.

Admiral Martin: The enemy knows it well. That's one of the bottlenecks he could use against us.

This had so many details in it that we were carrying out our primary objective and altering it only as necessary to accommodate more important visitors to come aboard, never accepting a serious change, one that would significantly diminish the value of the tactical thing that we were trying to prove.

This might be a good time to tell about the problem I had with Admiral Rickover.

John T. Mason: Norfolk?

---

* See the Naval Institute oral history of Vice Admiral Bernard M. Strean, USN (Ret.).

Admiral Martin: Norfolk, yes, Newport News. Admiral Rickover would come down about every two weeks or so, and I would invariably ask him to lunch and dinner for the time that he was there. He would never accept; then one time he did accept. I found out why he accepted my dinner invitation. He wanted to change my mind about the plans. It was his idea that this nuclear task group should go around the world in a minimum amount of time without anybody knowing where it was. It would just disappear. No one would know where we were. There would be no announcement until the day before they were to enter New York.

John T. Mason: So that it would be a complete test of the ships and their performance?

Admiral Martin: I didn't see that there was any test at all on that. Nobody doubted that they could steam long enough to go all the way around the world, but it left the tactical problems almost out of it, and it almost completely eliminated the visits by the various heads of state and our ambassadors.

John T. Mason: He saw this as of no import?

Admiral Martin: He saw it as a huge impact to announce this big thing, that here were three ships that went around the world at such and such speeds without anybody knowing where they were until now. Then they would come in with the fireboats and everything going, all the welcoming things that they do for a famous ship that's coming into port. He felt that would be worth it all, and I had strong disagreement with him on it. He told me on our last meeting before he left the ship for me to think it over until the next day. "Take all the time you want," he said, "but no later than 10:00 o'clock tomorrow you call the Chief of Naval Operations and tell him that you agree with me."

John T. Mason: Oh!

Admiral Martin: I said, "Admiral Rickover, I greatly admire you, and you're a distinguished man who will go down in history, but I really cannot agree with any part of your concept of this, because it eliminates so many very important things that it would not be possible to do in your plan."

John T. Mason: How did he respond to that?

Admiral Martin: Well, he obviously didn't like it. He'd been pretty friendly until I gave him a distinct down. We'd talked together before, and I think I told you about Arleigh Burke's handling of Admiral Rickover and Admiral Byrd—that they were distinguished men, and we should treat them that way.

He had talked to me, mostly on the phone, when I was Arleigh Burke's executive assistant, so we were not strangers to each other. I thought the way he did business sometimes was necessary to speed up what he was trying to do. He just didn't have time for all the little niceties and amenities of life. He was just too busy for them.

John T. Mason: It always helps, though, busy or not.

Admiral Martin: Yes, it does help.

I mentioned the various exercises that we did have while we were in there. One personal thing and probably the most important to me to date was when the *Enterprise* was in Cannes, France, I met my wife Friedel.[*] She was a widow, and she and her 12-year-old daughter were vacationing in Cannes. We met, I knew that was it, and, to shorten the story, I chased her for 19 months. She came from Europe over here, married me, and we've had over 14 perfect years together.

That was just a month before I left the Med, as a matter of fact. I was being relieved. Smoke Strean was leaving OP-33 in Washington to come over and relieve me. He'd been the most helpful person in the planning of this thing, providing charts and that sort of thing. I really wanted to take that force on what we called Operation Sea Orbit. It was going to be so continuously interesting, and in addition just the interest of making a round-the-world trip. Every segment was laid out to make great sense on specific tactical problems. I just thought that was going to be so very important.

---

[*] Friedel Opasinski of Hamburg, Germany, and Long Island, New York.

John T. Mason: What kind of reception did the idea meet with in the department?

Admiral Martin: It had very little opposition. It got favorable response from the beginning, and we got help from the beginning. The concept made so much sense. Here, for the first time, we had what you might call the minimum size of an attack carrier battle group. These three ships were about as minimum size that you'd get into trouble with anybody with, and two very able escorts, the *Long Beach* and the *Bainbridge*.

The three had been working together on tactical problems in the Med for a number of months, and so they were ready. They were well trained. The air wing on the *Enterprise* was exceptionally well trained to do this job.

John T. Mason: Can you substantiate the piece of the story that I got from Strean, I guess it was—substantiate it or not substantiate it—the fact that the principal proponent in the department was Admiral Ricketts. And once Admiral Ricketts had died, and the expedition was just getting under way, as I recall, then opposition began to develop, and even with Admiral McDonald, who was CNO.* He'd been in favor of it prior to that, but then he seemed to get very lukewarm at that point.

Admiral Martin: It's a scheduling problem, of course. We never have enough carriers. I can see where there might be some opposition from just the mechanics. The big problem of not having in your deployment schedule the commitments of keeping two attack carriers in the Western Pacific and two in the Mediterranean at all times, the long distances they had to travel to do that, and the exercises that were worked out by Second Fleet in the Atlantic and the First Fleet in the Pacific. I can see where it would throw a lot of long-planned other things into a cocked hat.

No, I really can't give you firsthand. I've heard that there were some problems. Smoke Strean could give you the details, because he was in the Pentagon when this was all happening and was there until just a matter of days before it left the Med to make this trip.

---

* The cruise began 31 July 1964. Admiral Claude V. Ricketts, the Vice Chief of Naval Operations, died on 6 July 1964. Admiral David L. McDonald, USN, served as Chief of Naval Operations from 1 August 1963 to 1 August 1967. His oral history is in the Naval Institute collection.

John T. Mason: You say there were two parts to this tour?

Admiral Martin: Two principal objectives, yes.

John T. Mason: First, the contingent was out for a certain time, then it had to go to Norfolk for some sort of servicing, and it was at that time that you had the conversation with Rickover, but then there was another segment to it?

Admiral Martin: We had already been doing the planning on this thing, and I really don't know how that changed the master schedule for the carriers and the escorts in the Pentagon. I know they always have a big problem of getting ships off in time to make these various deployments, but by the time I left there was no opposition. Maybe it was building up and I wasn't hearing about it. I didn't hear about it.

John T. Mason: Well, there were other aspects of your command in the Mediterranean.

Admiral Martin: For the most part, it was carrying out the Sixth Fleet schedule. Admiral Bill Gentner was the commander of the Sixth Fleet during that period.[*] Those schedules are made out a year in advance, so taking those three out of the Med required some rescheduling, but I don't think it was very serious.

John T. Mason: You were listed as also commander of the striking force.

Admiral Martin: Yes, that was a NATO job.

John T. Mason: Tell me about that.

Admiral Martin: I had two titles—three, actually. For organizational purposes I was Commander Carrier Division Two. For exercise purposes I was commander of the

---

[*] Vice Admiral William E. Gentner, Jr., USN, commanded the Sixth Fleet from 18 March 1963 to 2 June 1964.

nuclear task force. Then the NATO job was Commander Carrier Striking Force for the southern region of Europe. It was the Sixth Fleet's carrier striking force. They're probably called the attack carrier battle groups of the Sixth Fleet today. The attack carrier battle groups are part of NATO's southern striking force, and the Sixth Fleet Commander is the Commander of the Striking Force, Southern Region of NATO. So you have the two hats. There's not much difference whether you're one or the other, except when you have NATO you have ships of other countries that have to be coordinated and fitted into the various task groups.

John T. Mason: During your time there, did you have an exercise incorporating foreign navies?

Admiral Martin: Not I, because with a carrier task force the only places they could fit would be in the escorts, augmenting your antisubmarine activities on an exercise. No, there were other exercises where—for example, there was one called Fair Game, in which we operated against the French Air Force. At that time the French, although they were not a military part of NATO, even so they looked forward to these exercises against the Sixth Fleet, because we provided each other with the only really first-class air forces in that area. They would give us as many as 95 targets, some of them deep into France, that we could run off simulated nuclear missions into France, which would be opposed by their air force.

John T. Mason: De Gaulle must have been loath to do that.[*]

Admiral Martin: I believe these were kept from him. He may have known they were there, but they were not publicized. I used to get a lot of information from French friends, admirals and generals, that we needed to have these exercises. But I feel quite sure that Mr. de Gaulle did not know that there was this close cooperation. Also, the

---

[*] Charles de Gaulle was a general for the Free French in World War II. In 1958 he was called upon to form a government. He served from 1958 to 1969 as first President of France's Fifth Republic.

French would provide patrol craft covering large areas of the Mediterranean exercise area.

John T. Mason: Reporting to us?

Admiral Martin: Yes, reporting to us.

They weren't supposed to be a part of the military aspects of NATO, but in their exercises they welcomed them and were very cooperative. All the other nations we would fit into exercises that were appropriate to them. For example, Tunisia had a few mine craft, and they had a very small Navy, so I put a very small part of ours into an exercise with them. That came later, when I had the Sixth Fleet, but when I had the attack carrier striking force, with both the Sixth Fleet and NATO, on the NATO exercises we would attempt to get all the participation we could and fit them into the exercise, try to fit them in where they would most like to participate. They would frequently run out of fuel after two days of a four-day exercises, but they'd hang in there as long as they could. There were times when we provided fuel for them to finish an exercise. They'd come alongside our tankers and get a drink to finish the exercise.

John T. Mason: When you speak of the striking force and the NATO arm, is this a blue-water counterpart of the President's current push for a mobile force, a quick-reaction force?

Admiral Martin: It could be. The Navy and Marines have been providing that sort of thing for years, but nobody seems to know about it or appreciate it. That has always been one of what the Navy and Marines call an exclusive capability, to be able to deploy quickly this force which is able to carry out a lot of the small things or even something that's going to get big. As I mentioned earlier, the longer you delay it, the bigger it gets and the more forces you need. If you get there quickly, sometimes just your appearance there on the horizon can have a very stabilizing effect.

John T. Mason: That existing capability, why hasn't it been put forward at this point in the public mind?

Admiral Martin: I don't know. Maybe because—I don't know. There are service rivalries and service jealousies. I don't know. Because the Army and the Air Force, especially the Air Force, didn't have any part of it. They don't like it.

Interview Number 6 with Vice Admiral William I. Martin, U.S. Navy (Retired)

Place: Admiral Martin's home in Alexandria, Virginia

Date: Tuesday, 8 January 1980

John T. Mason: Well, Bill, before you begin this morning, I think it would be a delightful episode if you recounted those two things that Dave talked about in his letter during your time as executive assistant to Admiral Burke when he was CNO. First, the lighter-than-air episode.

Admiral Martin: Yes, that incident really had its beginning shortly after I came in as Admiral Burke's executive assistant.[*] He asked me to find some reasonably young fellow, not above the rank of captain, who would be the champion of lighter than air, because it was very clear that that program was coming to an end.[†] There were a number of high-type officers who'd been in lighter than air for their careers up to that point—so long, really, that they couldn't shift successfully into another career. So, with very good reason, the admiral wanted to know more about lighter than air. He wanted to go up in one of these lighter-than-air craft, and we tried this on two different occasions. Once at Lakehurst, New Jersey, when the wind was too high for the flight, and it had to be canceled. The other time was in Miami, when the weather was unsuitable for it. Then, a third time, we were in Cuba, and everything was calm, so we went up. A short time before this, I had re-qualified in all the Navy's latest jets, and this is by way of excusing my performance later with lighter than air.

I was asked if I'd like to take over the controls. The skipper of the ship was a friend of mine, and I declined. Admiral Burke teased me about that and called me a chicken. And so, finally, I took over the controls. I knew that the craft would be very sluggish and insensitive, but I had no idea how sluggish and insensitive. You would move the controls, big movements of the controls, and it was like the helm on a

---

[*] Captain Martin became Admiral Burke's executive assistant in January 1956.
[†] On 21 June 1961 the Secretary of the Navy announced the forthcoming termination of the Navy's lighter-than-air program. The last flight by a Navy blimp was on 31 August 1962. See Roy A. Grossnick, *Kite Balloons to Airships: the Navy's Lighter-than-air Experience* (Washington: Government Printing Office, 1986).

battleship. You'd count several seconds before anything would happen. I was accustomed to jets, which react when you almost have the thought, never a movement but just slight pressure on the controls. I must have looked very comical to anybody observing me. After a few minutes of that, I gave up. Admiral Burke has never let me up from that. He's continually reminding me of it, especially if there's somebody around to enjoy the story.

John T. Mason: What did he learn from this episode?

Admiral Martin: Well, from the total experience of not being able to fly lighter than air on two occasions, one thing that he learned was that a moderate amount of weather would cancel a mission in lighter than air. And on the one day in Cuba when I couldn't handle the controls, I think he might have seen the wide disparity between the techniques of flying a modern fixed-wing aircraft and the techniques for operating a lighter-than-air craft smoothly and safely.

Did you have something else in mind?

John T. Mason: Well, no, but he had, by his desire to go up and persisting in this desire, indicated some kind of interest in lighter-than-air craft, and at that stage of the game lighter than air was coming rather into disrepute, wasn't it?

Admiral Martin: Yes. It was considered that they were not worth the cost and the effort of doing it, because if you had an important mission for them to go on in good weather, they could do the job of ASW patrols better than anybody else, for the submarine areas, because they had great endurance, and they could stop when they wanted to.

John T. Mason: Just hover?

Admiral Martin: Hover, and they could take enough crew to stay out for long periods of time. There were many advantages that I think everybody would have liked to make use of, but this one thing of having to cancel meant that if they were assigned important missions, then you had to have a backup of something else that could go out on those occasions. Even today there's a limit to what you can do with them.

John T. Mason: How did Admiral Rosendahl, who was the formal spokesman for them, meet an argument of that sort?[*]

Admiral Martin: I really don't know. I was very much aware of the man, and I knew that he was a champion of them, but I don't know what his arguments were on the weather thing. It certainly existed and was so clear that I think Admiral Rosendahl may have been carried away with the advantages that I spoke of. If the weather is good, it does a better job than anybody else on antisubmarine patrols.

John T. Mason: Yes, as a matter of fact, in World War II, off the eastern coast, lighter-than-air craft did have a rather good record of attacking submarines.

Admiral Martin: Well, their big advantage, it seemed to me, was their search in the negative areas. A submarine that wanted to surface and fight it out, once they got surfaced and got a gun pointed at them, you present a tremendous target.

John T. Mason: The bag of helium would go up.

Admiral Martin: Exactly.

John T. Mason: And then the other incident?

Admiral Martin: Right. This was on my advice to Admiral Burke to take a nap in the middle of the day. He worked such long hours, and with good reason, especially his first year in office, because it was his policy to seek advice every place he could, especially

---

[*] Rear Admiral Charles E. Rosendahl, USN, was a pioneer in the Navy's airship program, starting in 1923. In 1943, after duty in the South Pacific as commanding officer of the heavy cruiser *Minneapolis* (CA-36), he became Chief of the Naval Airship Training Command at Lakehurst, New Jersey, and remained in that post through the remainder of World War II. He retired from active duty on 1 November 1946 and received a tombstone promotion to vice admiral.

from officers who had been senior to him, both active duty, of whom there were several, and retired.

John T. Mason: Now, this wasn't cosmetic on his part at all?

Admiral Martin: No, no. Not only did he have an open door to them, he would seek them out. This took a tremendous amount of time, and often it would be in the late evening. He'd be in the office from 7:30 in the morning until 8:30, 9:30, 10:30, 11:30. Frequently he went until 11:00 and almost midnight. He made sure that he didn't go into the next day, because he didn't want those who were working with him to brag about it, I guess, that they'd worked the whole night.

Because of these long hours, I was concerned about his health, although he was extremely healthy. He was just a very rugged person physically. In talking with the senior aides and executive assistants of other members of the Joint Chiefs, the Chief of Staff of the Army and the Air Force, I found that those officers were going down to the athletic department every day and getting a little exercise and usually taking a few minutes' nap. Maxwell Taylor, for example, would take a little exercise, and then he would invariably lie down and sleep for about 20 minutes, maybe more, depending on what his schedule was that afternoon.[*]

I thought that would be a very good thing and something that Admiral Burke should do to stay in good health and continue to compete with those people. He was so superior to all of them to begin with. He thought that was rather amusing, so after I'd discussed it with him seriously—when he would pass my desk, which he did frequently because he had to go to the head, to go into the back room to get a haircut, or for complete privacy—he would frequently ask me if I'd had my nap that day.

I remember one evening, it was late in the evening, well after dark, he came by, and I was looking out the window. As you know, in that part of the Pentagon, the windows look out on the Arlington Cemetery. He asked me what I was focusing on, and I told him I was looking out there at all the people who had worked the long hours that we were working. I really don't think Admiral Burke found that amusing.

---

[*] General Maxwell D. Taylor, USA, served as Army Chief of Staff from 30 June 1955 to 30 June 1959.

John T. Mason: Did you ever enlist the aid of his admirable wife in these efforts?

Admiral Martin: No, I didn't. I didn't have to. When she would call, especially if they had accepted an invitation to go someplace, she would tell him that she would be there to pick him up at a certain hour, and he would make it, because not only did he respect and love her, but we loved to have her along on trips because she could get him away from the long hours, talking all night, and getting him to bed at a reasonable hour. He responded to that sweet lady. When she laid down the law to him about getting away a little bit earlier and arriving at events that they had accepted, he would do it. Of course, he would take briefcases home with him at night, but he would be there.

John T. Mason: Now, last time you talked about the atomic task force and Sea Orbit, as it developed. Then you were deprived of the great pleasure and privilege of conducting this tour around the world. So you came back to Washington, did you?

Admiral Martin: I did come back to the Pentagon to be—they called them Assistant Chiefs of Naval Operations then.[*] Since that time the number-two various deputies are called the Assistant Deputies to the Chief of Naval Operations for Air, for Logistics, or whatever. So I was number two to Jimmy Thach, who was OP-05, DCNO (AIR).[†]

John T. Mason: You seemed always to get attached to charger types.

Admiral Martin: Yes, which was certainly an advantage, because you learn so much from those people. My acquaintance with Admiral Radford over the years was a very helpful thing. Since my experiences with Admiral Burke, when I look back sometimes on duties after that time, I can see where my experiences, what I had learned from people Like Radford, Burke, Thach, and others—just how much I drew on my experience with them in making difficult decisions easier later on.

---

[*] Rear Admiral Martin served from April 1964 to March 1967 as Assistant Chief of Naval Operations (Air).
[†] Vice Admiral John S. Thach, USN, served as Deputy Chief of Naval Operations (Air) from 8 July 1963 to 25 February 1965. The oral history of Thach, who retired as a four-star admiral, is in the Naval Institute collection.

John T. Mason: These were the top men in the profession in your generation.

Admiral Martin: Yes, they were, and I knew many of them. My first year in flag rank, when I was in Argentia, which I've already covered, Admiral Jerauld Wright was SACLant, CinCLant, and CinCLantFlt, and my experiences with him were very useful, very helpful.

    This is why I think it's so important for senior officers to set the example, because I certainly had examples set for me up there. I could recall later when I got into a difficult situation—it was almost like the old saying, "What would Farragut do?"* That passed through my mind in difficult situations many times.

John T. Mason: Tell me about your duty with Thach. How long a period was it?

Admiral Martin: It was two years.

John T. Mason: What was the scope of your duties?

Admiral Martin: I was sort of a chief of staff, taking care of details that would permit him to appear before the committees of Congress and to work more closely on the more important items where he was dealing directly with the Chief of Naval Operations, with the Secretary of Defense, with the Secretary of the Navy, and the offices of the Secretary of Defense, similar to the duties of an executive officer who tries to free the skipper for the more important things, to permit him, hopefully, time to cool his heels and do some planning without having to take care of details that could be handled at a lower level. The job was very similar to an executive officer's job, a chief of staff job, where you're dealing with a lot of people.

    All of those Deputy CNO jobs are big organizations. They do the same thing for the CNO that their assistants try to do for them. You're dealing with the highest level of

---

* David G. Farragut (1801-1870) was the senior Union naval leader in the Civil War; in 1862 he became the first officer in the U.S. Navy to hold the rank of rear admiral. He was particularly noted for his victory in the Battle of Mobile Bay in August 1864. He served in the Navy from the time he was a midshipman in 1810 until his death.

the Navy, and it goes outside Washington. It goes right out to the small units of the fleet. You deal with OpNav instructions, which are permanent instructions, and really the laws by which that particular subject is handled.

One of the things that was taking so much of our time at that time was the TFX, which had turned into the McNamara solution to the TFX, the F-111.[*] McNamara was insistent on the Air Force and the Navy using the same aircraft. On the surface it made some sense because of the commonality of parts, and you might take that all the way through to the coordination of training techniques and all that sort of thing. But, in practice, it had been tried before.

John T. Mason: It had been tried before?

Admiral Martin: Well, something like this. I guess many times they'd considered taking an Air Force plane that was successful and trying to adopt it to operate on aircraft carriers, but it had never been done successfully, and there are good reasons for that.

John T. Mason: And it always is in terms of economy, I suppose?

Admiral Martin: Always in terms of economy. The greater number you buy of a certain article—whether it's an airplane or a ship, a gun, a missile—the farther down the learning curve you go, the greater the production and the more efficient the production, and the less the cost.

For example, today these high-priced aircraft that we're buying now, it could make a difference of one to three or four million dollars for each one, depending on whether you're going to buy 100 or 500.

John T. Mason: Yes.

---

[*] The F-111—originally designated TFX—was a controversial fighter plane that Secretary of Defense Robert McNamara tried to develop in the 1960s for use by both the Air Force and the Navy. The Navy was eventually able to thwart its role as a carrier plane and developed the F-14 instead.

Admiral Martin: So it has those advantages, but the airplane that operates from an aircraft carrier is a different machine in so many areas. There are books written on this, Jack. There's a brochure on this that Grumman put out just two years ago, and they renew it each year to explain it to new members of Congress who are on the Armed Services Committee, because each year it comes up: why can't they use the same airplane?[*]

Now, it has worked the other way, where the Air Force has been able to take successful Navy planes and operate them very successfully on the field. The F-4, the Phantom, and the A-7, and the A-1.[†] Many of those have worked very effectively for them. On the Air Force version of those, they've been able to lighten them by eliminating the wing-folding devices, to take out the arresting hook, to leave off the catapult provisions, and that sort of thing. But it just won't work the other way around.

The airplane that operates from an aircraft carrier has to be designed from the bottom up. For example, the F-111A was to be the Air Force version. The F-111B would have been the Navy version. There were several things about that airplane that wouldn't have mattered too much with the Air Force. The fact that it was too big to get down the elevators on the aircraft carriers, and even after they shortened it 14 inches you still couldn't get it on the elevators with the prime mover, the tractor that tows it, on there with it. You'd have to put it on there, take the tractor off, and when it got down to the hangar deck put another tractor on to move it out. Things like very bad visibility over the nose, not being able to see the optical landing system or the landing signal officer because you just couldn't see over the nose well enough to see that. They made changes and attempts to correct that.

Another thing that had no adverse effect on a field was that it had a tendency to tip back and with a rolling ship—and this occurred on more than one occasion, the plane would tip back on its tail, and it would get out of hand and roll over the side. You'd lose this $13 million item.

---

[*] Following his retirement from active naval service, Vice Admiral Martin worked for the Grumman Aerospace Corporation.

[†] The McDonnell Douglas F-4 Phantom II was the Navy's primary carrier-based jet fighter of the 1960s and early 1970s. The Vought A-7 Corsair II was a carrier-based jet bomber used at the time in Navy and Marine Corps light attack squadrons. The Douglas A-1 Skyraider was a carrier-based propeller-driven attack plane.

John T. Mason: You were almost on the ground floor with it, weren't you?

Admiral Martin: Well, no. You see, they had been through the TFX thing, and McNamara had decided that this was the answer to the TFX. The F-111 was to be used by both the Navy and the Air Force.

I wrote a memorandum explaining it as I understood it. I thoroughly believed that the airplane was impossible for operations from an aircraft carrier. I got some reaction back on that.

John T. Mason: Did you? From the man himself?

Admiral Martin: Not directly from him, but it was fairly strong, even getting it indirectly. Then, just before I left that job, I wrote another one, a very lengthy memorandum, on just why it was utterly impossible, stating at the beginning that I thought the airplane would work very well for the Air Force, that I wouldn't criticize the F-111A for use by the Air Force, because they didn't have the limits on the size of their hangars, they didn't have the limits on the length of runways, the shop space that it was going to take, and many things that made it impossible to use on an aircraft carrier were not going to work adversely for operations from an airfield to a significant extent. But to use it on an aircraft carrier was utterly impossible, and I made it as strong as I could possibly make it, so strong that when I was called up to see the Secretary of the Navy—

John T. Mason: Who was that, Ignatius at the time?

Admiral Martin: No, it was Nitze.[*] I got the word at 7:30, and I thought it was pretty early for the Secretary to want to see me. He made a point of telling my office, whoever answered the phone, to be sure to tell me that the Chief of Naval Operations was with him on this. Just a few days after I had written the strongest possible memorandum I could compose on why the F-111 was impossible, I really and truly thought I was going to be sent to Timbuktu.

---

[*] Paul H. Nitze served as Secretary of the Navy from 29 November 1963 to 30 June 1967.

John T. Mason: Maybe you were in danger.

Admiral Martin: I thought that was going to be the subject, and I could hardly believe my ears when the Secretary said, "We would like for you to command the Sixth Fleet." Here I thought I was going to get fired, and instead I got promoted and sent to the best job in the Navy, without a doubt.

John T. Mason: But you got sent to sea.

Admiral Martin: Yes, that does become your second thought, you know, "What would they do to get me out of town?"

I'm sure that my views on the F-111B were shared by Admiral McDonald, who was CNO at that time, and shared probably by Secretary Nitze himself.[*] I had a great deal of respect for him. I still do.

John T. Mason: He didn't show it outwardly, however, did he?

Admiral Martin: Well, McNamara was overpowering, and I used to marvel at how Secretary Nitze would come back from McNamara, completely losing the objective that he'd gone up there with, particularly when it dealt with the F-111B. Every Friday morning he'd have breakfast with McNamara. Somebody would have breakfast each morning with McNamara, and it would be a sort of a continuous schedule. Friday morning was the Secretary of the Navy, and some other morning it would be the Secretary of the Air Force or the Army. On Thursdays we would brief him in great detail on what he should discuss with McNamara at breakfast the next morning.

I recall one time, this was near the end of my tour there, when our own Navy pilots, our own Navy aeronautical engineers, had dealt with the F-111 business. Our own pilots had flown it, and our own aeronautical engineers had rendered the data, and that was just so completely convincing to me. These people were not going to lie to us. They

---

[*] Admiral David L. McDonald, USN, served as Chief of Naval Operations from 1 August 1963 to 1 August 1967. His oral history is in the Naval Institute collection.

were going to tell the absolute truth, and they did. I thought that was so convincing, and we had briefed Secretary Nitze the evening before, and he said, "I finally see it, and I absolutely agree with you. Now we know. We have evidence, we have data that will stand up. This is extremely convincing, and I will take this up with Secretary McNamara tomorrow.

He got back around 11:00, and all the deputies would be up there. I'd frequently sit in for Admiral Thach, because he wasn't too well at that time. Also, when Thach was relieved by Paul Ramsey, Ramsey didn't come in for four months, and so I was the acting DCNO (Air), and I appeared before the congressional committees and so on.[*] As I say, he'd come back from breakfast with McNamara around 10:00 or 11:00 o'clock, and all the deputies wanted to be there, because he'd debrief us and give us every detail of it, but on the F-111B he was never able to convince McNamara.

John T. Mason: McNamara dug his heels in.

Admiral Martin: Completely, he'd just decided. I sometimes wondered, because Nitze was such an able man and had such a fine mind, he could be very convincing with me, but he didn't win many with McNamara that, as you say, McNamara had dug his heels in on. I don't think anybody did. This was the nemesis of members of Congress like Mendel Rivers, and other strong members of Congress, who weren't able to show up McNamara for what the guy was. This bothered them later. They weren't able to cut McNamara down to size. He had such a technique. First, he had a terrific memory, and he did a snow job that just wouldn't quit.

John T. Mason: He was in the driver's seat too.

Admiral Martin: He was in the driver's seat, but he was not necessarily in the driver's seat before the members of Congress, but they never did expose him. They wished later that they had. McNamara did a lot of damage, degradation—maybe that's not the word

---

[*] Vice Admiral Paul H. Ramsey, USN, served as Deputy Chief of Naval Operations (Air) from 31 March 1965 to 1 October 1966.

to use—but the loss of prestige of the man in uniform, his loss of authority to match his responsibility. That, I believe, started with McNamara.

John T. Mason: And you lay that against the background of the Vietnam struggle.

Admiral Martin: Yes. He'd never admit this, I'm sure, but he was anti-military. He didn't try to build up the morale and enthusiasm for serving. To me he destroyed it.

John T. Mason: How do you analyze the man?

Admiral Martin: Well, I really don't. Somebody might. It's surprising that there aren't books of all kinds around on what was wrong with McNamara. But I haven't read any that really exposed him in the way that books have taken other people apart. I just haven't read anything on that.

John T. Mason: Would you think perhaps the middle name to the man is a clue?

Admiral Martin: Strange? Yes. You know, they talked about what a failure he was at Ford. I've known people who knew important executives of the Ford Corporation who said how happy they were to get rid of him. The failure of the Edsel is laid at his door and other things like that, but he goes on.* Now he's head of the World Bank. I would expect that he would do a pretty good job there, because he is not dealing with people where he has to keep good morale. I don't think it's necessary for him to have good morale. Everything's rather cut and dried.

John T. Mason: Going back to the F-111, did you ever have an inclination, or did you have experience in flying one of these models?

---

* The Ford Motor Company, of which McNamara was briefly the president, introduced a new brand named the Edsel for the 1958, 1959, and 1960 model years. It sold poorly, resulting in losses for the company, and was dropped from production after only a few years.

Admiral Martin: No, I hadn't flown it, but I didn't need to fly it because, having been a test pilot for a number of years and having done test work even before I was doing it full time as an experimental test pilot, I knew something about what performance you could expect from an airplane without flying it. And, as I say, when I was really completely convinced and knew I was right was after our own test pilots, people I knew, had flown it and written their reports, and they were correlated, they agreed on all of these things. And our own aeronautical engineers—and we've had some wonderful aeronautical engineers of the year, both in uniform and out of uniform, civilians who were leaders in aircraft design.

People like George Spangenberg, with whom I worked very closely at the time.* He's retired now, but he was known as the most capable aircraft designer in the business and a very, very outspoken, a very courageous man. I greatly admire him, and there was another one in aircraft systems named Fred Gluckler, who was known as the best in aircraft systems. Terrific people, and they're the kind of people who turned out the F-4, the Phantom, the A-7, and now the F-14. I don't have to say this just because I'm still a consultant with Grumman, but the F-14 has been and still is the best fighter in the world today and will continue to be for the next eight or ten years, because it takes that long to come up with a new one. You can't even begin to think about it unless you've got $2 billion that you're ready to spend before it becomes operational in the squadron.

John T. Mason: Tom Connolly wanted to fly the F-111.†

Admiral Martin: He did.

John T. Mason: The F-111A he flew.

Admiral Martin: Yes, he did.

---

* George Spangenberg had a notable career in the field of aircraft acquisition. His oral history is online at http://www.georgespangenberg.com.
† Vice Admiral Thomas F. Connolly, USN, served as Deputy Chief of Naval Operations (Air) from 1 November 1966 to 31 August 1971. Admiral Connolly's oral history is in the Naval Institute collection.

John T. Mason: I guess maybe he did fly a model of the B too? He went down to Texas to fly the 111A.

Admiral Martin: I don't know. I know he flew the F-111A.

John T. Mason: And got into hot water.

Admiral Martin: Yes, he did. Tom described that airplane as, "She flies like a lady."
Tom was Deputy Chief of Naval Operations for Air for about two months before I left there.

John T. Mason: It was right at that time that he did fly it.

Admiral Martin: Well, it was after that, after I left. Nobody could fly that airplane at that time except the test pilots who were designated. It was after I left that it became available to other people. If I'd stayed on for another six months, I could have flown it.
The airplane has been a big disappointment to the Air Force until recently. They've lot so many where there was no explanation.

John T. Mason: It was almost a scandal in Vietnam, wasn't it?

Admiral Martin: It was. Now I think they've workrd most of that out. The airplane is going to be a very successful electronic warfare plane. It already is, but as a fighter, no. As a fighter-bomber they expanded it, and they look upon it now as a potential success, even for the longer-range mission.
Where are we right now?

John T. Mason: Well, that was one of the primary interests you had when you were with Thach, but there were others, I'm sure. Vietnam was hotting up at that point, when you went in in 1964.*

Admiral Martin: Right.

John T. Mason: Do you recall anything in that area?

Admiral Martin: Only that we weren't buying enough airplanes, and McNamara would not permit us to buy enough parts. There was a time when the Navy would buy airplanes, and they would buy lifetime supplies to support them, which, if you've got a very successful airplane, makes a lot of sense—to buy the spares while the factories are turning them out in numbers. They cost a lot less, and then you have them. The importance of doing that would be to get away from the tremendous effects of inflation that go on from year to year.

We had good aircraft, though. We had good aircraft carriers, and I thought they performed admirably. We had to be careful about lessons learned, though, because there was very little air opposition and no submarine opposition and no surface craft opposition. So you had to be careful about trying to glean the lessons that you learned from the Vietnam thing.

John T. Mason: Because the challenge wasn't there in that particular area?

Admiral Martin: No. The thing of defending yourself as you might in warfare in the Mediterranean, for example, where you'd be confronted with every possible vehicle that could attack the aircraft carrier and its aircraft: surface, subsurface, and air, and the missile business.

---

* On 2 August 1964, North Vietnamese patrol boats in the Tonkin Gulf attacked the destroyer *Maddox* (DD-731) in international waters during daytime. On the night of 4 August the *Maddox* and the destroyer *Turner Joy* (DD-951) reported being attacked by North Vietnamese craft. The question of whether the second attack occurred has since been generally refuted. The reports of the two attacks led to the congressional Gulf of Tonkin Resolution, which provided the legal basis for the commitment of U.S. armed forces in Vietnam.

John T. Mason: Did you go to Vietnam during this time?

Admiral Martin: No, I didn't. I left that job, as you know.

John T. Mason: But there must be other things. We were talking off-tape about the frustrations of this particular job.

Admiral Martin: Yes. For one thing, there are just limitless details that are never really dealt with to their final conclusion. In two years there—and I'd been in the Navy Department, I think, five times—you leave it feeling that you haven't accomplished anything. Then, a year or two later, you find out that you did. There were some OpNav instructions that needed to be written, some policy that needed to be changed, and so you do find that you've accomplished something, but while you're there you're never aware of packaging a project. It just doesn't seem to happen. A lot of these limitless details don't seem to be too important.

John T. Mason: Maybe that's because you're basically an activist.

Admiral Martin: Maybe that's it. I like to see something completed, especially at sea when you're operating and things are very interesting. I've never been at sea when I didn't find things interesting. You're either coming up with new tactics or improving old ones. There's always something to be done. There is an improvement program that's very clear that you want to accomplish, and you think of this when you first go to the job. But after you've learned as much as you need to know about it, where are the areas where you can improve it or change it, where are the areas where we're weak? Or in some cases, like when I was in the night business, there's an area in which you have no capability, so how can you accomplish? How can you develop some capabilities in areas where you have none?

I just don't see this thing happening, though, ashore. Some people are obviously brilliant, and they obviously do accomplish things ashore, especially in the Navy

Department, but I was never one who felt that I was accomplishing too much. As I say, after I left the job, I found out that I did do good in some areas.

John T. Mason: In this particular job as assistant to the chief, were you part of any kind of a kitchen cabinet of your own confreres who were assistants also?

Admiral Martin: No, not really. There was no place really to go out on an independent operation. I don't think it would have been proper anyway to do that without the DCNO (Air) knowing about it. I always kept him fully informed. On the other hand, there were areas that he did know about and that I would handle for him and in which I would be dealing with the various divisions and branches that wouldn't get up to him until it was ready to present. And if it wasn't going anyplace, it wouldn't get up to him at all.

John T. Mason: I think it was that particular period when Zumwalt was there with Nitze.

Admiral Martin: As his assistant.[*]

John T. Mason: Yes, as his assistant, and Ike Kidd was with McDonald, and Jerry Miller was with Rivero.[†] Those three were a kitchen cabinet and met daily for coffee and shared their experiences.

Admiral Martin: Well, from that point of view, yes. For example, the personnel division and branches within DCNO (Air), the aircraft programs, aircraft plans—I'd meet with the various branches frequently. But my door was always open, and they could come up and see me any time they pleased. But you just couldn't leave the door of the deputy open, because he had too many things that he was preparing himself for that were very important for his part in the Joint Chiefs' matters, or the big projects in the budget, the various things that take place in the CNO's Advisory Board—they call it the CAB.

---

[*] Captain Elmo R. Zumwalt Jr., USN, served as executive assistant to Secretary of the Navy Nitze, 1963-65. Zumwalt was later Chief of Naval Operations, 1970-74.
[†] Captain Isaac C. Kidd Jr., USN, was EA to the CNO, Admiral David L. McDonald, USN; Captain Gerald E. Miller, USN, was EA to the VCNO, Admiral Horacio Rivero, USN. The oral histories of McDonald, Miller, and Rivero are in the Naval Institute collection.

I felt that if I did my job properly, the most important thing I could do would be to relieve the deputy of as much detail as I could and still keep him fully informed.

John T. Mason: In the area of his duties with the budget, what were your duties in that connection?

Admiral Martin: Well, our part of the DCNO input in the budget would be developed and hammered at throughout the whole cycle. You started the new cycle before you'd actually finished with the previous one. It's a matter of working these out as convincingly as you can, as accurately as you can so far as cost is concerned, and defending them—first, with the Navy program itself, where they're always competing with something in either the submarine area, or—there's money for all the vested interests in the Navy. The things that you put as a very high priority might not be put as a high priority in other areas of the Navy. So you're always competing. That's not too bad, because it requires that you come up with proposals that are solid enough to survive the Navy competition, and then maybe they'll survive when they get down to OSD and when they get up to the Hill.[*]

It's a daily matter of scheduling these things so that you're going to have complete coverage. Then to allow time for the things that come up that you cannot schedule, the unexpected opposition or unexpected items in which you haven't been convincing. It's just a steady load. There's really never enough time to give to the things that you can't schedule.

John T. Mason: You said earlier, when you mentioned the fact that Thach was involved with the Hill and hearings, then there was an interim period of four months before Ramsey came in when you were acting. Do you want to talk about that area, the relationship with the Hill?

Admiral Martin: Well, I'd been up there before, so I wasn't too new. One thing I did find out was that some of the friendships I'd have up there, and I had a number of

---

[*] OSD – Office of the Secretary of Defense.

friends—my good old friend and mentor, Congressman Dewey Short had introduced me to his friends, and these were close friends, but when you're before their committee the friendships go out the door, and you may find yourself being asked some questions that you consider hostile.

John T. Mason: Not hostile personally?

Admiral Martin: Not personally, but hostile towards the subject matter under discussion. I recall appearing before Mendel Rivers's Committee on the Armed Services one day. I'd known Mendel and liked him a lot. He asked me a question to which I replied, "I believe it is so-and-so."

He interrupted me and said, "I don't give a damn what you believe. I want to know what you know."

John T. Mason: He was seeking facts.

Admiral Martin: He was seeking facts. I recall that the subject was the performance of a missile, and I had simply forgotten what its minimum range was if released at some particular altitude. I started to tell him what I thought it was, but he wanted the facts. After that I learned that when I didn't know I would say so and offer to supply it for the record.

John T. Mason: That's the regular procedure.

Admiral Martin: That's the regular procedure. You shouldn't guess at anything. But, all told, I thought that that was a very valuable experience. You develop a great respect for some of the members of Congress, and you fail to develop any respect for others.

John T. Mason: Did you submit yourself to some kind of rehearsal in preparation for these meetings?

Admiral Martin: Oh, always, what you call a meeting of the devil's advocates, in which you consider every question that you may be asked, including the bad ones.

John T. Mason: Especially the bad ones.

Admiral Martin: Especially the bad ones, yes, so that you at least had time to think about it and, if you've done this well, efficiently, then you won't be asked anything that you haven't already considered the answer to. Even if you've had plenty of time to prepare yourself, I think it's still a strain. I was never completely comfortable.

John T. Mason: Did you call on the assistance of JAG for any legal aspects of things?*

Admiral Martin: Not at our level we didn't. They'd get that further up, at the CNO's level and especially at the Secretary's level.

John T. Mason: During this time when you were appearing on the Hill, it was the McNamara regime, and there were certain strictures, were there not, laid down by DoD?

Admiral Martin: Right. You were expected to know the SecDef position, and you were expected to support it.

John T. Mason: Did you ever have an experience wherein you felt that you couldn't support it because it wasn't true?

Admiral Martin: Almost every aspect of the F-111B. As I say, I didn't go around talking about it, but when I was asked a question I'd give my honest feelings about it, and I offered them memoranda that were classified to advise my superiors, the Chief of Naval Operations and the Secretary of the Navy, and I'd be very open with those. I didn't hold anything back. That was, as I say, especially true after the Navy had its own information, and we weren't dealing with the results of the company's test pilots and the company's

---

* Officers of the Judge Advocate General's Corps are the Navy's uniformed lawyers.

aeronautical engineers, but our own Navy people in whom you had great trust, and you could be a lot more confident of your position.

John T. Mason: You never got called on the carpet by the Department of Defense, did you, for stating frankly your point of view before a congressional committee?

Admiral Martin: No, I wasn't, yet I think I gave some answers that they didn't like. But I never felt repercussions along those lines.

John T. Mason: During this assignment in the Pentagon with Admiral Thach I believe that your marriage occurred.

Admiral Martin: No, it was after Thach left. It was after Ramsey came in.

John T. Mason: But while you were still there.

Admiral Martin: Yes.

John T. Mason: Do you want to talk about that, put that on the record?

Admiral Martin: Well, years back, I guess, a divorce can be a pretty damaging thing, but that's changed now. For a flag officer to remarry could be especially difficult for the wife.

John T. Mason: Was that a factor? I didn't realize that.

Admiral Martin: I think it has been. I've been told of cases—I couldn't name one specifically, and, of course, the importance of the wife on the big responsible assignments is considerable.

John T. Mason: And sometimes, I understand, considered by the selection board too?

Admiral Martin: Maybe not openly, but it must be in the back of the minds of those that there is a wife who can't do her part; it might be. But a very fortunate thing happened to me. The day I was married, it was a Saturday, she had just arrived from Europe, and that very night we went to Ed Hidalgo's.* He was having a big party that night at his home, and he insisted on our coming the night we were married.

John T. Mason: What year was this?

Admiral Martin: This was in 1965.

He had a lot of important people there, Senator Packwood and another senator, members of Congress, and also the Secretary of the Navy, Paul Nitze, was there that evening, and he spent quite a bit of time in conversation with my wife Friedel.† I thought that was very fortunate for me, because within a year, when I was considered for the Sixth Fleet, an assignment where the wife has—as he told me, and as Dave McDonald told me—the Sixth Fleet is probably the most unusual command in any of the services because about half the job is on the diplomatic side, and the wife has certain responsibilities. They are unwritten, but they are there, and I'm sure the background investigation of my wife, back in Europe, in Germany, was very detailed and very complete. I thought it was a real compliment to her that I was given command of the Sixth Fleet after just one year of marriage.

As a matter of fact, Secretary Nitze reminded me just before I left that the wife did have responsibilities, so much so that the Navy provided an airplane and a crew to take her where she should go. He said, "You take Friedel wherever you go, because she represents the United States better than you do."

I quite agreed with him, and so she did. She was superb on that assignment, because where were many times when I had to be at sea, and the diplomatic side of it had to be taken care of. I would arrive late in port, and she was there to take care of our

---

* Edward Hidalgo was a special assistant to the Secretary of the Navy in the mid-1960s. He later served as Secretary of the Navy.
† Robert W. Packwood, a Republican from Oregon, served in the Senate from 3 January 1969 until his resignation, effective 1 October 1995.

responsibilities on the social side, protocol and so on. She entertained beautifully. She had knowledge of a number of languages that she could handle, not fluently.

John T. Mason: Yes, but it's a tremendous asset, really.

Admiral Martin: A tremendous asset.

John T. Mason: You discovered very quickly then that there was no hindrance because it was a second marriage.

Admiral Martin: That's true, nor was it a disadvantage that she was a foreigner. Within a week or so after we were married, I was considered for the Seventh Fleet. The Seventh Fleet Commander, who name was Brick Blackburn, had gotten pretty seriously injured in a catapult accident, and they felt that he might be hospitalized more than a month, so they were considering replacing him.[*] When I was asked how long it would take me to pack, and I asked, "To go where?" They said command of the Seventh Fleet, and I said, "I'm already packed for that job." But I said, "I do have a little problem here, because my wife isn't naturalized yet, and she couldn't go with me unless she is, so I would like to have some help to speed up the process." So they did that.

She had only ten days, and there was a stack of books a foot high that she was given to study for the examination.

You may not want all this.

John T. Mason: Yes, it's very interesting.

Admiral Martin: English was not her second-best language then either. So I thought it would be almost impossible for her to go through those books and take the exam. So I went through them myself with colored crayons and scratched out everything—I used a yellow felt pen, you could still read through it. I marked those areas that I thought she

---

[*] Vice Admiral Paul P. Blackburn Jr., USN, served as Commander Seventh Fleet from 1 March 1965 to 7 October 1965.

should not study, because she wouldn't have time. For example, on the Civil War—have I told you this before?

John T. Mason: No.

Admiral Martin: I said, "I'm not proud of this period in our history, the War Between the States, and I just can't believe that on a rushed-up exam like this you will get a single question on the Civil War."

John T. Mason: Was this a verbal examination?

Admiral Martin: A verbal exam.

Ten days later, I went with her to the exam. I couldn't go into the examining room, but I could hear the exam.

John T. Mason: This was in the State Department?

Admiral Martin: This was on the fifth level of the Old Post Office Building at 12th and Pennsylvania. I could hear what was going on in there, and he asked her three questions about the Civil War. The first two she had right off. She had the answers to them, and I was amazed. I couldn't understand how she would know that, because I just knew that she hadn't had time to study it. The third question, though, was a Civil War question, and the answer was Abraham Lincoln. I can remember so well her saying to the examiner, "Sir, his name was Abraham," and she couldn't bring up Lincoln. And she said, "Sir, he's right behind you." There was a bronze bust of Lincoln sitting right behind the examiner.

He immediately called the Director of Naturalization. His name was Barton, and he came from Missouri, I found out later. He called Barton and said, "We have a lady down here who's making over 100%. So Director Barton came right down, and he asked her some questions. He was speaking in a low voice, and I couldn't hear what he said. But when he came out—

John T. Mason: You must have been very nervous.

Admiral Martin: I was. I said, "Mr. Barton, how does one make over 100% on a naturalization exam?"

"Well," he said, "in the case of this lady, it's simple. She gives you back more than you ask for. For example, I asked her how many of the original colonies she could name, and she named all 13 in the proper order in which they came in. Things that I couldn't answer. I also asked her if she could name four former Presidents of the United States, assuming that she knew the current one. She started with George Washington and gave the first and last names in proper sequence right up to the current one, which is Nixon. That's the way you make over 100%. You give back more than you've been asked."

Well, that word got around, too, you know, and probably, a few months later had something to do when I was given the job. It turned out that Blackburn recovered in time to go back to it.

John T. Mason: Yes, I realize he did.

Admiral Martin: Yes, and eventually Johnny Hyland went to that job. And so, when I was considered, I'm sure, for the Sixth Fleet, that also could have made a difference, the fact that she loved this country so much and was so interested in it, and she made over 100% on her naturalization examination.*

John T. Mason: At some point, however, she must have wondered what she was getting into, that she had to go through all of this.

Admiral Martin: You know, though, Jack, I think a lot of people who are naturalized, who have come here, have a deeper, day-to-day appreciation of this country than some of us whose forebears have been here for generations.

---

* Vice Admiral John J. Hyland, USN, served as Commander Seventh Fleet from 13 December 1965 to 6 November 1967. The oral history of Hyland, who retired as a four-star admiral, is in the Naval Institute collection.

John T. Mason: We just take it for granted.

Admiral Martin: We do take it for granted, and they don't. Her mother is the same and her daughter. They're just more enthusiastic about this country and more defensive about it. They become extremely active when this country is criticized, more than most of us.

Yes, that was an important part of that assignment in the Pentagon.

John T. Mason: Tell me how you were sprung loose from the Pentagon for sea duty. This was in 1967?

Admiral Martin: Yes, 1967. I don't think it was recorded, this story I told you about getting the assignment?

John T. Mason: This would be a continuation of what you told me about being called up to the Secretary's office and the CNO was present.

Admiral Martin: Yes. This was in April of 1967.[*] So we went to the Mediterranean. The Navy always provided—I think this was the custom and maybe it still is—an airplane to take the prospective fleet commander and his family and the personal items that he's going to need—all his uniforms and things of that kind—as soon as he gets there.

John T. Mason: You were succeeding whom?

Admiral Martin: I was succeeding Dick Ashworth.[†]

When we arrived, the flagship and the fleet commander's staff and the dependents they had with them were just completing the move from Villefranche to Gaeta, Italy. Monsieur de Gaulle had invited the United States to leave France, and all other

---
[*] Vice Admiral Martin commanded the Sixth Fleet from 10 April 1967 to 14 August 1968.
[†] Vice Admiral Frederick L. Ashworth, USN, commanded the Sixth Fleet from 9 May 1966 to 10 April 1967. His oral history is in the Naval Institute collection.

foreigners—foreigners to de Gaulle—to pull their military out of France. The homeport for the commander of the Sixth Fleet had been Villefranche since it began.

John T. Mason: This was only the homeport for the commander, though, wasn't it? It wasn't much of a fleet base for us, was it?

Admiral Martin: No, but his flagship and the families that were there, the ones that had come on, about 1,200 altogether. They were just completing the move to Gaeta when we arrived, so things were very unsettled ashore. I didn't get into much of that, because things began to happen within hours after I had told Admiral Ashworth, "I relieve you, sir."

The Greek coup, when the four colonels took over the Greek Government. Within another two weeks, because they had taken over and were in control with such confidence that the argument with Turkey over Cyprus boiled up again.[*] That was in April and May. Then, near the end of May, around the 26th, I was convinced that there were going to be hostilities between Israel and Egypt.

John T. Mason: Well, you wanted an active command.

Admiral Martin: Yes, I did. As a matter of fact, I don't think before I left that I had looked at the Sixth Fleet Commanders who'd been there. All of them loved the job and didn't want to leave. The ones who had stayed the longest were there when there was a lot of trouble, like Cat Brown.[†] He was there longer than anybody else. I had jokingly said I was going to stir up some trouble when I got there in order to stay as long as possible, but it was already stirred up. I really had nothing to do with it.

John T. Mason: What was it ordinarily, a two-year tour?

---

[*] King Constantine II became the Greek monarch in 1964. Colonel Georgios Papadopoulos led a bloodless coup against him on 21 April 1967. Constantine retained his title but was powerless. In December of that year he tried to overthrow the military junta but failed, at which point he and his family fled the country and went to Italy. Papadopoulos declared himself Premier in 1968 and President in 1973. He was ousted in a counter coup in 1973.
[†] Vice Admiral Charles R. Brown, USN, commanded the Sixth Fleet from 4 August 1956 to 30 September 1958. He was in the job during the 1956 Suez Crisis and the 1958 landings in Lebanon.

Admiral Martin: Ashworth was there 12 or 13 months. It depended, I guess. Others had been there for a year and a half. I think Cat Brown was the only one who'd been there as long as two years. Maybe it's because it was such a desirable job, and there's always somebody standing in the wings, eager to get in there.

As I say, about the 26th of May I was absolutely certain in my own mind that there were going to be hostilities between the Arabs and the Israelis. So I started moving some fleet units, which you could do at that time without asking questions. Being a protégé of Arleigh Burke, I took advantage of that, and I had the fleet moving towards the Eastern Mediterranean, that is, the units that we were going to need.

John T. Mason: How many carriers did you have?

Admiral Martin: Two.

John T. Mason: One on either side of the Med?

Admiral Martin: Sometimes they'd operate together. Under normal conditions, you just do the scheduling with available liberty ports. You would have them spread, but they would often get together for exercises, especially the big NATO exercises, we'd have them both there.

I got a call from Jack McCain, who was in London as CinCUSNavEur, and he said, "Bill, I've got Secretary Rusk on the other line, on the hotline."* I'm a little ahead of the story, because this was on the day the destroyer, which I believe was the first of June. That was the first day of the famous Five-Day War.† After hostilities had started, he called me and said—we were talking back and forth by teletype. That's really the best way to carry on a conversation, because you've got a record of it later.

---

* Admiral John S. McCain, Jr., USN, served as Commander in Chief U.S. Naval Forces Europe and Commander in Chief U.S. Naval Forces Eastern Atlantic from May 1967 to July 1968. Dean Rusk served as Secretary of State from 21 January 1961 to 20 January 1969.
† It is generally known as the Six-Day War of June 1967. It grew out of Egypt's action in closing the Gulf of Aqaba and moving troops into the Sinai Peninsula. Israel initiated the war on 5 June with air attacks on airbases in Syria, Jordan, and Egypt. In the days that followed Israeli forces completely defeated their Arab opponents and occupied the Golan Heights, West Bank of the Jordan River, the Sinai, and the east bank of the Suez Canal.

"Secretary Rusk wants to know where the major units of the fleet are." I think he said, "What's the center of gravity of the fleet?"

So I said, "Well, Jack, everything we're going to need is east of Crete, except for the amphibs, and they're on the way." They were slower.

He told this to Rusk. Then he called me again and said, "The Secretary wants to know where the fleet commander himself is. Where are you?"

I said, "I'm aboard my flagship, of course, east of Crete."[*]

So he told Rusk, and the story is—I've heard this from somebody besides McCain—that Dean Rusk said, "Thank God, Martin didn't ask permission, because if he had asked permission, he would have been told no or wait, and he would have been waiting a hell of a long time."

It points up one of the advantages of naval forces. You can move without disturbing any other nation. You're going to remain in international waters, and there is no permission required to do that.

John T. Mason: Provided you aren't checkmated by the White House.

Admiral Martin: Well, unless you are—yes, you could be checkmated there.

We were in a position, and we had the forces there if they had been needed, and really drew up our own set of rules that we would not go closer than 100 miles to any of the areas of the conflict—Egypt, Israel. We stayed 90 miles outside of Cyprus, at least 50 miles from Syria. We set our own limits in order that we wouldn't get the United States into an embarrassing situation. We weren't committed, but we were there if we had been committed. And that's another one of the uses of naval forces. The fact that you're there, even though you're not committed to either side, you're available if your country decides to side with one or the other. You're in position, and I'm sure it has a very decided stabilizing effect, the fact that you're out there.

---

[*] The guided missile light cruiser *Little Rock* (CLG-4) was Sixth Fleet flagship from 25 January 1967 to 22 August 1970.

Among the interesting things that happened there was the request that I received from news people to get aboard some ship of the fleet. They all wanted to get aboard the flagship. I really didn't need any of them. I personally didn't want any of them.

John T. Mason: What is the policy, actually?

Admiral Martin: The policy at that time was laid down by Mr. McNamara, who told me through the Navy that I would have exactly 14 members of the media and what countries would be included.

John T. Mason: Would the correspondents make their own selections?

Admiral Martin: I think that was done back in the Pentagon. They came out to me. There were four Americans; there were two British; and representatives from Italy, Spain, France. Well, they filled out the other 14.

John T. Mason: This in spite of de Gaulle's recent action, the French were still invited?

Admiral Martin: Yes. As a matter of fact, it made very little difference so far as our relationships back and forth were concerned. In the exercises that we had, French forces and our forces would operate together. In fact, the biggest exercise we had was with the French, and it appeared almost that de Gaulle didn't know anything about it.

These 14 newsmen were all gentlemen except two of the Americans who were very young and very ambitious, and they've become very well known since then.

John T. Mason: As investigative reporters?

Admiral Martin: There's nothing to be gained by mentioning their names.

John T. Mason: Did they turn out to be investigative reporters?

Admiral Martin: They were determined to find controversial things. For example, from the very beginning until past the end of their stay aboard, they stated that the Sixth Fleet had taken part in that Israeli war on the side of the Israelis. Even right up to the end, when everybody knew that this wasn't the case and the other 12 tried to explain that to them, curb them, and hold them down—but right up to the day they left, they weren't saying it directly, but they were making statements that left no doubt that they believed that we had taken part in that war.

John T. Mason: How long did you entertain all these reporters?

Admiral Martin: I didn't want to entertain them at all. As of matter of fact, I sent them all to the carrier, the *America*, because they could take better care of them; they had more space.[*] I really didn't have additional space.

John T. Mason: They were out from under foot too.

Admiral Martin: I would bring them over to the flagship, three or four at a time. I provided every detail that I could possibly dream up to convince these two that we were not taking part in that war on either side, using such things as letting them observe the loading of aircraft, letting them see the combat information center, which would give the radar plots of the aircraft that we had in the air, because we had to keep on training. It just had to be done. We had to fly. They could see from the radar plot that none of these aircraft came closer than 100 miles to any of the disputed areas. I finally brought up the two chiefs in charge of the catapults with their records to show that the planes that we had launched during this whole period could not have been launched combat loaded. They were launched for training flights only, because the pressures they used couldn't have gotten a fully loaded with ordnance—they couldn't have taken off with that.

John T. Mason: That sounds a little too technical for them.

---

[*] Captain Donald D. Engen, USN, was commanding officer of the aircraft carrier *America* (CVA-66) during the Six-Day War. The oral history of Engen, who retired as a vice admiral, contains discussion of the newsmen on board his ship during that period.

Admiral Martin: Well, it does, but they could ask the chiefs what is the pressure that's required to launch, let's say, an F-4 or an A-4 combat loaded. They'd give that to them, and the pressures required to launch these aircraft for a normal training flight. They were able to confirm that, but it still didn't impress them.

John T. Mason: What does this say about the unbiased nature of the profession?

Admiral Martin: I don't know, but as I told them—there were two Americans on there, and I do remember them. I remember all four of these. Bob Goralski.*

John T. Mason: Was he a reporter too?

Admiral Martin: He was a good one, yes. And Bill Gore. They were the two good ones, and they tried their best to convince these other two and told them, along with myself, that they were really unpatriotic, that they were doing their country a disservice to leave any doubt that the Sixth Fleet had taken part in that war on either side.

John T. Mason: Did they represent papers or—?

Admiral Martin: One of them represented *The New York Times*, and the other one represented the Associated Press. As I say, they've become well known since then, and they've both tried to contact me even recently. They were doing books, and I wouldn't have anything to do with them. As a matter of fact, I tried to get them discredited, and McNamara wouldn't do it.

That was the only big problem I had during that period, dealing with the press. The rest of it was a matter of keeping the forces trained and sharp, also doing some pretty unusual things at that time to take care of the maintenance that had to go on. A broken-down ship normally had to go all the way back into Naples, so I ordered the destroyer into Crete so they wouldn't have to go that far. We had to send a number of ships in there for repairs.

---

* Robert A. Goralski was a correspondent for NBC News from 1961 to 1975.

John T. Mason: What facilities in Crete?

Admiral Martin: Well, Souda Bay was available to us and would permit us to use the airfield and permit us to use the anchorage. The Greeks were very cooperative at that time, and there was no problem really at all of getting clearance to move the destroyer tender in there and operate.

John T. Mason: I take it that our initial problems with the colonels had been resolved?

Admiral Martin: Yes. I spent quite a bit of time with them after that and almost had them convinced that if they had come up with a constitution and free elections, we could probably get back together. They were complaining because we had stopped all military support and, I guess, had imposed other restrictions on them. As a matter of fact, Papadopoulos, who was the head of them, asked me, "Do you believe that this administration is pro-NATO?'

I said, "Yes, I believe that's true."

"Do you believe that it's especially pro-United States?"

I said, "I'm convinced that you are."

"Do you believe that this country is more peaceful than it was previously?"

I said, "I only know what I've read about the riots that you were having over here, the problem with transportation and utilities, but I believe that's true because certainly everything seems to be in order now. The buses run on schedule and things of that kind."

John T. Mason: Were they at that time opposed to the return of the King?

Admiral Martin: I don't know. I think so, but he said, "Well, in view of this, what kind of an ally does the United States want?"

I said, "We want to make sure that you are going to be a democracy and if you will complete this constitution that you said you're working on and you come up with free elections and you find yourselves still in elective positions, I think you're going to find the attitude of the United States quite different."

I seemed to get a response form that that indicated that they intended to do it. From what I've read since that time, though, I'm sure a lot of things were going on that I did not know about. Political prisoners were being taken and put off on one of the islands out there, and there were no doubt some abuses, some things going on that were not being reported in the news.

John T. Mason: At that time, were you, indeed, being the voice of he State Department?

Admiral Martin: No, I was just asked my personal opinion, and I'm sure I made I very clear that this was my personal opinion.

John T. Mason: Let me ask one other personal opinion.

Admiral Martin: Were you implying that I was speaking beyond my—?

John T. Mason: No, no, indeed, no. Seemingly, the general policy of the United States in insisting with various non-democratic governments that they set up a democracy seems to me to be a little unrealistic.

Admiral Martin: It is limiting. It isn't always in the nation's best interest to hold off for that. I agree with that, but I do believe that this was the policy, yes.

John T. Mason: Very often it is, in Latin America and other places where it seems that democracy couldn't function, at least democracy as we know it couldn't function.

Admiral Martin: This is true in several countries. My best friends in Spain, for example, said, "We need a strong leaders. We need another Franco. It's just our nature. We have to have a strong person."* And I think this is true in Iran.† It's quite clear that they need a strong central guy who can pull them together, because it's just a bucket of worms right now, and there's nobody in control.

John T. Mason: Yet we seem to be insisting that they have free elections and do all these things, and they're not compatible with—

Admiral Martin: That is the desire, but I see what your point is, and I quite agree with it. It's frequently in the nation's best interest to support a stable government, no matter what its leanings politically are. We've proven that we get along pretty well with Yugoslavia.‡ They haven't done anything to harm us. There have been some problems in South America in which we have insisted on our concept of democracy that was not in their best interest, because they need a strong leader.

John T. Mason: Well, that was a diversion I couldn't resist.
　　Going back to the facilities for the fleet repair and that sort of thing, you were talking about Souda Bay.

Admiral Martin: Yes, that was a big help to us on logistics of maintaining the fleet forces outside of normal logistic support terminals like Naples.

John T. Mason: Did we have access to Malta too?

Admiral Martin: Yes, we did then, because Dom Mintoff hadn't come in yet.§ Yes, we had access there. As a matter of fact, we would rotate the destroyer tender that had

---

* Francisco Franco was dictator of Spain from 1936 until his death in 1975.
† When the Shah left Iran in January 1979, the Ayatollah Ruhollah Khomeini seized power and declared the nation to be an Islamic republic. On 4 November 1979, about two months prior to this interview, Iranian militants seized the U.S. embassy in Teheran and took the staff members there as hostages. The hostages were ultimately released on 20 January 1981.
‡ In 1945 Josip Broz Tito established a Communist government in Yugoslavia. He broke ties with the Soviet Union in 1948. He remained the nation's ruler until his death in 1980.
§ Dom Mintoff was the leader of the Malta Labour Party from 1949 to 1984. He served as the nation's Prime Minister from 1955 to 1958 when it was still a British Crown Colony. Following Malta's independence from Britian, Mintoff was again Prime Minister from 1971 to 1984.

normally been at Naples for the entire deployment. We would move him back to Malta, just so they would get used to our being there and to continue our welcome there. It was not a big problem to send the destroyer tender down there. I've forgotten which one it was right now, but they did a wonderful job. Those ships had tremendous talent. If they couldn't get a certain part, they'd manufacture it. Just remarkable.

John T. Mason: Floating factories, weren't they?

Admiral Martin: Floating machine shops. It was very good. During my entire period with the fleet, I was so impressed with the capabilities and efficiency of our supply system, including the supply officers who were doing it, very high types. As a matter of fact, I was impressed with the Marines we had there.

On another occasion we kept those Marines at sea for over 30 days down off Cyprus, staying 90 miles out.

John T. Mason: This was earlier on?

Admiral Martin: No, this was later. They couldn't get ashore. We rigged up this deal of allowing them to come over to the aircraft carriers for liberty, and we'd open up the stores for them. We would provide means for them to play basketball and things like that. After two weeks of that, we arranged for them to go into Malta. We took a poll, and the men would rather come aboard the aircraft carrier than go to Malta.

John T. Mason: Well, Valletta didn't have much to offer, did it?

Admiral Martin: Apparently not, but they could get on terra firma. There are so many things you can do with a fleet that has that kind of capability and flexibility, even up to providing a form of liberty for them.

John T. Mason: That's rather imaginative.

Admiral Martin: It worked too.

John T. Mason: Was this something of your innovative skill?

Admiral Martin: At this point I don't know whether I thought it up or somebody on the staff did. Frequently, some guy on the staff has a concept, and the admiral buys it. I wouldn't claim it. I don't know whether it was mine or not. I thought it would work, though, and it did.

To get back to the situation in Gaeta, just before we left we had completely moved into our quarters. The fleet commander now has quarters for him, and one of the first things I did was ask for this kind of permission to establish quarters for the fleet commander so he didn't have to go through this thing of looking for a place to live when he's busy. It was sort of proof in my case because I went to sea and stayed there for quite a while shortly after I arrived.

John T. Mason: What did Mrs. Martin do at that point?

Admiral Martin: I was going to tell you about that. She had us settled in a penthouse that was overlooking the nicest beach in all of that part of the Mediterranean, called Serrapo Beach, and when I came back we were living in a farmhouse outside of a little place called Formia, and here's how that happened.

She found out—this was after I had gone to sea for this five-day war thing—that the enlisted men and most of the junior officers had their families there, both the staff and the ship, were making plans for them to come back to the United States because they simply couldn't pay their rentals. The rentals had gone up by a factor of three or four.

John T. Mason: Simply because the fleet was looking for a place?

Admiral Martin: Because everybody was looking for a place to live. The mayor of Gaeta had stated—nobody had questioned him too closely on this—that everyone connected with the Sixth Fleet staff and the Sixth Fleet flagship had to live in Gaeta, and he claimed that he had it in writing.

John T. Mason: From whom?

Admiral Martin: Well, this is part of the story. So my wife had made an appointment to see him. I was gone. She didn't know this, but I was going to be gone for over a month. She talked to him about the difficulties that they were having finding places to rent, and asked him finally, "Mr. Mayor, I want to see this document that you say you have that says that everybody connected with the flagship of the Sixth Fleet and the Sixth Fleet staff has to live in Gaeta," a small community. He went over to the desk and picked up a document in Italian that looked very official, brought it back, and handed it to her, not knowing she could read it. She handed it back and said, "Mr. Mayor, I am ashamed of you. This isn't even on the same subject. You do not have a document that says that, and just to prove to you that we don't have to live, all of us, in Gaeta, I've got to set an example. I am moving out of my penthouse with the next two days, as soon as I can find a place to live, and it's going to be outside of Gaeta. I'll let the others know for sure that they're not in trouble if they move out of Gaeta."

And she did. She found a little farmhouse outside of Formia, which was eight miles from Gaeta. I came back, expecting to be in this penthouse, and I was in this farmhouse over in Formia.

John T. Mason: The mayor didn't object at this point?

Admiral Martin: He couldn't. He was speechless. He was absolutely speechless.

You know what happened? The prices came down even more than they had been before, because they really wanted to keep us there because, you know, we'd do our marketing there and that sort of thing.

John T. Mason: Sounds like they had a monopoly.

Admiral Martin: They had a monopoly, and it was all through his statement that he had a document that said we had to.

The morale of the dependents when I came back was just unbelievable, and Mrs. Martin could do no wrong after that. They canceled their plans to go back to the States, and we had a very happy arrangement. As I say, the ones who stayed in Gaeta were able to get places that were even below what they had been before we moved in there in the first place. It was a good thing all the way around, because it opened up a lot of available rentals and spread the marketing around, so that there was some competition. It worked out very well. The mayor became very cooperative and very supportive after that.

John T. Mason: That's a remarkable incident, bearing out what Mr. Nitze said about her.

Admiral Martin: Exactly.

Well, let's see. When that settled down—things didn't really settle down, because all the Arab countries were closed to the Sixth Fleet. We had no liberty ports in Northern Africa.

John T. Mason: This was the immediate result of the Six-Day War?

Admiral Martin: Immediately.

John T. Mason: To that point we did have?

Admiral Martin: Yes, we could go into Libya, Tunisia, Algeria.

John T. Mason: We used Wheelus?[*]

Admiral Martin: We used Wheelus and were on very good terms with the head of state in Tunisia and with old King Idris.

---

[*] Wheelus Air Force Base in Libya.

VADM William I. Martin, Interview #6 (1/8/80) – Page 283

John T. Mason: Idris was in Libya.*

Admiral Martin: Yes, and this wild man Qaddafi took over while he was out of the country.

John T. Mason: He was in Turkey. I've often wondered whether he stayed in Turkey, or is he still alive?†

Admiral Martin: I didn't hear. He was old, and he was feeble at the time. He was not in good health, and I think one of the reasons he left was for his health.

We'd been on good terms with Morocco for a long, long time, and Morocco was one of the first ones to open up again. Before I left there, Morocco was available to us. We could go into Tunisia. Algeria was not too friendly.

John T. Mason: There was Boumedienne.‡

Admiral Martin: Yes. The name of the big base he had there was underground facilities for submarines and that sort of thing.

John T. Mason: Was that Bizerte?

Admiral Martin: No.

John T. Mason: Mers-el-Kebir?

Admiral Martin: Yes, a very useful port if we could have used it.

---

* Colonel Muammar el-Qaddafi became Libya's head of state as the result of a bloodless coup that seized power on 1 September 1969 and cast out King Idris I. Qaddafi proclaimed a republic but set himself up as a dictator and held power until he was killed by revolutionaries on 20 October 2011.
† King Idris died in exile in Cairo, Egypt in 1983 at the age of 94.
‡ Houari Boumedienne, supported by an army supplied with Soviet weapons, became head of state of Algeria in a bloodless coup in 1965. He declared himself President in 1976 and governed until his death in 1978.

John T. Mason: The French had just recently turned that over to them, hadn't they?

Admiral Martin: Yes, and then they in turn were turning it over to the Russians. They were able to go in there. It didn't become an accomplished fact until later.

Lebanon offered to open up if we'd buy so many thousands of barrels of apples. But by the time I left there, we still hadn't gone back in there. Plans were under way to go back in, and we have been in since that time.

John T. Mason: It was a costly Six-Day War for the fleet, wasn't it?

Admiral Martin: Yes, it was, but we continued to have successful small-scale operations with the small Tunisian Navy and the Moroccans, but not into Libya, of course, and, of course, friendly developments with Egypt took place quite some time after that.

John T. Mason: We want to mention the fact that there was such a ship as the *Liberty* because, I mean, if we're dealing with the Six-Day War we can't just overlook the fact that there was an incident of that sort, even though we're not going to comment on it.[*] I still want to mention the fact that this only heightened the difficulties for the commander of the Sixth Fleet.

Admiral Martin: Yes.

John T. Mason: This occurred on the seventh, eighth, and ninth of June.

Admiral Martin: That was a tragic thing. I believe there were 34 people killed and, as I recall, 191 injured. I flew over there as soon as I could. I took the flagship at high speed within range of a helicopter flight, went over, and was lowered away by cable to the deck of the *Liberty*.

---

[*] On 8 June 1967, during the Six-Day War between Israel and Egypt, Israeli aircraft and torpedo boats made a number of attacks on the U.S. communications intelligence ship *Liberty* (AGTR-5). Of the ship's crew of 297, 34 were killed and 171 wounded. Israel claimed that the attack on the *Liberty* was a case of mistaken identity and apologized. Many in the ship's crew were skeptical of the claim.

John T. Mason: How soon was this—?

Admiral Martin: After she was shot up, this was the next day.

When that ship was under attack, the first we knew about it was when my operations officer and my communications officer came up and told me what they were hearing on the radio, that there was a young voice down there that said that he was on a U.S. ship that was under attack. They recommended that I go down to communications, what we called the radio shack, and find out, so I could hear for myself.

Of course, none of these messages were being authenticated, which would be normally the case, that authenticates that this is a valid message, the authenticators on the beginning and end of the message. None of those were authenticated. They only had one circuit that was available to them, and there was this young voice that was telling that this U.S. ship was under attack. After listening to that for just a few minutes, three or four minutes, I was convinced, along with them, that it was, in fact, a U.S. ship that was under attack.

John T. Mason: Was it identified by name?

Admiral Martin: It was, yes.

John T. Mason: But you didn't even know it was there?

Admiral Martin: No.

Within ten minutes I had jets, both attack and fighters, launched and on their way down. They got about halfway there when this flash message came in from Tel Aviv.* It was a short message. As I recall, it was three paragraphs. It started out: "We have attacked a U.S. ship in error."

Paragraph two: "We are very, very sorry that we made this mistake."

And paragraph three: "What can we do to help the injured?" and so on.

---

* "Flash" is the highest precedence for Navy message traffic.

So I recalled this flight. It turned around and came back. I wondered what might have happened. I do know that if this had happened, they would have shot down everything in sight.

John T. Mason: Your planes would have?

Admiral Martin: Our planes would have shot down everything in sight. They'd have done everything necessary to protect that ship, and they'd have sunk the torpedo boats that were there. It would have really been a massacre.

John T. Mason: But, according to the story, Washington got in on this.

Admiral Martin: According to the story, they did, but I know very, very little about it, and I don't think that I would contributed anything worthwhile if I told what little I do know about it. As a matter of fact, I've just about done it.

We got the ship out of there and got doctors aboard.

John T. Mason: Where was she taken?

Admiral Martin: She was trying to get 100 miles out under her own power and finally went into Malta. That's where the court of inquiry was held, and Ike Kidd headed up the court of inquiry.* Ike may not want to talk about this either.

John T. Mason: Were you present for that?

Admiral Martin: Oh, no. I had to stay with the fleet.

John T. Mason: But you did later recommend that the skipper get the Medal of Honor?

---

* Rear Admiral Isaac C. Kidd Jr., USN.

Admiral Martin: Yes, because it was perfectly clear when I got aboard that he was seriously injured, but he was still in command of that ship.

John T. Mason: This was McGonagle?

Admiral Martin: Yes. He was a commander, later made captain.[*]

All of these late things that are being written about the *Liberty*—there are a lot of things in there that are new to me and some things I doubt. I don't think anything's to be gained by getting into that controversy.

John T. Mason: There was another incident, or another event. This was in the following year, and this might occasion some comment. In the middle of the year, I guess, you celebrated the 20th anniversary of the Sixth Fleet.

Admiral Martin: Yes.

John T. Mason: Do you want to talk about that?

Admiral Martin: That was my idea. I thought it would be so appropriate because I was so proud of the fleet and so convinced of the good it was doing by simply being there. I'd had these wonderful messages from various nations, in most cases from the head of state, expressing their appreciation for the fleet's presence and how much it had meant to them. One of them was very flowery in describing the ships that were out there, and he knew that this was indeed what we were calling: power for peace.

So we decided to have an anniversary. I had such terrific talent. There was Captain George Rodgers, who's a neighbor of mine here now.[†] He was my public relations officer. During World War II he was a very classy fighter pilot and was a reserve. I came to admire his work when I was Chief of Naval Air Reserves in Glenview, and he came out to be my public affairs officer there. I had to make special arrangements

---

[*] Commander William L. McGonagle, USN.
[†] Captain George F. Rodgers, USNR.

to get him to go to the Sixth Fleet, and he came down a couple of months later. The present Chief of Information, Admiral David Cooney, was a commander at that time, and was the public relations officer.* We had some differences at the beginning, but I came to admire him very much. The things that he told me I would get into trouble if I did, turned out to be exactly right. I did get into trouble.

John T. Mason: You mean over this celebration?

John T. Mason: No, it was something else. I know I'm jumping around here, but Admiral Ashworth had asked me would I honor and carry out a speaking commitment that he had made in Rome, to talk to the American Club there.

John T. Mason: Were those businessmen in the community?

Admiral Martin: Most of them were Americans in Rome or strong friends of America in Rome. I really don't know what the eligibility for membership was, but there were a couple of hundred people there.

What I decided to do was discuss what a fleet commander must do when he reports to a new job, reviewing his operation plans and that sort of thing. The situation at that time required a plan to be open-ended, because we really didn't know who were going to be our friends and who were going to be our enemies, and to consider some rather farfetched things that might happen so that we could take these under consideration like a contingency and at least have some plans for dealing with what might have otherwise been the unexpected and there be unprepared.

I was just walking them through this and made some statements that the Soviets didn't like. The Italian press was 30% Communists at the time, and they picked this up and headlined it. So, by the time I got back from Rome to the flagship, the Chief of Naval Operations wanted to talk to me directly on the phone, and he said, "Bill, what the hell did you say in Rome today? It's all over the press here."

---

* Rear Admiral David M. Cooney, USN, served as the Navy's Chief of Information from February 1975 to August 1980.

I gave him the gist of it, and he said, "Well, send me a copy of it, your remarks."

I said, "Admiral, I can't do that, because I talked from rough notes."

So he said, "Well, reconstruct it, put it on the wire right now, and send it back to me," which I did. But the Communist newspapers never let up on that.

Then *Pravda, Izvestia,* and *Red Star*, the Soviet press, picked this thing up and continued using it up to a couple of years ago. The last time they mentioned "Warmonger Martin" was two years ago.

John T. Mason: Indelible stamp you had.

Admiral Martin: Yes, that's right.

But the strong thing and what really took the heat off that was that at the same time I was speaking in Rome, Brezhnev was speaking in Czechoslovakia, at a luncheon there, and he was speaking very truculently on why the United States would have a fleet in the Mediterranean.* Why did the United States even dream that they were welcome in the Mediterranean, because they were not? He brought up the differences and distances of how far we were from the United States, and there we were acting like we were the biggest power in that part of the world, so far away. He asked for Czechoslovakian support on this, to demand that the United States withdraw their ships from the Mediterranean.

At that very moment, they were pouring ships from the Black Sea, through the Dardanelles, and into the Mediterranean. They built up from 12 ships to about 50, because we had 48 total in there at the time. When they'd finished, within a week or so of that, they had more ships than we had—I mean naval ships, combatants.

It was that realization that took the heat off of my speech in Rome, because they were building up at the time that they were demanding that we withdraw.

John T. Mason: And turn it over to them.

---

* Leonid I. Brezhnev served as general secretary of the Central Committee of the Soviet Union's Communist Party from 1964 until his death in 1982.

Admiral Martin: Yes.

John T. Mason: Well, to go with your story about the celebration, how you developed that.

Admiral Martin: Yes, the plans for it were drawn up, and they looked very good. I asked General Lemnitzer—*

John T. Mason: He was in Paris?

Admiral Martin: He was SACEur, and he, by this time, had moved out of France to Brussels. So General Lemnitzer, a wonderful man, came down. He was the reviewing officer, and I believe that every NATO country was represented, in many cases by what corresponds to our Chairman of the Joint Chiefs of Staff. We had a lot of high-level people aboard.†

John T. Mason: Where did the celebration center?

Admiral Martin: It was in the Eastern Mediterranean.

John T. Mason: You had traffic signals for the Russian fleet, did you?

Admiral Martin: Well, they joined up on us. They had their trailers, as we called them. Before I got there, they had been using trawlers that had a maximum speed of 16 knots. If you wanted to get away from them, you went about 16 knots and left them behind.

During the Arab-Israeli thing, because they really wanted to observe especially what we were doing on the carriers, they put destroyers in that could keep us with us, sometimes a cruiser. I made the headlines on that, too, because they were so close to us

---

* General Lyman L. Lemnitzer, USA, served as NATO's Supreme Allied Commander Europe from 1963 to 1969.
† The event was on 25 June 1968. Lemnitzer was on board the fleet flagship *Little Rock* (CLG-4) to watch the fleet pass in review.

when we were operating and maneuvering. We were just about to finish refueling, and two of them were right inside our formation. I sent them a message in Russian by voice and by dispatch telling them that they were endangering not only our forces but their own forces, that we would complete refueling in a few minutes, and then we would be maneuvering at high speed on various courses at various speeds. I pointed out that they'd been inside our formation, following us wherever we went all morning, and it was obvious that they were following us. It was not a coincidence that they happened to be passing through our formation. I just told them to get out; it was unsafe. The headlines back here were that the commander of the Sixth Fleet told the Soviets to get lost. Others said told to go to hell, which I hadn't, but I felt that way about it.

John T. Mason: Did they respond in message form?

Admiral Martin: No, they didn't come back at us.

John T. Mason: Did they get out?

Admiral Martin: Yes.

John T. Mason: You had a Russian interpreter on board.

Admiral Martin: Yes. It took him just a short while to draw up this message so I could release it, and he could give it to them in Russian over the tactical circuit. I'm sure they got it.

John T. Mason: You didn't really know; he might have told them to go to hell.

Admiral Martin: Maybe he felt stronger about it than I was willing to express. I hadn't thought about that. It's possible.

This parade we had just went off perfectly. The weather was good, every ship carried out what he had to do with excellent timing and excellent distances. General

Lemnitzer said then, and has said since, that in all of the times that he's seen military parades and ceremonies, that was the best.

John T. Mason: What role did CinCSouth have in this celebration?

Admiral Martin: He was there as a guest. We had a lot of guests. I guess CinCSouth was Rivets Rivero at the time.*

John T. Mason: Yes, it was in 1968, so it was borderline.

John T. Mason: Yes, because he relieved Don Griffin.†

John T. Mason: What sort of reaction did you get in the United States and the Navy to that?

Admiral Martin: Photographs of it and messages we got from several sources. Almost everybody in NATO came through with a congratulatory message on how well it was done, especially their appreciation for having been invited.

I really don't know the extent of media coverage that it got here at home. I know that people sent me clippings, though, that showed some of the photographs here, so it must have been pretty good.

John T. Mason: It must have been a fillip to the morale of the fleet too?

Admiral Martin: Yes, they were very proud, very proud, indeed.

I can see General Lemnitzer now. We had this platform up on top of number-one turret. Navy carpenters can do anything. It's just amazing, the talent that you have on a ship. They built this nice platform there that would seat all of the upper level of our

---

* Admiral Horacio Rivero, USN, served as Commander in Chief Allied Forces Southern Europe from January 1968 to May 1972. His oral history is in the Naval Institute collection.
† Admiral Charles D. Griffin, USN, served as NATO's Commander in Chief Allied Forces Southern Europe from March 1965 to January 1968. His oral history is in the Naval Institute collection.

guests and provide a place for Lemnitzer to stand where he could be seen as these ships were coming down on either side. We were steaming at good speed right down the middle. These columns were only 1,000 yards apart, so we were at 500 yards. A breakdown in the steering of the flagship would have been a pretty interesting and exciting event!

John T. Mason: A risk you had to take.

Admiral Martin: A risk we had to take.

Everything went off so well. Lemnitzer was so proud, as he stood and saluted each one of these ships as it came by, and they saluted. They had the rails manned, and they all saluted as they went by. He turned to me one time and said, "Why can't the Army put on something like this?" He was still saluting.

That was a day that the Sixth Fleet really deserved.

John T. Mason: Have there been subsequent celebrations?

Admiral Martin: I don't know. That was 11 years ago.

John T. Mason: They could have done it the 30th.

Admiral Martin: There could have been, yes, 25th and 30th.

John T. Mason: That causes me to ask what was the status of the Royal Navy in the Mediterranean at that point?

Admiral Martin: Sometimes there were no ships at all of the Royal Navy, and at other times two or three would be in there for a specific exercise. There were none in there permanently.

John T. Mason: After Suez, they began to move out, did they?

But still at that point they had control of the facilities in Malta, didn't they?

Admiral Martin: Yes, at that point.

John T. Mason: And Gibraltar?

Admiral Martin: And Gibraltar, yes. They had a governor general in Malta, and they had a governor general in Gibraltar and a flag officer there, a fellow named Davenport.

John T. Mason: FOIC, I guess he is.

Admiral Martin: Exactly, flag officer in command.
    But the Italians, the Greeks, and sometimes the Turks would take part in the NATO exercises we'd have in the Eastern Mediterranean. They would sometimes run out of funds and have to pull out of the exercise before it was over, although on a couple of occasions we refueled them ourselves, because it was important that they stay until the end of the exercise.

John T. Mason: Unreliable allies who run out of funds and depart.

Interview Number 7 with Vice Admiral William I. Martin, U.S. Navy (Retired)

Place: Admiral Martin's home in Alexandria, Virginia

Date: Friday, 18 January 1980

John T. Mason: Well, sir, after having talked about your being in the Mediterranean as commander of the Sixth Fleet, now, in 1968, you shifted your flag and came back to the Atlantic as Deputy CinCLant.[*]

Admiral Martin: Right. Eph Holmes had the big titles there.[†] He was SACLant, CinCLant, and CinCWestLant. I came back as his Deputy CinCLantFlt. Shortly after I retired, they made that assignment Deputy CinCLant and Deputy CinCLantFlt, one title.

John T. Mason: Just as a footnote, how does it happen that CinCLant is also CinCLantFlt when, in the Pacific, CinCPac is different from CinCPacFlt?[‡]

Admiral Martin: There are two reasons for that, I think. In CinCPac, all three of the services have sizable forces, so it is a joint command of the services, whereas in the Atlantic neither the Army nor the Air Force has forces permanently assigned to CinCLant. Certain op orders include them, but they're always provisional. There are operations plans that involve other forces, because the op order would be derived from the broader paper, and the plan would be for a specific operation. Those existed, but I'm not too familiar with them, because, as I say, I was the deputy for CinCLantFlt but not for

---

[*] Vice Admiral Martin served from August 1968 to February 1971 as Deputy Commander in Chief, U.S. Atlantic Fleet; Chief of Staff to Commander in Chief Atlantic Fleet; and Chief of Staff to Commander in Chief Atlantic.

[†] Admiral Ephraim P. Holmes, USN, served as Supreme Allied Commander Atlantic, Commander in Chief Atlantic, and Commander in Chief Atlantic Fleet from 17 June 1967 to 30 September 1970.

[‡] For a number of years prior, one four-star U.S. admiral simultaneously held the posts of Supreme Allied Commander Atlantic (SACLant), a NATO billet; Commander in Chief Atlantic Command (CinCLant), a joint-service U.S. billet; and Commander in Chief Atlantic Fleet (CinCLantFlt), a Navy-only U.S. billet. In 1985, the commands were divided, with one four-star admiral serving as SACLant and CinCLant and another four-star admiral as CinCLantFlt and Deputy CinCLant. The nominee for the SACLant/CinCLant job required international and U.S. Joint Chiefs of Staff approval because it was not Navy-only. In October 1999, the name of Atlantic Command changed to United States Joint Forces Command to emphasize the command's role leading transformation of U.S. military forces.

CinCLant. He had a small staff that took care of the joint matters. He was gone so much that there was plenty for me to do on the fleet side.

The SACLant job required him to go over to Brussels.

John T. Mason: That's what took him away so much, wasn't it, the NATO end of it?

Admiral Martin: Right. It was an extremely busy job, with the places he was supposed to appear, the titles he had, and he had an entirely different staff doing the NATO business, Supreme Allied Commander Atlantic. That staff had a number of foreigners on it, carefully selected, all of them outstanding officers. Jim O'Grady, a vice admiral, was his deputy for the NATO side of his job, the SACLant side of his job.[*]

As I say, I rarely got into the details of it, although Jim O'Grady and I were good friends, and we'd certainly keep each other informed of matters where there was a need for coordination.

But, to get back to your original question, why the different organizations in the Pacific command and the Atlantic command. I think service politics got into it also. From where I was looking at it, it appeared to me that SACLant really had to be a naval officer, because there was really so little for the Army and the Air Force to do initially, and they were just opposed to assigning forces to a basically naval command. I think that's always been true.

John T. Mason: At the time of the missile crisis, of course, CinCLant had another had, did he not, and he had large forces, Army and Air Force, under him?

Admiral Martin: At that time, that is true, and it was one of those occasions in which SACLant would break out some of his plans and derive some op orders from it that would involved the assignment of Army and Air Force forces.

I think Corky Ward was very much involved in that.[†]

---

[*] Vice Admiral James W. O'Grady, USN.
[†] Vice Admiral Alfred G. Ward, USN, commanded the Second Fleet from October 1962 to August 1963. The oral history of Ward, who retired as a four-star admiral, is in the Naval Institute collection.

John T. Mason: Yes, Corky was Second Fleet at that point, and, of course, Dennison was—*

Admiral Martin: CinCLant.

John T. Mason: And Dennison at one point had half a million troops under his command.

Admiral Martin: Yes. It was still basically a Navy show, though.

John T. Mason: Yes.

Admiral Martin: As it is right now, like today. The forces that they could move in, visible, viable forces that could be moved into the Persian Gulf-Indian Ocean area, where they could do any good at all were naval forces. They could move simply by a U.S. order, because they stay in international waters, and they don't have to go through a second or a third country at all to get permission to move. It is that flexibility that gives navies such exclusive capability.

That's why, of course, the blockade was almost exclusively a naval action in the Cuban Missile Crisis.

John T. Mason: Well, to revert to your job, tell me about the scope of it. What were you expected to do?

Admiral Martin: As I said, because Eph Holmes was gone so much of the time, I, as the deputy, took over his duties while he was gone. It was a matter of providing the op plans and the op orders for the Atlantic Fleet forces, of coordinating the various commands that support the fleet—Commander Service Force, Commander Naval Air Force, the Marines that were assigned—the branches that supported the fleet, together with the operating forces. They involved not only the exercises that were scheduled, we were running into

---

* Admiral Robert L. Dennison, USN, served as Supreme Allied Commander Atlantic, Commander in Chief Atlantic, and Commander in Chief Atlantic Fleet from 28 February 1960 to 30 April 1963. His oral history is in the Naval Institute collection.

periods where there were insufficient operating funds to do what we wanted to do. Then it was a matter of working out the priorities for that so that we got the most out of what we were putting operational money in there for.

John T. Mason: I would imagine that you were drained somewhat by what was going on in Vietnam, were you not?

Admiral Martin: Yes. There were forces that were assigned to the Pacific.

John T. Mason: Your own fleet forces?

Admiral Martin: Yes. We'd keep up with what was going on in the Vietnam War, but we had no direct responsibilities, of course, for it.

John T. Mason: How many carriers, for instance, did you maintain in the Atlantic at that time?

Admiral Martin: There were supposed to be six, but there were times when we'd have only five. Two of them were always deployed to the Mediterranean, to the Sixth Fleet, and we'd usually have one or two under repair or overhaul. That's almost always the case. They do that intentionally, to stagger them so that they will be able to put one in for a big overhaul that will take months. Then there are others that go in just to do patch-up as necessary to wait for a time when they can afford to put it out of commission long enough for a big overhaul.

It's been proven that to keep one carrier deployed and on station continuously requires a total of three to fill that job, but it's rare that you have that kind of backup.

John T. Mason: Does that pertain to the nuclear-powered ones too?

Admiral Martin: I think it does.

John T. Mason: They can go for much longer periods without—

Admiral Martin: Well, that's true, but, of course, they do a lot of things in the overhaul besides power plant.

John T. Mason: Oh, yes.

Admiral Martin: The periods of overhaul are different between nuclear powered and conventional powered, but different only from the standpoint of the power plant.

CinCLantFlt has capable force commanders, like Commander Service Force, a flag officer; Commander Naval Air Force, a flag officer; three-star Commander Amphibious Force. He had a two-star Marine directly on his staff, but for certain op plans, the Commander Fleet Marine Force Atlantic, who was a three-star, a lieutenant general, would, of course, come under him on occasion. And to it was a matter of having highly capable flag officers at the head of the various forces. It was a matter of coordination then and not a difficult one either, because I thought they got along fine, kept everything in balance. There seemed to be no argument about insufficient support for a certain operation, arguments about who was going to provide it and how much, and that sort of thing. It was a very well balanced staff in that regard, so this matter of CinCLantFlt, I thought, was one of monitoring the coordination and of providing support as necessary.

John T. Mason: Tell me about some of the significant events that happened in that tour.

Admiral Martin: Before you came, I was thinking about some of the significant events. From the point of CinCLantFlt, there were no special deployments. There were exercises that would take place. We had Pickles Heinz down there with the amphibs.[*] The amphibious commander would be the principal in some of the exercises we had, especially those that were coordinated with the Marines. Some of them would be in the

---

[*] Vice Admiral Luther C. Heinz, USN, Commander Amphibious Force Atlantic Fleet.

Caribbean, Puerto Rico, and some of them would be down on the coast of Carolina. There would be other exercises that would go up into the North Atlantic.

These were all well thought out and well planned, and once they were under way, here again it was a matter of CinCLantFlt monitoring from then on because they were always under the designated task force commander with forces assigned. Things went off so well that I really don't remember anything, any snags that we had.

John T. Mason: Did you have to maintain any kind of vigilance in the Cuban water area?

Admiral Martin: No, even that didn't come up. This plane that got everybody so upset didn't happen when I was there. You remember there was a Cuban who flew into Florida. Nobody knew he came in there until he'd come in. I wasn't there at the time, but that got everybody stirred up because I don't think the Air Force wanted to provide the forces from the Air Defense Command for that sector, because the possibilities of that happening in any significant force would require constant forces assigned to defend against it, just as it is not today. It might change now. They've got some advanced MiGs down there now. I understand that they claimed that they are not outfitted to carry heavy ordnance.

John T. Mason: We don't necessarily believe that, though?

Admiral Martin: I'm not convinced that we have any way of finding out for sure, because the external configurations just don't show up without very close examination by someone who knows what to look for.

The Air Defense Command has been getting less and less important, and less and less funds are being put into it. At the time the Air Defense Command was formed, there seemed to be a reason for it. The principal attack might be manned bombers, but it never came about. The big missiles took over, and the manned aircraft interceptors are not capable of handling defense against the big missile.

John T. Mason: Did CinCLantFlt have any cognizance over the training facilities at Guantánamo?*

Admiral Martin: Yes, he did. Of course, that's been established for a long, long time, and there was also the establishment at Roosevelt Roads on Puerto Rico, which is a very important training ground.† The argument about the use of Culebra and the other islands there—‡

John T. Mason: Vieques?§

Admiral Martin: Vieques was just getting heated up at that time.

Here again, there were some dissidents. Almost every place we'd have trouble, it seems to me that when we finally get the truth of it, it's Communists trying to stir up trouble, if they can, because that's when they make their big gains, when there's a lot of trouble.

John T. Mason: It certainly proves to be the case. When there is trouble, why don't we go right to the root of the matter?

Admiral Martin: Well, that's just it, and this is one of the biggest concerns. Everyone seems to have a reason to know that doing away with important elements of CIA and the downgrading that has happened there results in our not getting the kind of information we

---

* Guantánamo Bay, on the south coast of Cuba, near the eastern end of the island, for many years provided a fleet anchorage and training area for U.S. Navy ships.
† U.S. Naval Station Roosevelt Roads was located at the eastern edge of Puerto Rico. Its land mass consists of 31,000 acres: 8,600 acres on the island of Puerto Rico and 22,400 acres on Vieques Island, seven and one half miles southeast of the main station. The facility was completed in 1943, and Roosevelt Roads was commissioned as a U.S. Naval Operations Base. It served as both a training facility and base for Navy ships until being closed in 2004.
‡ Culebra, an island in the Caribbean, is 17 miles west of Puerto Rico. In 1939, the U.S. Navy began using the island as a target for gunnery and bombing practice. That lasted until 1975, when the target practice moved to the island of Vieques.
§ Vieques is a Caribbean island off the east coast of Puerto Rico. For many years the Navy and Marine Corps used it as a training site for amphibious landings and shore bombardment. In 2001 Puerto Rico's Governor Sila María Calderón Serra signed an agreement for the U.S. military to vacate the island. The U.S. departure began on 1 May 2003.

want.* I think we're going to have to build that up again with certain individuals. You can call it a spy organization if you want, but there's important information that you don't get any other way, the political elements that are involved. How do you find this out from a satellite or from aerial reconnaissance? You just don't find it out that way. There's a lot of information you can get only through having an agent underground working with the masses.

There's a lack of understanding, however, on just how important those training areas were to us. We looked for alternate areas, and they just weren't available. Of course, the areas where you can have—fenced off, so to speak—and use live ordnance, they've almost gone. Areas where you can have air-to-air training and that sort of thing. There are very few of those left. There was a time, not too many years back either, where we could operate on air-to-air exercises, training weapons, off our East Coast and off of Florida, Key West. There's still an area there that can be used, but it gets smaller and smaller. The military has to make more and more concessions to civil aviation and, of course, that's beginning throughout the Caribbean now. Civilian air traffic has so greatly increased, commercial air. There just was not an alternate area where you could establish the kind of fleet training area that permitted you to use the ordnance with training heads on it, and where you could put Marines ashore with the forces that were necessary to get them ashore, sustain them while they're ashore, and to defend the area against all sorts of threats, submarine and surface.

The loss of that training area was very serious. There just wasn't any other in the Atlantic that was available to us.

John T. Mason: What efforts did the Navy make, if any, to offset the fact that these areas were being taken away from them and the agitation that was going on to have them taken away from the Navy? What efforts did the Navy make?

Admiral Martin: We tried to make the point, to be as convincing as we could, of how valuable those areas were to us, and to study possible alternates, to show that there wasn't really an adequate fallback position.

---

* CIA – Central Intelligence Agency.

John T. Mason: Whom did the Navy have to convince, the State Department?

Admiral Martin: Well, the secretariat. There was a fellow named Graimes, who was an assistant to the Assistant Secretary of the Navy. We were dealing through our own secretariat and with the Office of the Secretary of Defense. We had people who were working very closely with them all the time, trying to make our case. It was a very difficult thing to do, because it didn't seem to me that our own secretariat was as convinced as I thought they should be of the importance of that area.

John T. Mason: When you had exercises at Culebra and places like that, did you invite DoD people down there to observe them, so that they would have firsthand knowledge?

Admiral Martin: Yes, we did. I would say that Eph Holmes in the periods that he was back in this country, back in his headquarters, that took up a lot of his time. Except for trying to show, as you say, through the exercises where they could come down and see for themselves, we made a very conscientious search for alternatives, and there were none. You could come back to a fallback position using a small area projecting out from the west coast of Puerto Rico, but it couldn't take the place of the instrumentation that had already been done. To try to establish that in another area and get the sea-lanes cleared for the period in which you were going to exercise and things like that was a very unsatisfactory alternate to the training grounds that we had out at Roosevelt Roads.

John T. Mason: Roosevelt Roads is still—?

Admiral Martin: It's still active.

John T. Mason: What actual threat was there to the Puerto Rican population on these islands? Was there any?

Admiral Martin: No. I don't remember all the details, but at the time that this first came up, it seems to me that there were fewer than 100 families involved in the whole island of

Culebra, and they were far better off with the Navy in there than they had ever been before, and they were far better off than they were going to be if the Navy pulled out. Yet you had these big demonstrations and riots that occurred then and I understand still occur down there. What stirred them up, I don't know. The governor at that time was a person to whom you could talk, and it seemed to me that he was agreeing with us, but he had this element that he still had to listen to.

John T. Mason: That was still Muñoz Marin, wasn't it?*

Admiral Martin: Yes. It was an unsolvable problem, just a problem without solutions. We weren't getting the support in our own Congress that we should have. There were some softheaded people who seemed to take the side of the opposition, the dissenters, without looking at what little they had to really complain about. It was no nearer solution when I left, when I was really familiar with it, than when we started, and I think it still goes on.

John T. Mason: What was the relation of CinCLantFlt with some of the Latin-American navies? What kind of cooperation would you attempt with them?

Admiral Martin: Well, we had this operation called UNITAS at the time.

John T. Mason: That was Arleigh Burke's creation, wasn't it?

Admiral Martin: Yes, it was Burke's creation. I think it was very well laid out from the beginning. Here's another case where it took very little of our time, because that operation went off so smoothly. The headquarters were in Puerto Rico, and he had his little force assigned. It was patterned for the smoothest kind of operations with the small navies that they would encounter if they went down around South America. You wouldn't take an aircraft carrier or a big cruiser on an operation like that, because you've

---

* Luis Muñoz Marin was Governor of the Commonwealth of Puerto Rico from 1 January 1949 to 2 January 1965.

got to match the forces to get the maximum participation with their navies. I don't recall any problems that they had.

John T. Mason: What were the attitudes within CinCLantFlt on the ability, in case there was a necessity to utilize some of these Latin-American naval forces—what credence would you place in them?

Admiral Martin: We didn't expect them to be capable of doing much more than defend offshore from their own borders. In fact, that was quite a goal for them to shoot at, to be able to contribute to the defense of their own waters. Their ASW efforts were the most important of all, and they were capable of doing some of that. Their equipment was obsolete from our standards, but the reports we'd get back were that most of those navies were quite capable of covering, protecting, their own waters, surveillance of those waters. Without exception, the commanders of the UNITAS forces made very valuable connections and developed good relationships with the head of the Navy, with the armed forces people, in those countries. It worked out just about the way Arleigh Burke expected it to.

John T. Mason: There was a command centered in San Juan, too, was there not, a naval command, a flag officer?*

Admiral Martin: I don't think so, Jack. There was a senior captain who had Roosevelt Roads and the admiral who had the UNITAS force. I don't remember a flag officer at Roosevelt Roads.

John T. Mason: Would you talk about antisubmarine warfare and the efforts of CinCLantFlt in that area? This became a paramount thing after the missile crisis, when we were suddenly alerted to the fact that the Soviets had submarines in that part of the world.

---

* The Tenth Naval District, commanded by a U.S. rear admiral, was headquartered at San Juan, Puerto Rico, from 1 January 1940 until it was disestablished on 30 September 1980.

Admiral Martin: They formed an ASW Forces Atlantic command. Vice Admiral Paul Masterton had that job at that time. It seems to me that his greatest value was operating various ASW forces in exercises and as the fleet contact point for the ASW deputy under the Chief of Naval Operations, where they worked in ASW across the board—air, surface, and subsurface.* That was under his cognizance as well—air, surface, and subsurface.

Frequently on the big exercises they would take part as part of the task force, especially if they were working at some distance from our coast. Those forces would be assigned as part of the bigger operation in the North Atlantic. Also, keeping track of submarine contacts, the unknowns, that they'd run across in the Atlantic, ones that were apparently being kept on station by the Soviets.

John T. Mason: This called for vigilance in the North Atlantic, up in the Iceland area and the channels that they would use.

Admiral Martin: Yes. Of course, those contacts were very classified then. I don't know whether they are now or not. I just mention that, but we were able to keep track of the submarines that came out of the northern areas, Murmansk and around the northern capes and down through the Greenland-Iceland-U.K. gap, and attempt to keep them plotted.

It was just the beginning, I believe, of the submarines that they had that were capable of long-range missiles.

John T. Mason: Were there any flights sponsored by NASA that had to be monitored or dealt with in your tour down there?†

Admiral Martin: No, I'm not aware of them. I don't recall where we had any responsibilities.

---

* Vice Admiral Turner F. Caldwell Jr., USN was then Director of Antisubmarine Warfare Programs in OpNav.
† NASA – National Aeronautics and Space Administration.

John T. Mason: What provision did you make for VIP visits to the fleet, the entertainment of them, the effort to educate them to the value of the fleet?

Admiral Martin: That wasn't too difficult to handle, because usually their schedule would be gone over in OpNav, sometimes Chinfo. The Chief of Information would be the principal, but when it would come to us, we would assign it to whatever force they were going to visit. We would draw up the schedule, and then we'd turn the part that was for ComNavAirLant over to him. If it was an amphibious matter, we'd turn that over to the commander of the amphibious forces. We had a small public relations staff—it was never big—that would monitor what they were doing and provide, as necessary, people to accompany for the fleet commander. Each of the various force commanders had his own show to put on, so it was just really a matter of turning it over to them and coordinating, if they were going to more than one force.

John T. Mason: Sometimes when the visiting dignitary was of sufficient stature, a head of state or something of that sort, it did involve the high command, didn't it, briefings in his presence and that sort of thing?

Admiral Martin: Yes. Here was another program that Arleigh Burke started, the visiting flag officers who would come from South America and from Europe, from all over the world. We had an auditorium where we were equipped and had sufficient talent to brief them and to entertain them while they were there. We had so much talent to call on that we tried to pattern the schedule, if it wasn't already made out by someone in Washington, to cover the areas that were of greatest interest to them. If their principal value would be in the ASW business, that's where they would spend most of their time; that was where they'd get their briefing. This was true of most of the small navies. ASW was not only the area of greatest interest to that country, their coastline, but the forces that they could afford were not capable of doing much more than ASW.

It was rare, of course, that you'd get anybody who was coming only to this one place, because the visiting Chiefs of Naval Operations from these various countries would have a schedule that would take them to five or six major places while they were on the visit, frequently starting with Washington and sometimes ending there.

John T. Mason: But your command would have a particular interest in delegations from Congress, because that's where your lifeblood came from.

Admiral Martin: That's right.

Paul Stillwell: How did you treat them?

Admiral Martin: Well, we'd always use the updated part of the sea-power presentation that Jack McCain first did. Have you talked to Jack yet?

John T. Mason: Yes.

Admiral Martin: Which is really getting into the basics of the exclusive capabilities of sea power. We could make that pitch. You had to be a little careful not to overdo it, perhaps, because I'm sure that that's what they got in Washington, too, the advantages of a navy. If it was a CNO from our area, from the Atlantic area, we would try to cover what they might contribute to a threat in their area, where they might fill in, supplement the forces that we might be putting in.

John T. Mason: You're talking about the foreign navies?

Admiral Martin: Yes, I'm talking about the foreign navies. For the members of Congress, you would try to show them, knowing what was in our budget, try to help the CNO's effort to convince them of the necessity of those forces or for the new systems that we were trying to get. It could be very supportive. We would be able to take them out aboard the ships and show them the areas where we wanted their support. Sometimes they'd make their own requests. Some of the members, especially those from the House or Senate Armed Services Committee, would come down sometimes at their own request, and they wanted to see certain specific things. It was not necessary for the CinCLantFlt staff to go with them, because we had so much talent in the various forces—amphibious force, air force, sub force, ASW forces, and the Marines—that would handle the details of those.

John T. Mason: Did you personally have any time for flying?

Admiral Martin: No. The Office of the Secretary of Defense had tried to eliminate what they call proficiency flying. In the days when I was a junior officer, every aviator had to fly at least four hours a month for pay purposes.

John T. Mason: Yes, flight time.

Admiral Martin: Flight time, and the Office of the Secretary of Defense decided that that was a place where they could save some money, so they kept whittling away at that, and the changed the requirement so that it was not necessary to fly four hours. It was not necessary on the part of any aviator to fly four hours a month, or even one hour a month. They would provide support only for those who were in active billets or who would likely go back to active billets. You'd provide proficiency flight time for a commander only if he had passed his aviator physical, and if he was likely to be reassigned to an active flying assignment.

There were not too many, and very few captains, but they were the ones who laid it out, and so they almost cut out the proficiency flying. I think it was a bad thing, because that's one of the complaints that you're hearing today, one of the reasons why aviators don't want to stay in the service, because they don't get to fly as much as they want. That's why they came in the service to begin with, and for them to be so restricted and limited in flying that it took the fun out of it for a while. Also, it kept them from maintaining proficiency. You'd have to give almost every one of them a refresher course if they were to go back into active flying.

John T. Mason: Does this mean that when you were deputy down there you didn't fly at all?

Admiral Martin: No, but I wasn't required to fly.

John T. Mason: But you did occasionally?

Admiral Martin: Yes, especially if I was in a multi-engine or multi-place aircraft going someplace where I could take over the flying. But there was not a requirement. For the first four years I was a flag officer, I did keep up my proficiency. But I had to do it on my own time, in the evenings, weekends, and at my own initiation. It was not a requirement, but it was something that I thought was valuable, and I still do. I think that they should permit a few of the pilots who want do to it—there are not that many of us who want to do it, really—the ones who really want to do it to the point of using their own time after hours, weekends, and nights. There are few enough that I think it would be valuable to do it, so that you have senior captains and flag officers, a few of them at least, who really keep their proficiency up and know what the youngsters are up against. I think it's extremely valuable to do that. But, no, it wasn't a requirement that I do it. I would when I could.

John T. Mason: Did you have to make many trips to Washington in that time?

Admiral Martin: I would fill in for the CinCLantFlt on certain conferences that were being held in Washington. There weren't too many. The home schedule would be made out so that on the big occasions, that you could forecast that he should attend, commanders' conferences and things like that, that the Chief of Naval Operations would call for, he'd try to arrange his schedule to be there for it, if it was important that he do it. But there were very few occasions, actually, surprisingly so. We had a lot of people from Washington visiting us.

John T. Mason: Where did you reside, in Norfolk?

Admiral Martin: Yes. They used to call it Admirals' Row—I guess they still do—these old buildings that were constructed by the various state in the exposition of '07.* These were built by the states at their expense to represent whatever architecture they wanted to represent. Almost all of the southern states, the houses that they had there—Maryland, Virginia House, West Virginia House. There were over 20 of those that were constructed for that exposition, all on Dillingham Boulevard down there. I think there are between 15 and 20 that are still being used.

John T. Mason: Virginia House is occupied by CinCLant, isn't it?

Admiral Martin: Virginia House is now occupied by CinCLant. At that time he was in Missouri House, and the commandant of the district was in Virginia House.

Eph Holmes's relief was Charlie Duncan, and Charlie came down before he moved down, looked over the situation, and decided that he preferred going to Virginia House, so the commandant was assigned to another set of quarters.† He was assigned to New Hampshire House, and they did quite a bit of renovating on the Virginia House before he moved in there.

John T. Mason: Yes, Charlie showed me a lot of pictures of it, of the interior. It was quite elegant.

Admiral Martin: It was. Missouri House was very nice too.

John T. Mason: And where did you live?

Admiral Martin: I first was in New Hampshire House. Then, when Charlie decided he wanted to go in Virginia House, it was decided that the deputy would be assigned to the Missouri House, which were the next most prestigious quarters. The fact is I thought

---

* The most senior U.S. naval officers in Norfolk live in houses that were built for the Jamestown Colony tricentennial exposition of 1907.
† Admiral Charles K. Duncan, USN, served as Supreme Allied Commander Atlantic, Commander in Chief Atlantic, and Commander in Chief Atlantic Fleet from 30 September 1970 to 31 October 1972. His oral history is in the Naval Institute collection.

that, taking into account everything, the grounds as well as the structure, the Missouri House was more desirable.

John T. Mason: Were you there in Charlie's time?

Admiral Martin: Only for two months, and shifting the senior quarters was quite a shakeup there. It took about two months to get things squared away. There was no big change between Charlie Duncan and Eph Holmes. They were both highly capable, both of them gentlemen of the highest order, good to work with, very pleasant to work with, and they certainly treated me like the deputy, because when they were gone I felt that I could resort to the old saying, "What would Farragut do? What would Holmes do? What would Duncan do?" It wasn't difficult to come up with decisions that couldn't wait for them.

John T. Mason: Well, your tour of duty with the Atlantic Fleet came to an end in 1971. This was your last tour of duty.

Admiral Martin: Early in '71—I had really come to a decision about four months prior to that, that in '71 I would have less than two years to serve before I would hit the age of 62, which was the mandatory retirement age. And that, together with not being too pleased with the way things were going in the Navy—I considered Admiral Zumwalt a friend, but I did have some basic disagreements with him.*

John T. Mason: On the content of the Z-grams?

Admiral Martin: Some of those, yes, Z-grams that seemed to be lowering our standards as far as so many things that were traditional. The uniform had gotten so terribly bad and

---

* Admiral Elmo R. Zumwalt, Jr., USN, served as Chief of Naval Operations from 1 July 1970 to 29 June 1974. During his tenure he made a great many dramatic innovations that attempted to deal with such issues as enlisted rights and privileges, equal opportunity, and Navy families. Junior personnel generally viewed the changes much more favorably than did their seniors. Z-grams were consecutively numbered policy directives from Chief of Naval Operations Zumwalt that attempted to deal with such issues as enlisted rights and privileges, equal opportunity, and Navy families. Junior personnel viewed them much more favorably than did their seniors. See *U.S. Naval Institute Proceedings*, May 1971, pages 293-298.

the general appearance, but also the thing that disturbed me most of all was that he encouraged everyone, regardless of status in the Navy, to write directly to him about complaints. This had the effect of undermining commanding officers and terribly so.

John T. Mason: Was this noticeable in the Atlantic Fleet?

Admiral Martin: Very much so, yes. As deputy commander in chief, they would come to me, especially if they were officers who had served with me before and knew that I would treat it with confidence. They would tell me what was happening. Here would be a commanding officer spending a large part of his time answering complaints that some of his enlisted personnel had written direct to the Chief of Naval Operations, with the encouragement of the Chief of Naval Operations. He was defending himself against complaints that had very little basis, complaints that, had they been brought up to him, I'm sure he was the kind of an officer who would have straightened them out in time. This was not just one officer but several.

When you undermine the commanding officer, you further undermine the chief petty officers, and that can do a great deal of damage to a service like the Navy that operates on mutual trust.

John T. Mason: The first thing is demoralization, isn't it?

Admiral Martin: Demoralization, terrible demoralization.

I'd always felt that if I couldn't be 100%, especially if I were a flag officer and I couldn't operate 100% loyal, totally loyal to the Chief of Naval Operations, it would be time to get out, and so I planned to retire. About that time I got a letter from Admiral Zumwalt that indicated that that was his desire, too, and so at least we were in harmony on my resignation, which I did on the first of February 1971.

John T. Mason: Tell me. During your time with the Atlantic Fleet, did you also have these minority reps on the ships? That was part of his endeavor, wasn't it?

Admiral Martin: I think it was just beginning. It hadn't materialized as yet, but there were some racial outbreaks that were of a type that we hadn't seen before. Here again, it was the result of tolerating dissenters who were not being treated unfairly. But when you start giving more attention and more concessions to dissenters than you do to those who are complying, things get out of hand.

There are so many examples that I could give you, but it would take too long to give them. They were mostly within this line. The rules about haircuts and general behavior that didn't appear to be too important of themselves, but they all tied in to changes that I thought were moving us from a tradition of first class in everything—first class in appearance, first class in performance, first class in results, to a downhill situation.

John T. Mason: Yes, I've heard men talk about the appearance, as you say, of the enlisted personnel in the Navy. Traditionally, they'd been looked upon as some kind of ambassadors in foreign lands, when they went ashore on liberty, and then turn out to be a ragtag kind of navy.

Admiral Martin: Exactly. It was just like an old saying that comes from my area, maybe before my day, that a really first-class outfit that put out a first-class performance also looked like a first-class outfit, and I believe that's true. I think that one is in harmony with the other, and I think if you don't have one, it will drag down the other. You cannot drag down performance, and therefore appearance becomes important.

I loved the Navy, and that's what I had wanted to do since I was nine years old, to become a naval officer, and it wasn't a happy thing to leave it, but it seemed the thing to do and, as it turned out, if I was going to leave the Navy, I left it at a very good time.

John T. Mason: How did Friedel feel about your getting out of the Navy?

Admiral Martin: She hadn't been in the Navy very long, but she loved the Navy and, if I may say so, the Navy loved her. She had a reputation of her own and had become so knowledgeable and so respectful of the Navy's customs and traditions that the same things that were bugging me were bugging her. But she's a very adaptable person and agreed with me that it was time to go. Long before I had mentioned to anybody that I might retire soon, I began to get letters from some interesting opportunities on the outside where I would be able to work.

John T. Mason: Your unexcelled experience with airplanes was a tremendous asset.

Admiral Martin: Well, not only in those areas, the aerospace areas, but also in a position where I would still be connected with the Navy in a way in which I might be able to serve it along with earning a living, and it turned out that way.

I had a number of offers, four of them that were very interesting, from aerospace companies in areas in which I could contribute and in which I could work probably with considerable flexibility.

I selected the one that I had the most respect for and that operated on principles that were very similar to my own.

John T. Mason: Which one was that?

Admiral Martin: That was Grumman Aerospace Corporation. I'd flown so many of their aircraft, and I'd flown a number of them under conditions that they were no longer expected to fly, they were so damaged, so I had a great respect for them. I had felt for some time that if I went with an aerospace company it would probably be Grumman, because I did have so much respect for them. It turned out that way, and I've had a very flexible situation with them. I've never been asked to do anything that was in conflict in any way with the rules and regulations of the Secretary of Defense or with my own principles. I've been able to operate mostly on my own initiative and to operate across the board.

John T. Mason: You're still with them?

Admiral Martin: Yes, I'm still with them. When I passed 65, I was told that there was no age limit in my case. We'll find out, though, this spring because I'll be 70. Sixty-five was their age limit, and we'll find out if 70 is their age limit.

John T. Mason: The law has changed, so—

Admiral Martin: Yes. In May we'll find that out.

I've been happy with what I've been able to do for the Navy through Grumman, and for Grumman through the Navy, and others who were in their customer line, without being or even appearing to be a lobbyist and without forcing my way or imposing my way in the hallowed halls of the Pentagon or Crystal City or Capitol Hill.[*] The fact is I go to those places only when I'm invited, and that turns out to be quite frequently enough. But I must say that the training that I had in the Navy has served me well. I've been able to work harmoniously with various segments of industry, operating on the same principles that I thought were wonderful principles of the Navy. So the training that the Navy gave me has been extremely useful.

John T. Mason: Well, that's a very fine statement to make.

Admiral Martin: And here's where Grumman has been very kind to me too. There were some things that I wished to do voluntarily. They were not going to pay me anything except the pleasure of working in those areas. The work I've done for the National Air and Space Museum and with the Naval Air Test Center at Patuxent River, Maryland, and evaluations that I continue to perform for the Naval Academy—these are things that I would like to do if no one was paying me anything, and I would be doing them. But very happily Grumman encourages me to work in those areas. So it's a little bit like being paid for your hobbies, and it turns out to be of value all the way around. If the chairman of the board and the president really meant it when I passed 65, telling me that I had no age limit, perhaps I'll be working for them several more years.

---

[*] Crystal City is the name for a large modern office complex in Arlington, Virginia, not far south of the Pentagon.

John T. Mason: Well, good, I hope you are, because I'm sure you can make a real contribution, and I do thank you for this series.

Admiral Martin: It's been a pleasure for me, Jack, I can really assure you.

Launched in 1969, the U.S. Naval Institute's award-winning oral history program is among the oldest in the country. Used in combination with documentary sources, oral histories offer a richer understanding of naval history through candid recollections and explanations rarely entered into contemporary records. In addition, they help depict the atmosphere of a particular event or era in a manner not available in official documents.

The nonprofit Naval Institute accomplishes its history projects through contributed funds and gratefully accepts tax-deductible gifts of all sizes for this purpose. This support allows the Institute to preserve the life experiences of today's service men and women so they may enlighten and inspire future generations.

For information about opportunities to underwrite Naval Institute oral history projects, please contact the Naval Institute Foundation at 291 Wood Road, Annapolis, Maryland 21402; by phone at (410) 295-1054; or by e-mail at foundation@usni.org.

Index to the Oral History of
Vice Admiral William I. Martin, U.S. Navy (Retired)

AJ Savage
Aircraft developed in the late 1940s for delivery of nuclear weapons, 91-92

Air Development Squadron Six (VX-6)
In 1961 a ski-equipped LC-130 from the squadron rescued an ill Russian scientist from Antarctica, 187-188

Air Force, U.S.
Controversial congressional hearings in 1949 about the B-36 bomber, 105-115
In the late 1950s ran the DEW Line and North American Air Defense Command to detect incoming Soviet bombers, 182-186, 208
Storage of inactive aircraft at Davis-Monthan Air Force Base in Arizona, 219-220
Navy opposition to Secretary of Defense Robert McNamara's attempts in the 1960s to make the TFX a carrier plane, 250-257, 263-264

Airships
Martin and CNO Admiral Arleigh Burke rode a blimp in the mid-1950s, 244-245
Blimps had advantages for ASW but also drawbacks, 245-246

Alcohol
During World War II, pilots drank on board aircraft carrier *Enterprise* (CV-6) to relax after missions, 74-76

***America*, USS (CVA-66)**
News media representatives boarded the ship during the Six-Day War of June 1967, 274

Amphibious Warfare
Support of the U.S. amphibious landing at Saipan in June 1944, 58-65
Atlantic Fleet exercises in the late 1960s, 299-300

Antarctica
In 1961 a ski-equipped LC-130 from VX-6 rescued an ill Russian scientist from Antarctica, 187-188

Antiair Warfare
Martin was shot down during a dive-bombing attack on Saipan in June 1944, 39, 58-67, 76-77
In the summer of 1945 Commodore Arleigh Burke got Martin ordered to the U.S. Fleet staff for anti-kamikaze experimental work, 78-80
The Atlantic Barrier Wing was a Navy-run patrol between Argentia, Newfoundland, and the Azores in the late 1950s to detect incoming Soviet bombers, 180-195

By the late 1970s the role of the North American Air Defense Command had diminished, 300

Antisubmarine Warfare
Blimps had advantages for ASW in the mid-1950s but also drawbacks, 245-246
Carrier Division 19 ASW operations in the Pacific in the late 1950s, 196-204
By the Atlantic Fleet in the late 1960s-early 1970s, 305-306

Arctic
Cold-weather training course conducted in the early 1950s by Canada's McGill University, 131-135

Argentia, Newfoundland
In 1958-59, Martin commanded the Atlantic Barrier Wing at Argentia, 124, 133, 180-195

***Arkansas*, USS (BB-33)**
Midshipman cruise to Europe in the summer of 1931, 8-12

Army, U.S.
Role in the 1949 inter-service squabbles, 113

Ashworth, Vice Admiral Frederick L., USN (USNA, 1933)
Commanded the Sixth Fleet, 1966-67, 269-271, 288

Atlantic Barrier Wing
Navy-run patrol between Argentia, Newfoundland, and the Azores in the late 1950s to detect incoming Soviet bombers, 180-195

Atlantic Fleet, U.S.
The Atlantic Barrier Wing was a Navy-run patrol between Argentia, Newfoundland, and the Azores in the late 1950s to detect incoming Soviet bombers, 180-195
Involvement in the 1962 Cuban Missile Crisis, 296-297
One of three command hats for Admiral Ephraim P. Holmes, 1967-70, 295-297
Coordination of type commanders in the late 1960s, 297-300
Diminishing training areas for the fleet since the 1960s, 301-304
Antisubmarine warfare activities in the late 1960s-early 1970s, 305-306
Coordination of VIP visits to the fleet in the late 1960s-early 1970s, 307-308

Aurand, Lieutenant Commander Evan P., USN (USNA, 1938)
Involved in testing air-to-air rockets in 1945 as possible anti-kamikaze weapons, 79-80

Aviation Cadets
Valuable assets in fleet squadrons in the 1930s, 223

Azores

The Atlantic Barrier Wing was a Navy-run patrol between Argentia, Newfoundland, and the Azores in the late 1950s to detect incoming Soviet bombers, 180-195

B-36 Peacemaker

Controversial congressional hearings in 1949 about this Air Force bomber, 105-115

Bainbridge, USS (DLGN-25)

Vice Admiral Hyman Rickover's involvement in the ship's design in the 1950s, 170-171

Operations in 1963-64 included being part of a nuclear-powered task force, 229-240

Barbers Point, Hawaii, Naval Air Station

Site of the Fleet All-Weather Training Unit Pacific (FAWTUPAC) in the late 1940s, 103-104, 115-116, 135

Blackburn, Vice Admiral Paul P. Jr., USN (USNA, 1930)

Briefly commanded the Seventh Fleet in 1965, 266

Blake, Lieutenant (junior grade) Albert P., USNR

Flew from the aircraft carrier *Enterprise* (CV-6) during the invasion of Saipan in June 1944, 64-66

Blimps

Martin and CNO Admiral Arleigh Burke rode a blimp in the mid-1950s, 244-245

Blimps had advantages for ASW but also drawbacks, 245-246

Bombs/Bombing

Use of TBF Avengers from Torpedo Squadron Ten (VT-10) for bombing attacks in 1944, 34-39, 58-65, 76-77

Support of the U.S. amphibious landing at Saipan in June 1944, 58-65

A kamikaze damaged the aircraft carrier *Enterprise* (CV-6) in May 1945, 71-73

U.S. Army Air Forces planes bombed Japan with nuclear weapons in August 1945, 70-71, 81-82, 91

Post-World War II Navy plans for nuclear weapons delivery, 85, 91-92

Controversial congressional hearings in 1949 about the Air Force's B-36 bomber, 105-115

The Atlantic Barrier Wing was a Navy-run patrol between Argentia, Newfoundland, and the Azores in the late 1950s to detect incoming Soviet bombers, 180-195

Bradley, General of the Army Omar N., USA (USMA, 1915)

As Chairman of the Joint Chiefs, was critical of the Navy during 1949 congressional hearings, 113

Brezhnev, Leonid
    In the late 1960s the Soviet leader criticized the U.S. naval presence in the Mediterranean, 289-290

Budgetary Considerations/Issues
    Naval aviation budget in the mid-1960s, 261

Bureau of Aeronautics (BuAer)
    Relationship with the Naval Air Test Center in the late 1940s, 101

Burke, Admiral Arleigh A., USN (USNA, 1923)
    Wife Roberta, 164, 248
    In 1944-45 served as chief of staff to Vice Admiral Marc Mitscher, 150
    In the summer of 1945 got Martin ordered to the U.S. Fleet staff for anti-kamikaze experimental work, 78-81
    As a member of the General Board in 1947-48 kept in touch with the Naval Air Test Center, 84-85, 91-92
    In 1949 headed OP-23 during the Navy's fight against the Air Force, 112-114
    Sudden elevation to CNO in 1955 over flag officers who had been senior, 157-158
    In 1955 got Martin command of an aircraft carrier, 137-139
    In 1956-57 Martin served as his executive assistant, 128-129, 148-177, 244-248
    Relationship with foreign navies, 173-174, 212, 304-305
    In 1959 asked flag officers for suggestions to improve the Navy, 194-195
    Involved in Martin's billet assignments in 1959-60, 196-201, 205-206
    Philosophy on quick response in operational assignments, 230-231

Byrd, Rear Admiral Richard E., USN (Ret.) (USNA, 1912)
    Complaints from and about in the mid-1950s, 149-151, 169-170, 238

C-130 Hercules
    In 1961 a ski-equipped LC-130 from VX-6 rescued an ill Russian scientist from Antarctica, 187-188

Canada
    Cold-weather training course conducted in the early 1950s by McGill University, 131-135
    In 1958-59, Martin commanded the Airborne Early Warning Wing at Argentia, Newfoundland, 124, 133, 162, 180-195

Canadian Navy
    Antisubmarine operations in the Pacific in the late 1950s-early 1960s, 199

Carl, Major Marion E., USMC
    Superb pilot who flew at the Naval Air Test Center in the late 1940s, 99-100

Carrier Division Two
    Operations in the Mediterranean in the early 1960s included a nuclear-powered task force, 229-240
    Involvement in exercises with foreign nations in the early 1960s, 241-243

Carrier Division Five
    Operations in the Pacific in the late 1950s, 177-178

Carrier Division 19
    Antisubmarine operations in the Pacific in the late 1950s, 196-204

Chaplain Corps, U.S. Navy
    In the mid-1950s Chaplains James Kelly and John O'Connor worked on a moral leadership program for CNO Arleigh Burke, 161

Christensen, Captain Ernest E. Jr., USN (USNA, 1934)
    Commanded the aircraft carrier *Hornet* (CVS-12) in 1959-60, 197

Clark, Captain Thurston B., USN (USNA, 1927)
    Served as senior aide to the Chief of Naval Operations in the mid-1950s, 148-149

Coast Guard, U.S.
    Iceberg patrols in the North Atlantic in the late 1950s, 180-183

Coffin, Lieutenant Albert P., USN (USNA, 1934)
    Commanded Torpedo Squadron Ten (VT-10) in the autumn of 1942 in the Guadalcanal campaign, 49

Cold Weather Operations
    In the late 1940s the Naval Air Test Center did experiments flying a patrol plane in icing conditions, 121-124
    Cold-weather training course conducted in the early 1950s by Canada's McGill University, 131-135

Commercial Aircraft
    As a Naval Academy midshipman in the early 1930s, Martin flew home to Missouri in a Ford Tri-Motor, 14
    In the lat 1940s a KLM pilot alerted the Navy on icing conditions, 121-122

Communications
    In February 1959 the Soviet trawler *Novorossisk* cut transatlantic underwater cables near Newfoundland, 188-193
    Radio report in June 1967 from the U.S. intelligence ship *Liberty* (AGTR-5) while under attack, 285
    Message from Israel that its forces had attacked the *Liberty*, 285

Congress, U.S.
    Representative Dewey Short helped Martin get a Naval Academy appointment in 1940, 3-4
    Controversial congressional hearings in 1949 about the Air Force's B-36 bomber, 105-115
    Strong support for Navy programs over the years, 212
    Relationship with the Naval Air Reserve in the early 1960s, 218-219
    Relationship with Secretary of Defense Robert McNamara in the 1960s, 254-255
    Naval aviation testimony in the mid-1960s, 261-263
    Visits to the Atlantic Fleet in the late 1960s-early 1970s, 308-309

Conn, Lieutenant Lannie, USN (USNA, 1927)
    Flight instructor at Pensacola in the late 1930s, 24

Connolly, Commander Thomas F., USN (USNA, 1933)
    Served as first director of Test Pilot School at Patuxent River, 1948-51, 86-87, 96
    As Deputy Chief of Naval Operations (Air), 1966-71, opposed the TFX, 256-257

Conolly, Vice Admiral Richard L., USN (USNA, 1914)
    As president of the Naval War College, 1950-53, 128, 130

Cooney, Rear Admiral David M., USN
    In the late 1960s was Sixth Fleet public affairs officer, later Chief of Information, 1975-80, 288

Corpus Christi, Texas, Naval Air Station
    Site of flight training at the beginning of World War II, 28-29

Crete
    Souda Bay Served as a logistics base for U.S. Sixth Fleet ships in 1967, 275-278

Crommelin, Captain John G., Jr., USN (USNA, 1923)
    Provided information to the congressional committee investigating the Air Force's B-36 bomber in 1949, 109-115

Cuban Missile Crisis
    Array of U.S. forces involved in the October 1962 event, 296-297

Culebra Island, Puerto Rico
    Diminishing Atlantic Fleet training facilities in the area since the 1960s, 301-304

Dace, Lieutenant (junior grade), Carl C., USN
    Young test pilot at the Naval Air Test Center in the late 1940s, 96-97

Davis, Captain William V., Jr., USN (USNA, 1924)
Involved in the establishment of Test Pilot School at Patuxent River in the late 1940s, 86

Day, Lieutenant Colonel Karl S., USMCR
Around 1940 wrote a book on instrument flying, 28

Defense Department
Cut back on proficiency flying for senior naval aviators in the 1960s, 309-310

De Gaulle, General Charles
In 1967, at the behest of French President de Gaulle, the U.S. Sixth Fleet moved its flagship's homeport from France to Italy, 269-270

Discipline
At the Naval Academy in the early 1930s, 7, 14-15

Doyle, Vice Admiral Austin K., USN (USNA, 1920)
In the early 1930s promoted aviation to Naval Academy midshipmen, 12
In the mid-1930s served on board the battleship *Idaho* (BB-42), 17, 147
In the mid-1950s was Chief of Naval Air Training, 146-147

Duncan, Admiral Charles K., USN (USNA, 1933)
Served 1970 to 1972 as Commander in Chief Atlantic Fleet, 311-312

Duncan, Admiral Donald B., USN (USNA, 1917)
Served 1951-56 as Vice Chief of Naval Operations, 162-163

Egypt
Positioning of the U.S. Sixth Fleet during the Six-Day War of June 1967 between Egypt and Israel, 271-276

Eisenhower, President Dwight D. (USMA, 1915)
Relationship in the 1950s with CNO Arleigh Burke, 174-176

Empire Test Pilots' School, England
Association in the late 1940s with the Naval Air Test Center, 97-98, 101

Enlisted Personnel
Martin's two TBF crewmen were killed when their TBF was shot down at Saipan in June 1944, 66-67
Yeomen took dictation from CNO Arleigh Burke in the mid-1950s, 153

Enterprise, USS (CV-6)
Took part in the Guadalcanal campaign in autumn 1942, 44-50

Lieutenant Commander Butch O'Hare was killed in November 1943 while doing night fighter experiments, 42-43

Ship from which Torpedo Squadron Ten (VT-10) operated in 1943-44, 33-39, 49-50, 58-67, 75-76

Treatment of a wounded Japanese destroyer skipper on board the carrier in June 1944, 76-77

Operated in 1944-45 as a night carrier with Night Air Group 90, 40-44, 52-57, 67-70

A kamikaze damaged the ship in May 1945 and knocked her out of the war, 71-73

During World War II, pilots drank on board to relax after missions, 74-76

Enterprise, USS (CVAN-65)
Operations in 1963-64 included being part of a nuclear-powered task force, 152, 171, 229-240

FH Phantom I
Used in night interception tests at the Naval Air Test Center in 1949, 108-109

FR Fireball
Combination jet-propeller plane the Navy operated briefly in the mid-1940s, 90

F3D Skyknight
Night fighter flown at the Naval Air Test Center in the late 1940s, 108-109, 117-118

F4U Corsair
Used in 1945 tests of rockets as anti-kamikaze weapons, 79-81

F7F Tigercat
Fighter that Martin used in the late 1940s to visit various air stations and talk about all-weather flight requirements, 93-94

F-14 Tomcat
Capability in the 1970s when equipped with radar and the Phoenix missile, 117-119

F-111 Aardvark
Navy opposition to Secretary of Defense Robert McNamara's attempts in the 1960s to make the TFX a carrier plane, 250-257, 263-264

Felt, Admiral Harry D., USN (USNA, 1923)
In the late 1930s commanded Bombing Two (VB-2) on board the aircraft carrier *Lexington* (CV-2), 128

Served in the early 1950s as deputy to the president of the Naval War College, 128, 130

As Vice Chief of Naval Operations, 1956-58, 128-129, 165-166

Fleet All-Weather Training Unit Pacific (FAWTUPAC)
Instrument training, 1948-50, 103-104, 115-116

In the mid-1950s moved from Hawaii to San Diego, 135-136

Flight Training
Martin received flight training at Pensacola Naval Air Station, 1937-38, 21-26
Martin was an instructor at Pensacola in 1940-41, 27-28
Martin served 1941-42 as a flight training instructor at Corpus Christi, 28-29

Ford Trimotor
Commercial aircraft in which Martin flew home from the Naval Academy in the early 1930s, 14

France
In 1967, at the behest of French President Charles de Gaulle, the Sixth Fleet flagship moved its homeport from Villefranche to Gaeta, Italy, 269-270

French Air Force
Involvement in NATO exercises in the early 1960s, 241-242

French Navy
Involvement in NATO exercises in the early 1960s, 241-242

Gaeta, Italy
In 1967 became the homeport of the Sixth Fleet flagship, 269-270
Housing situation for U.S. Navy personnel and dependents in 1967, 280-282

Gallery, Rear Admiral Daniel V., Jr., USN (USNA, 1921)
Vetoed by General Lauris Norstad in 1959 for the post of deputy chief of the U.S. Military Assistance Advisory Group to West Germany, 204-205

General Board of the U.S. Navy
As a member of the General Board in 1947-48, Arleigh Burke kept in touch with the Naval Air Test Center, 84-85, 91-92

Germany
Role of the U.S. Military Assistance Advisory Group in aiding West Germany in the early 1960s, 204-212

German Navy
Role of the U.S. Military Assistance Advisory Group in the early 1960s, 209-212

Glenview, Illinois, Naval Air Station
In the early 1960s was the base for the Chief of Naval Air Reserve Training, 213-229

Gray, Captain James S., USN (USNA, 1936)
In the early 1950s headed the all-weather flight desk in OP-05, 120

Greece
    Military coup in 1967, 270
    Relationship with the U.S. Sixth Fleet in 1967, 275-278

Grumman Aerospace Corporation
    In the 1970s published brochures to explain carrier planes to new members of Congress, 251
    Martin worked for the company after his retirement from active naval service in 1971, 315-317

Guadalcanal
    Battle of Santa Cruz Islands, October 1942, 44-46
    Martin landed on the island in the autumn of 1942 when he couldn't get back to the carrier *Enterprise* (CV-6), 47-48

Gunnery-Naval
    Exercises by the battleship *Idaho* (BB-42) in the mid 1930s, 18-19
    Naval gunfire support in the invasion of Saipan in June 1944, 62-63

Hall, Captain Grover Budd H., USN (USNA, 1921)
    Commanded the aircraft carrier *Enterprise* (CV-6) in 1944-45, 75

Hamilton, Commander Thomas J., USN (USNA, 1927)
    Served in the mid-1940s as executive officer of the aircraft carrier *Enterprise* (CV-6), 36

Harlow, Bryce
    In 1949 served as chief counsel to the House Armed Services Committee, 110-111

Hartwig, Lieutenant Commander, USN (USNA, 1924)
    Commanded the destroyer *Russell* (DD-414) when she rescued survivors at the Battle of Santa Cruz Islands, October 1942, 46

Helicopters
    In 1955 the aircraft carrier *Saipan* (CVL-48) used helos to provide post-hurricane rescue and relief for the area of Tampico, Mexico, 143-145

Hidalgo, Edward
    Hosted a party in 1965 the day Martin and his second wife were married, 265

Hollandia, New Guinea
    Role of Torpedo Squadron Ten (VT-10) in supporting the U.S. landing at in April 1944, 49-52

Holmes, Admiral Ephraim P., USN (USNA, 1930)
Served as Supreme Allied Commander Atlantic, Commander in Chief Atlantic, and Commander in Chief Atlantic Fleet from 1967 to 1970, 127, 295-297, 303

Hornet, **USS (CV-8)**
Sunk in the Battle of Santa Cruz Islands in October 1942, 44-46

Hornet, **USS (CVS-12)**
Served as flagship for Carrier Division 19 during ASW operations in the Pacific in 1959-60, 196-197, 201-204

Hurricanes
In 1955 the aircraft carrier *Saipan* (CVL-48) provided post-hurricane rescue and relief for the area of Tampico, Mexico, 140-146

Hyland, Admiral John J., USN (USNA, 1934)
Served as a Navy test pilot during World War II, 86
Commanded the Atlantic Barrier Wing in 1959-60, 182-183, 197
Commanded the Seventh Fleet, 1965-67, 268

Idaho, **USS (BB-42)**
Modernization at Norfolk Navy Yard, 1931-34, 16
Operations in the mid-1930s, including gunnery and floatplane aviation, 15-20

Independence, **USS (CVA-62)**
In 1958 Martin was slated to be her first commanding officer but was selected for flag rank instead, 139, 179

Information, Navy Office of (Chinfo)
Support for the Naval Air Reserve in the early 1960s, 222-223

Indianapolis, **USS (CA-35)**
An SOC floatplane from the ship rescued Martin in June 1944 after he had been shot down off Saipan, 63-65, 76-77

Instrument Flying
Martin's interest in the discipline developed in the late 1930s at Pensacola, 26-27
Martin wrote a book in the early 1940s on instrument flying for carrier pilots, 28-29
Use of in Torpedo Squadron Ten (VT-10) in 1943-44, 33, 49-52
Projects at the Naval Air Test Center in the late 1940s, 83-84, 96-97
In the late 1940s Martin visited various naval air stations to talk about all-weather flight requirements, 93-95
Role of the Fleet All-Weather Training Unit Pacific (FAWTUPAC) in the late 1940s, 103-105, 115-116
In the early 1950s aviator students of the Naval War College got their instrument training at Quonset Point, 120, 129-131

In the early 1950s OP-05W put out an OpNav instruction on instrument flying, 125-126

Intelligence
After being shot down at Saipan in June 1944, Martin gathered information about the island, 61

Isley, Lieutenant Commander Robert E., USN (USNA, 1933)
Killed by Japanese antiaircraft fire while bombing Saipan in June 1944, 58-59

Israel
Positioning of the U.S. Sixth Fleet during the Six-Day War of June 1967 between Egypt and Israel, 271-276
Israeli attack on the U.S. intelligence ship *Liberty* (AGTR-5) in June 1967, 284-287

Issit, Commander Donald K., USN
In 1949 trained Admiral Arthur Radford in instrument flying, 104

Italy
In 1967 Gaeta became the homeport of the Sixth Fleet flagship, 269-270, 280-282

Japan
U.S. carrier-plane attacks on the home islands in early 1945, 70-71
U.S. Army Air Forces planes dropped atomic bombs on Japan in August 1945, 70-71, 81-82
Potential use of kamikazes if the United States had invaded the home islands, 70-71

Japanese Navy
Was short on experienced carrier pilots after heavy losses at Midway in June 1942, 42-43
Treatment of a wounded Japanese destroyer skipper on board the aircraft carrier *Enterprise* (CV-6) in June 1944, 76-77
A kamikaze damaged the aircraft carrier *Enterprise* (CV-6) in May 1945, 71-73

Joint Chiefs of Staff
CNO Arleigh Burke's participation in JCS meetings in the mid-1950s, 156-157
Access to the President diminished, beginning in the 1960s, 174-177

Kamikazes
Potential use of if the United States had invaded the home islands of Japan during World War II, 70-71
A kamikaze damaged the aircraft carrier *Enterprise* (CV-6) in May 1945, 71-73
In the summer of 1945 Commodore Arleigh Burke got Martin ordered to the U.S. Fleet staff for anti-kamikaze experimental work, 78-81

Kane, Lieutenant Commander William R., USN (USNA, 1933)
 Commanded Fighting Ten (VF-10) from the aircraft carrier *Enterprise* (CV-6) during the invasion of Saipan in June 1944, 61-62

Kauffman, Lieutenant Draper L., USN (USNA, 1933)
 Led an underwater demolition team during the U.S. invasion of Saipan in June 1944, 60-63

Kelly, Commander James W., CHC, USN
 In the mid-1950s worked on a moral leadership program for CNO Arleigh Burke, 161

Kidd, Rear Admiral Isaac C., Jr., USN (USNA, 1942)
 Conducted a court of inquiry in 1967 into the Israeli attack on the intelligence ship *Liberty* (AGTR-5), 284-287

King, Vice Admiral Ernest J., USN (USNA, 1901)
 Served as Commander Aircraft Battle Force, 1938-39, 29-30

Koch, Rear Admiral George P., USN (USNA, 1933)
 Served from 1963 to 1965 as Chief of Naval Air Reserve Training, 227-228

Korte, Lieutenant Commander Ernest J., USN
 In 1959 commanded the radar picket destroyer escort *Roy O. Hale* (DER-336), which sent a boarding party to a Soviet trawler that cut underwater cables near Newfoundland, 188-193

Lang, Captain James G., USN (USNA, 1930)
 In the mid-1950s commanded the aircraft carrier *Saipan* (CVL-48), 140-141, 147

Leave and Liberty
 For midshipmen on a summer training cruise to Europe in 1931, 8-10
 Arab liberty ports in the Mediterranean were closed down to Sixth Fleet ships following the Six-Day War in 1967, 282-284

Lee, Vice Admiral Fitzhugh, USN (USNA, 1926)
 In the late 1950s commanded Carrier Division Five, 177-178
 In the early 1960s served as Chief of Naval Air Training, 227

Lemnitzer, General Lyman L., USA (USMA, 1920)
 As NATO's SACEur, attended the Sixth Fleet's 20th anniversary celebration in 1968, 290-293

Leonard, Captain William N., USN (USNA, 1938)
 Test pilot who testified to Congress in 1949 hearings on the B-36 bomber, 107

Liberty, USS (AGTR-5)
  Israeli attack on the U.S. intelligence ship in June 1967, 284-287

Libya
  Coup installed a new government in 1969, 282-283

Lighter-Than-Air
  Martin and CNO Admiral Arleigh Burke rode a blimp in the mid-1950s, 244-245
  Blimps had advantages for ASW in the mid-1950s but also drawbacks, 245-246

Little Rock, USS (CLG-4)
  Served as Sixth Fleet flagship during the Six-Day War of June 1967, 272, 284
  Reviewing ship for the Sixth Fleet's 20th anniversary celebration in 1968, 290-293

Lockheed Corporation
  Worked with the Navy in the late 1940s in testing patrol planes in icing conditions, 121-123

Long Beach, USS (CGN-9)
  Operations in 1963-64 included being part of a nuclear-powered task force, 229-240

Malta
  Served as a logistics base and liberty port for U.S. Sixth Fleet ships in 1967, 278-279

Mann, Commander Hoyt D., USN (USNA, 1936)
  In the early 1950s served as an instrument training instructor at Quonset Point, 131

Manson, Lieutenant Commander Frank A., USN
  Public affairs officer who was a speechwriter for CNO Arleigh Burke in the mid-1950s, 154

Marianas Islands
  Martin was shot down during a dive-bombing attack on Saipan in June 1944, 39, 58-67, 76-77

Marine Corps, U.S.
  Air operations from Guadalcanal in autumn of 1942, 44

Martell, Vice Admiral Charles B., USN (USNA, 1930)
  Chided Martin for performing better at sea than ashore, 127

Martin, Vice Admiral Harold M., USN (USNA, 1919)
  Served as ComAirPac, 1952-56, 136-137

Martin, Vice Admiral William I., USN (Ret.) (USNA, 1934)
  Parents, 1-4

Siblings, 2-3
Second wife Friedel, 10, 238, 264-269, 280-282, 314-315
Children, 77
Boyhood in Missouri in the 1910s and 1920s, 1-2
Attended the University of Oklahoma and University of Missouri, 1938-40, 3-4
As a Naval Academy midshipman, 1930-34, 5-15
Served 1934-37 in the battleship *Idaho* (BB-42), 15-20
Received flight training at Pensacola Naval Air Station, 1937-38, 21-26
Served 1938-40 in Scouting Squadron Two (VS-2), 29-32
Served 1940-41 as a flight training instructor at Pensacola, 26-27
Served 1941-42 as a flight training instructor at Corpus Christi, 28-29
Served 1942-43 as executive officer/commanding officer of Scouting Squadron 10 (VS-10), 44-49
Commanded Torpedo Squadron Ten (VT-10), 1943-44, 30-39, 49-52, 58-67, 76-77
Commander Night Air Group 90, 1944-45, 40-44, 52-57, 67-77
In the summer of 1945 served on the U.S. Fleet staff for anti-kamikaze experimental work, 78-81
From 1945 to 1948 served as a test pilot at the Naval Air Test Center, Patuxent River, 82-102, 121-124
Served 1948-50 as executive officer of the Fleet All-Weather Training Unit Pacific (FAWTUPAC), 103-119
As a student at the Naval War College, 1950-51, 120, 128-131
Attended a cold-weather training course conducted in the early 1950s by Canada's McGill University, 131-135
From 1951 to 1953 was all-weather flight coordinator in OP-05W, the Air Warfare Division of OpNav, 119-120, 125-126
Served 1953-55 as commanding officer of the Fleet All-Weather Training Unit Pacific (FAWTUPAC), 135-137
Commanded the aircraft carrier *Saipan* (CVL-48) in 1955-56, 138-147
In 1956-57 Martin served as CNO Arleigh Burke's executive assistant, 128-129, 148-177, 244-248
Served 1957-58 as chief of staff to Commander Carrier Division Five, 177-180
In 1958-59, commanded the Airborne Early Warning Wing at Argentia, Newfoundland, Canada, 124, 133, 162, 180-195
Commanded Carrier Division 19 in the Pacific, 1959-60, 196-204
In 1960-61 was deputy chief of the U.S. Military Assistance Advisory Group in West Germany, 205-210
Served 1961 to 1963 as Chief of Naval Air Reserve Training, 212-229
Commanded Carrier Division Two, 1963-64, 152, 229
Served as Assistant CNO (Air) from 1964 to 1967, 248-250
Commanded the Sixth Fleet, 1967-68, 265-290
From 1968 to 1971 was deputy and chief of staff for Commander in Chief Atlantic Fleet, 295-315
Post-retirement work for Grumman Aerospace Corporation, 315-317

Masterton, Vice Admiral Paul, USN (USNA, 1933)
Commanded Antisubmarine Warfare Force Atlantic Fleet in the late 1960s, 305

McCain, Vice Admiral John S., USN (USNA, 1906)
Commanded Task Force 58 in 1944-45, 73

McCain, Admiral John S. Jr., USN (USNA, 1931)
Service in OpNav in the 1950s included presentations on sea power, 112, 160
Served as CinCUSNavEur during the Six-Day War of June 1967, 271-272

McDonald, Admiral David L., USN (USNA, 1928)
Served as Chief of Naval Operations, 1963-67, 252-253

McGonagle, Commander William L., USN
Commanded the intelligence ship *Liberty* (AGTR-5) when she was attacked by Israeli forces in June 1967, 284-287

McKechnie, Rear Admiral Arnold W., USN (USNA, 1927)
In 1961 was relieved early as Chief of Naval Air Reserve Training because of a heart attack, 212-213

McNamara, Robert S.
Position on the controversial TFX aircraft in the mid-1960s, 250-257, 263-264
Martin's assessment of McNamara as SecDef, 254-255
Relations with Congress, 254-255

Medical Problems
Treatment of a wounded Japanese destroyer skipper on board the aircraft carrier *Enterprise* (CV-6) in June 1944, 76-77
In 1955 Martin had surgery to remove World War II shrapnel, 137-140

Mexico
In 1955 the aircraft carrier *Saipan* (CVL-48) provided post-hurricane rescue and relief for the area of Tampico, 140-146

Miles, Rear Admiral Milton E., USN (USNA, 1922)
In October 1955 commanded U.S. hurricane relief in the area of Tampico, Mexico, 144-145

Military Assistance Advisory Group
Role in advising the West German armed forces in the early 1960s, 204-210

Miller, Rear Admiral George H., USN (USNA, 1933)
Service in OpNav in the 1950s, 112-113, 154, 160

Miller, Captain Shirley S., USN (USNA, 1927)
    At the Naval War College in the early 1950s, 130

Mitscher, Vice Admiral Marc A., USN (USNA, 1910)
    Commanded Task Force 58 in 1944-45, 73, 78-79

Mumma, Rear Admiral Alfred G., USN (USNA, 1926)
    As Chief of the Bureau of Ships, briefed CNO Arleigh Burke in the mid-1950s, 160-161

National Advisory Committee for Aeronautics (NACA)
    Interaction in the late 1940s with the Naval Air Test Center, 95-96

Naval Academy, Annapolis, Maryland
    Plebe year in 1930-31, 5-7
    Academics in the early 1930s, 6-7, 10-11
    Summer training cruises in the early 1930s, 8-13
    Aviation orientation in the early 1930s, 12
    Only half the class of 1933 graduated that year; others came back later, 23
    First-class year in 1933-34, 13
    Discipline in the early 1930s, 7, 14-15

Naval Air Test Center, Patuxent River, Maryland
    Site of flight testing from 1945 to 1948, 82-102
    Testing of foreign planes after World War II, 89-90, 98-99
    Establishment of Test Pilot School in 1948, 85-87, 96
    Relationship with aircraft manufacturers in the late 1940s, 100-101, 121-124
    Involved in controversial congressional hearings in 1949 about the Air Force's B-36 bomber, 107-109

Naval Ordnance Test Station, Inyokern, California
    Testing of 4½-inch air-to-air rockets at China Lake in the summer of 1945 as possible anti-kamikaze weapons, 79-81

Naval Reserve, U.S.
    Role of the Chief of Naval Air Reserve Training in the early 1960s, 213-229
    Call-up of reservists to active duty in the 1940s-60s, 225-226

Naval Reserve Officer Training Corps (NROTC)
    Training at various universities in the early 1960s, 224

Naval War College, Newport, Rhode Island
    In the early 1950s aviator students of the college got their instrument training at Quonset Point, 120, 129-131
    Leadership in the early 1950s, 128
    Curriculum, 130

Navigation
On board the aircraft carrier *Saipan* (CVL-48) in 1955, 142-144

Needham, Rear Admiral Ray C. "Bud," USN (USNA, 1931)
Served in the Bureau of Naval Personnel in the late 1950s, 178-179

Newcomer, Commander Lloyd E., USN
Served on the Atlantic Barrier Patrol in the late 1950s, 187
In 1961 commanded an LC-130 mission that rescued an ill Russian scientist from Antarctica, 187-188

New Guinea
Role of Torpedo Squadron Ten (VT-10) in supporting the U.S. landing at Hollandia in April 1944, 49-52

News Media
Coverage of the Sixth Fleet during the Six-Day War of June 1967, 273-275
Negative coverage of a speech Martin made to Americans in Rome in the late 1960s, 288-289
Covered ceremonies for the Sixth Fleet's 20th anniversary in June 1968, 292

Newton, Lieutenant Commander Walter H. Jr., USN (USNA, 1933)
During World War II served on the staff of Rear Admiral John W. Reeves Jr., 204-205

Night Flying
Martin began doing tactical development work in 1938-40 in Scouting Squadron Two (VS-2), 29-32
Use of the TBF Avenger for night operations in 1943-44, 32-39
Lieutenant Commander Butch O'Hare was killed in November 1943 while doing night fighter experiments, 42-43
Role of Night Air Group 90 on board the aircraft carrier *Enterprise* (CV-6), in 1944-45, 40-44, 52-57, 67-70
Projects at the Naval Air Test Center in the late 1940s, 83-84, 96-97, 107-109, 121-124
In the late 1940s Martin visited various naval air stations to talk about all-weather flight requirements, 93-95
Role of the Fleet All-Weather Training Unit Pacific (FAWTUPAC) in the late 1940s, 103-105, 115-116
Training for pilots of Carrier Division 19 in 1959-60, 202-203

Nitze, Paul H.
As Secretary of the Navy in the mid-1960s had difficulties in dealing with Secretary of Defense Robert McNamara, 252-253
In 1965, on the day of Martin's second marriage, Nitze sized up his new wife, 265, 282

Norden Bombsight
Used in Navy torpedo planes in the late 1930s-early 1940s, 30-31

Norfolk Naval Base
Admirals' Row quarters for senior officers in the late 1960s-early 1970s, 310-312

Norstad, General Lauris, USAF (USMA, 1930)
As NATO Supreme Allied Commander Europe in 1959, vetoed Rear Admiral Dan Gallery for the U.S. Military Assistance Advisory Group in Germany, 204

North American Air Defense Command
In the late 1950s had the mission of detecting incoming Soviet bombers, 182-183
By the late 1970s its role had diminished, 300

North Atlantic Treaty Organization (NATO)
Role of the U.S. Military Assistance Advisory Group in aiding West Germany in the early 1960s, 204-210
Involvement of the U.S. Sixth Fleet in exercises with foreign nations in the early 1960s, 241-243
General Lyman Lemnitzer, SACEur, attended the Sixth Fleet's 20th anniversary celebration in June 1968, 290-293
From 1967 to 1970 Admiral Ephraim P. Holmes served as SACLant, 295-296

Nuclear Power Program
Admiral Hyman Rickover's involvement with the frigate *Bainbridge* (DLGN-25) and carrier *Enterprise* (CVAN-65) in the 1950s and 1960s, 170-171
Operations in 1963-64 of the nuclear-powered task force of *Enterprise* (CVAN-65), *Long Beach* (CGN-9), and *Bainbridge* (DLGN-25), 229-240

Nuclear Weapons
U.S. Army Air Forces planes bombed Japan in August 1945, 70-71, 81-82, 91
Post-World War II Navy plans for nuclear weapons delivery, 85, 91-92

O'Connor, Lieutenant John J., CHC, USN
In the mid-1950s worked on a moral leadership program for CNO Arleigh Burke, 161

O'Grady, Vice Admiral James W., USN (USNA, 1936)
In the late 1960s served as deputy to NATO's Supreme Allied Commander Atlantic, 296

O'Hare, Lieutenant Commander Edward H., USN (USNA, 1937)
Killed in November 1943 while doing night fighter experiments, 41-42

OP-05
Martin's work from 1951 to 1953 was all-weather flight coordinator in the Air Warfare Division of OpNav, 119-120, 126

In the early 1950s OP-05W put out an OpNav instruction on instrument flying, 125-126

Activities of the office in the mid-1960s included the TFX squabble, 248-257, 263-264

Impact of the Vietnam War and other issues on naval aviation in the 1960s, 258-260

Naval aviation budget in the mid-1960s, 261

Testimony to Congress in the mid-1960s, 261-263

OP-23
The Organizational Research and Policy Division of OpNav during the Navy's 1949 fight against the Air Force, 112-114

P2V Neptune
Forerunner of this plane was tested in the late 1940s to ascertain its ability to fly in icing conditions, 121-123

Patuxent River, Maryland, Naval Air Station
Site of flight testing from 1945 to 1948, 82-100

Pearson, Lieutenant (junior grade) Charles B., USNR
Killed on a torpedo attack near Palau Island in March 1944, 38

Pensacola, Florida, Naval Air Station
Site of flight training in the late 1930s-early 1940s, 21-27

Homeport for the aircraft carrier *Saipan* (CVL-48) in the mid-1950s, 140, 146-147

Phillips, Lieutenant Commander John L. Jr., USN (USNA, 1933)
Was the commanding officer of Torpedo Squadron Ten (VT-10) in the carrier *Enterprise* (CV-6) when Lieutenant Commander Butch O'Hare was killed in November 1943, 41-42

Planning
Preparation in 1963-64 for Operation Sea Orbit, the around-the-world cruise by a nuclear-powered task force, 233-240

Polaris Missile Program
Involvement of CNO Arleigh Burke in the mid-1950s, 167

Program Evaluation Review Technique (PERT)
Used for the Polaris program in the late 1960s, 167-168

Promotion of Officers
In the late 1950s Martin was deep-selected for rear admiral and denied command of the aircraft carrier *Independence* (CVA-62), 178-180

Public Relations
On behalf of the Naval Air Reserve in the early 1960s, 222-223, 226
In the late 1960s Martin made a controversial speech to Americans in Rome, 288-289

Puerto Rico
Diminishing Atlantic Fleet training facilities in the area since the 1960s, 301-304

Quilter, Lieutenant (junior grade) Edward S., USNR
Flight instructor at Pensacola in the late 1930s, 25

Quonset Point, Rhode Island, Naval Air Station
Instrument training site for Naval War College students in the early 1950s, 120, 129-131

Raborn, Rear Admiral William F., Jr., USN (USNA, 1928)
Frequent calls to the CNO's office in the mid-1950s concerning the Polaris program, 149-150, 167-169

Racial Issues
In the early 1970s in the Atlantic Fleet, 313-314

Radar
Used on board TBF Avengers for night operations in 1943-44, 32-34, 37, 41-42
Role of in night fighter operations in the late 1940s-early 1950s, 116
Capability of the F-14 Tomcat in the 1970s when equipped with radar and the Phoenix missile, 117-119

Radford, Admiral Arthur W., USN (USNA, 1916)
As Vice Chief of Naval Operations in the late 1940s, directed Martin to visit various naval air stations to discuss all-weather flight operations, 93-95
As Commander in Chief Pacific in 1949, qualified as an instrument pilot, 104-105
In 1949 sent Martin to Washington for the congressional hearings on the Air Force's B-36 bomber, 105-115
Personal relationship with Martin, 136

Ramsey, Vice Admiral Paul H., USN (USNA, 1927)
In the mid-1930s served on board the battleship *Idaho* (BB-42), 17, 103
In the late 1940s commanded the Fleet All-Weather Training Unit Pacific (FAWTUPAC), 103-104, 115
In 1965-66 was Deputy Chief of Naval Operations (Air), 17, 254

Reeves, Rear Admiral John W. Jr., USN (USNA, 1911)
    Commanded Task Group 58 from the aircraft carrier *Enterprise* (CV-6) in 1944, 65-66, 74, 204-205

Rescue at Sea
    An SOC floatplane from the heavy cruiser *Indianapolis* (CA-35) rescued Martin in June 1944 after he had been shot down off Saipan, 63-66
    Rear Admiral John W. Reeves organized rescue teams during air operations in 1944, 65-66

Revolt of the Admirals
    Controversial congressional hearings in 1949 about the Air Force's B-36 bomber, 105-115

Rickover, Vice Admiral Hyman G., USN (USNA, 1922)
    Complaints from and about in the mid-1950s, 149-152, 237-238
    Involvement with the nuclear power program in the 1950s and 1960s, 170-171, 229-230, 236-238
    Got into areas that were not his direct responsibility, 171-172
    Miffed because his plan for Operation Sea Orbit was not accepted, 236-238

Rivers, L. Mendel (Democrat-South Carolina)
    Congressional questioning of Martin during testimony in the mid-1960s, 262

Rockets
    Testing of 4½-inch air-to-air rockets at China Lake in the summer of 1945 as possible anti-kamikaze weapons, 79-81

Rodgers, Captain George F., USNR
    In the late 1960s served as public affairs officer for Commander Sixth Fleet, 287-288

Rosendahl, Vice Admiral Charles E., USN (Ret.) (USNA, 1914)
    Advocate for airships for many years, 246

***Roy O. Hale*, USS (DER-336)**
    In 1959 sent a boarding party to investigate a Soviet trawler that cut underwater cables near Newfoundland, 189-193

Royal Navy
    Diminished ship presence in the Mediterranean in the late 1960s, 293-294

Ruddy, Commander Joseph A. Jr., USN (USNA, 1930)
    In the early 1950s served as an instrument training instructor at Quonset Point, 131

Ruge, Vice Admiral Friedrich O.
    Headed the West German Navy in the early 1960s, 209-210

Rusk, Dean
    As Secretary of State in 1967, asked for the position of the Sixth Fleet in the run-up to the Six-Day War between Egypt and Israeli, 271-272

***Russell*, USS (DD-414)**
    Rescued survivors after the sinking of the aircraft carrier *Hornet* (CV-8) at the Battle of Santa Cruz Islands, October 1942, 46

S2F Tracker
    Operations from the ASW carrier *Hornet* (CVS-12) in 1959-60, 202-203

SOC Seagull
    An SOC floatplane from the heavy cruiser *Indianapolis* (CA-35) rescued Martin in June 1944 after he had been shot down off Saipan, 63-65

Saipan, Marianas Islands
    Martin was shot down during a dive-bombing attack on Saipan in June 1944, 39, 58-67, 76-77

***Saipan*, USS (CVL-48)**
    In 1955 provided post-hurricane rescue and relief for the area of Tampico, Mexico, 140-146
    Ship handling in the mid-1950s, 140-142, 146-147

Santa Cruz Islands, Battle of
    Involvement of the aircraft carriers *Enterprise* (CV-6) and *Hornet* (CV-8), 44-50

***Saratoga*, USS (CV-3)**
    Operated briefly as a specialized night carrier in February 1945, 68

Scouting Squadron Two (VS-2)
    Operated from the aircraft carrier *Lexington* (CV-2), 1938-40, 26, 29-30

Sea Orbit, Operation
    Planning in 1963-64 for this around-the-world cruise by a nuclear-powered task force, 233-240

Selection Boards
    Deep selection to rear admiral in 1958 for three members of the Naval Academy class of 1934, 178-180

Sheely, Lieutenant Donald M., USN (USNA, 1951)
    In 1959 was executive officer of the radar picket destroyer escort *Roy O. Hale* (DER-336) and led a boarding party to a Soviet trawler that cut underwater cables near Newfoundland, 188-193

Sherby, Commander Sydney S., USN (USNA, 1936)
    Involved in the establishment of Test Pilot School at Patuxent River in the late 1940s, 86, 96

Ship Handling
    On board the aircraft carrier *Saipan* (CVL-48) in the mid-1950s, 140-142, 146-147

Short, Representative Dewey J.
    Helped Martin get a Naval Academy appointment in 1930 and remained a friend, 3-4, 262
    Involved in controversial congressional hearings in 1949 about the Air Force's B-36 bomber, 105-115

Six-Day War
    Positioning of the U.S. Sixth Fleet during the war of June 1967 between Egypt and Israel, 271-276
    Israeli attack on the U.S. intelligence ship *Liberty* (AGTR-5) in June 1967, 284-287
    News media coverage of the Sixth Fleet during the war, 273-275

Sixth Fleet, U.S.
    Operations in the Mediterranean in the early 1960s included a nuclear-powered task force, 229-240
    Involvement in exercises with foreign nations in the early 1960s, 241-243
    In 1967 shifted the flagship's homeport from Villefranche, France, to Gaeta, Italy, 269-270, 280-282
    Mrs. Martin served as a hostess when her husband commanded the fleet in 1967-68, 265-266
    Generally the fleet commander's tour is short, 270-271
    Positioning of the Sixth Fleet during the Six-Day War of June 1967 between Egypt and Israel, 271-276, 290-291
    Israeli attack on the U.S. intelligence ship *Liberty* (AGTR-5) in June 1967, 284-287
    Arab liberty ports in the Mediterranean were closed down to Sixth Fleet ships following the Six-Day War, 282-284
    Ceremonial celebration in June 1968 of the 20th anniversary of the Sixth Fleet, 287, 290-293

Sonobuoys
    Used by aircraft from the antisubmarine carrier *Hornet* (CVS-12) in 1959-60, 203-204

Soucek, Rear Admiral Apollo, USN (USNA, 1921)
    Commanded the Naval Air Test Center from 1947 to 1949, 88, 98-99, 108

Souda Bay, Crete
    Served as a logistics base for U.S. Sixth Fleet ships in 1967, 275-278

South America
    UNITAS combined exercises in the 1950s-1970s involved U.S. and South American navies, 173-174, 304-305

Soviet Navy
    Operations in the Pacific in the late 1950s-early 1960s, 199-200
    Increase of ship presence in the Mediterranean in the late 1960s, 289-291
    Submarine operations in the late 1960s-early 1970s, 305-306

Soviet Union
    The Atlantic Barrier Wing was a Navy-run patrol between Argentia, Newfoundland, and the Azores in the late 1950s to detect incoming Soviet bombers, 180-195
    In February 1959 the Soviet trawler *Novorossisk* cut transatlantic underwater cables near Newfoundland, 188-193
    In 1961 a ski-equipped LC-130 from VX-6 rescued an ill Russian scientist from Antarctica, 187-188
    In the late 1960s Soviet leader Leonid Brezhnev criticized the U.S. naval presence in the Mediterranean, 289-290

Spangenberg, George A.
    Navy aeronautical engineer who criticized the TFX as a potential carrier plane in the 1960s, 256

Spruance, Admiral Raymond A., USN (USNA, 1907)
    Talked with Martin after Martin was shot down at Saipan in June 1944, 65

Strauss, Franz Josef
    Served as West Germany's Defense Minister from 1956 to 1962, 210-212

Strean, Rear Admiral Bernard M., USN (USNA, 1933)
    In 1964 commanded Operation Sea Orbit, the around-the-world cruise by a nuclear-powered task force, 236-239

Stump, Admiral Felix B., USN (USNA, 1917)
    From 1945 to 1948 served as Chief of Naval Air Technical Training, 135
    From 1953 to 1958 commanded the Pacific Fleet and Pacific Command, 135-136

Suez Crisis
    Actions of CNO Arleigh Burke in response to this 1956 event, 175-176

TBF Avenger
    Flown by Torpedo Squadron Ten (VT-10) in 1943-44, 33-39, 49-52, 58-60
    Modified in 1944 for extended range as part of Night Air Group 90, 52-56
    Ruggedness of the airplane, 39

TFX
Navy opposition to Secretary of Defense Robert McNamara's attempts in the 1960s to make this Air Force fighter into a carrier plane, 250-257, 263-264

TV-1 Seastar
The Air Force version, the XP-80, flew at the Naval Air Test Center in the late 1940s, 99-100
The first Pacific Fleet jets went to Fleet All-Weather Training Unit Pacific (FAWTUPAC) in the late 1940s, 1104

Tactics
Martin began doing tactical development work in night flying in 1938-40 in Scouting Squadron Two (VS-2), 29-32
Role of radar in night fighter operations in the late 1940s-early 1950s, 116

Taddeo, Lieutenant (junior grade) Alfred, USNR
Flew from the aircraft carrier *Enterprise* (CV-6) during the invasion of Saipan in June 1944, 64-66

Tate, Lieutenant (junior grade), Hugh J., USN
Young test pilot at the Naval Air Test Center in the late 1940s, 96-97, 108

Taylor, General Maxwell D., USA (USMA, 1922)
Served as Chief of Staff of the Army, 1955-59, 247

Test Pilots
Experimental work in 1945-48 at the Naval Air Test Center, 82-103
Selection of test pilot candidates in the late 1940s, 101-102

Test Pilot School, Patuxent River, Maryland
Inaugurated in 1948, 85-87, 96-97
Selection of test pilot candidates in the late 1940s, 101-102

Thach, Vice Admiral John S., USN (USNA, 1927)
Commanded Antisubmarine Warfare Force Pacific, 1960-63, 198
Served as Deputy Chief of Naval Operations (Air) from 1963 to 1965, 248-250, 254

Torpedoes
Unreliable performance when dropped by Torpedo Squadron Ten (VT-10) in 1943-44, 33-34, 37-38

Torpedo Squadron Ten (VT-10)
Training at Seattle in 1943, 33
Did mostly bombing rather than using torpedoes, 1943-44, 30-38
Use for night operations in 1943-44, 32-36
Support of the New Guinea landings in April 1944, 49-52

Support of the Saipan landings in June 1944, 58-67, 76-77

Trapnell, Captain Frederick M., USN (USNA, 1923)
Did test pilot work both during and after World War II, 85-88, 96-103

Towers, Vice Admiral John H., USN (USNA, 1906)
As Deputy CinCPacFlt, was consulted in 1944 on modifying TBF Avengers for extended night operations, 52-56

Tunisia
Involvement in NATO exercises in the early 1960s, 241-242

Turner, Vice Admiral Frederick C., USN
Young test pilot at the Naval Air Test Center in the late 1940s, 84, 96-97, 109
Served 1976-79 as DCNO (Air Warfare), 84, 96

Turner, Lieutenant Stansfield, USN (USNA, 1947)
Served as a briefer for CNO Arleigh Burke in the mid-1950s, 155

Truk Atoll, Caroline Islands
Attacked by U.S. carrier planes and surface ships in February 1944, 34-37

Tuzo, Lieutenant Paul B. "Squeak" Jr., USN (USNA, 1925)
Tough flight instructor at Pensacola in the late 1930s, 24-25

UNITAS
Combined exercises in the 1950s-1970s that involved U.S. and South American navies, 173-174, 304-305

VS-2
See: Scouting Squadron Two (VS-2)

VT-10
See: Torpedo Squadron Ten (VT-10)

VX-6
See: Air Development Squadron Six (VX-6)

Vieques Island, Puerto Rico
Diminishing Atlantic Fleet training facilities in the area since the 1960s, 301-304

Villefranche, France
In 1967, at the behest of French President Charles de Gaulle, the Sixth Fleet flagship moved its homeport from Villefranche to Gaeta, Italy, 269-270

Vinson, Representative Carl, (Democrat-Georgia)
Led controversial congressional hearings in 1949 about the Air Force's B-36 bomber, 105-115

WV Warning Star
Lockheed-built airborne early warning plane that joined the fleet in the mid-1950s, 121, 125
Patrols in the late 1950s to detect incoming Soviet bombers, 180-195

Weather
Relationship over the years between the Navy and the weather bureau, 124-125
In the late 1940s the Naval Air Test Center did experiments flying a patrol plane in icing conditions, 121-124
VW Warning Star aircraft flew into hurricanes in the 1950s, 125
In 1955 the aircraft carrier *Saipan* (CVL-48) provided post-hurricane rescue and relief for the area of Tampico, Mexico, 140-146
Coast Guard iceberg patrols in the North Atlantic in the late 1950s, 180-183
Difficult flying weather at Argentia, Newfoundland, in the late 1950s, 185, 187

Weschler, Commander Thomas R., USN (USNA, 1939)
Served as aide to Chief of Naval Operations Arleigh Burke in the mid-1950s, 152, 159, 166

Whitehead, Captain Richard F., USN
Commanded support aircraft for the invasion of Saipan in June 1944, 61-62

Wilkins, Sir George Hubert
Battleships *Arkansas* (BB-33) and *Wyoming* (BB-32) went to the rescue of Wilkins's planned polar expedition in mid-1931, 8, 134

Wright, Admiral Jerauld, USN (USNA, 1918)
As Commander in Chief Atlantic Fleet, kept in touch with Martin in the late 1950s, 193, 249

***Wyoming*, USS (AG-17)**
Midshipman summer cruises in 1931 and 1933, 8, 12-13

XP-59 Airacomet
Jet fighter considered by the Navy in the 1940s, 100

Zumwalt, Admiral Elmo R. Jr., USN (USNA, 1943)
Impact of his policies and style during his initial months as Chief of Naval Operations in 1970, 312-314